Poisonous Plants and Fatal Fungi

© Jessica Weiser

About the Author

Sandra Kynes spent the early part of her life exploring the wonders of New York City while studying, working, and raising her son. She has since lived in Europe, England, and now Midcoast Maine, where she resides with her family and cats in a mid-nineteenth-century farmhouse surrounded by meadows and woods. Sandra loves connecting with nature through gardening, hiking, bird-watching, and kayaking. On occasion, she misses New York. Visit her website at www.kynes.net.

Poisonous Plants and Fatal Fungi

The Lore and Lure of Deadly Botanicals

SANDRA KYNES

First Edition
First Printing, 2025

Book design by Rordan Brasington
Cover design by Kevin R. Brown
Interior illustrations by Llewllyn Art Department

Library of Congress Cataloging-in-Publication Data (Pending)
ISBN: 978-0-7387-7861-7

Llewellyn Publications
A Division of Llewellyn Worldwide Ltd.
2143 Wooddale Drive
Woodbury, MN 55125-2989
www.llewellyn.com

Printed in the United States of America

GPSR Representation:
UPI-2M PLUS d.o.o., Medulićeva 20, 10000 Zagreb, Croatia
matt.parsons@upi2mbooks.hr

Other Books by Sandra Kynes

From Llewellyn Worldwide

The Witches' Encyclopedia of Magical Plants (2024)

Magical Faery Plants (2022)

Tree Magic (2021)

Beginner's Guide to Herbal Remedies (2020)

Magical Symbols and Alphabets (2020)

Llewellyn's Complete Book of Essential Oils (2019)

365 Days of Crystal Magic (2018)

Crystal Magic (2017)

Plant Magic (2017)

Bird Magic (2016)

Herb Gardener's Essential Guide (2016)

Star Magic (2015)

Mixing Essential Oils for Magic (2013)

Llewellyn's Complete Book of Correspondences (2013)

Change at Hand (2009)

Sea Magic (2008)

Your Altar (2007)

Whispers from the Woods (2006)

A Year of Ritual (2004)

Gemstone Feng Shui (2002)

From Crossed Crow Books

The Avian Oracle (2024)

Forthcoming Book by Sandra Kynes

Fairy Trails (2026)

Disclaimer

The material in this book is for informational and entertainment purposes only. It is not intended as a plant or mushroom identification guide or medical resource. This book is sold with the understanding that the publisher and author are not liable for the misconception, misinterpretation, or misuse of any information provided. If you suspect a poisoning, get professional medical help immediately.

This book is dedicated to Joyce Koehnlein,
dear friend and longtime supporter.

Contents

Introduction

Plants are our allies. Since the dawn of human time, we have relied on them for almost everything: food, medicine, wood for building shelters, fibers for making clothing, and a wide range of other domestic necessities. They also serve as memorials, placed or grown on the graves of our loved ones. Plants fascinate and enchant us with their beauty and fragrance; we enjoy them so much that we give them as gifts. The enthusiastic Victorians created an interpretation of plant meanings with a language of flowers. As children, many of us delighted in the charming drawings of English illustrator Cicely Mary Barker (1895–1973) that showed flower fairies playing amongst an endless array of beautiful plants.

But all was not bucolic splendor. In childhood, we also learned that some plants and fungi have a dangerous side and can be put to sinister use. We don't know the ingredients of the recipe called Sleeping Death that the Evil Queen used to poison Snow White, but the delivery device was a shiny red apple. In *Barbar the Elephant*, the pachyderm king died after eating a poisonous mushroom, and in *The Wizard of Oz*, as Dorothy and her friends walked through a poppy field, the dangerous effects of the flowers made her (and Toto, too) fall asleep. And then there's Alice, who fell down a rabbit hole and encountered a hookah-smoking caterpillar that suggested she partake of a mushroom on her rather psychedelic trip through Wonderland. Even before we could read these stories for ourselves, we learned to associate poisonous plants with the inviting and curious realm of the fairy tale, which increased their potential to fascinate us.

But there's more to it than childhood stories. From penny-dreadful novels, murder mysteries, and true crime television programs to the popularity of Halloween, we seem to have a penchant for ghoulishness. And though we may fear it, we also have a fascination with the mystery of death. Poisonous plants and fatal fungi fit into and feed this dark enchantment like a gothic charm. Some of them have a sinister beauty that piques the imagination and makes us wonder how something so alluring could be so dangerous. Sometimes we delight in the things that scare us and sometimes we are fascinated by the things that horrify us. We like getting scared. In fact, we're hardwired for it.

Whether bungee jumping or watching a horror film, getting scared is a full-body experience. Fear makes the heart rate go up and the fight-or-flight response kick in with a rush of adrenaline, which in turn triggers the release of endorphins and dopamine. But unlike real danger, we know we're safe and, with the chemicals the body has released into the bloodstream, we even feel good.

As with the scary fairy tales of childhood, a little bit of fear keeps us on our toes. It keeps us alert to the dangerous world out there beyond our cozy homes, but more importantly, we also learn about ourselves and how we might deal with threats. Although reading about poisonous plants may not elicit the same chemical cocktail response in the body as riding an amusement park roller coaster, like other similar activities, it may appeal to a sense of the macabre that sometimes allows us a little glimpse of our own dark sides. A true crime television show or murder mystery novel may prompt us to think like a killer or ponder how best to carry out a poisoning. For a little while we get to be the villain, we get to pretend, but then we come back to ourselves knowing that we are not the bad guys, nor do we want to be. We get to enjoy a little escapism that is not only entertaining, but also helps reinforce social guardrails.

However, not all the tales told throughout this book are ghoulish fun; many are dark, and some rather miserable, but then, poisoning is serious business. From a distance we are safe to look down the dark rabbit holes of other people's lives. While their stories may affect us, perhaps more than feeling sad, they leave us thankful for our own circumstances.

What Makes a Plant Poisonous?

Since plants cannot run away or hide from predators, they have developed special types of defense mechanisms. Some plants have a structural defense, such as thorns, prickles, or rough hairs on their stems, while others produce chemical toxins, which can be just as or even more effective. Stinging nettle is armed with both; nature's belt-and-braces approach. It has stiff hairs that break off, prick the skin of the animal or human that brushed against it, and then release an unpleasant cocktail of histamine, formic acid, and serotonin. Although stinging nettle is not deadly, it can produce an uncomfortable to severe allergic reaction. The chemical defenses of many plants and fungi are meant to repel, deter, and sometimes kill.

Phytochemicals are compounds produced by plants that are important to their functioning and survival. Some phytochemicals are defensive compounds that protect a plant against infections, infestations, and predators. Some defensive compounds are harmful to humans if ingested or inhaled; others, if they touch the skin. An entire plant may be poisonous, or only parts of it may be harmful.

Defensive toxins produce an assortment of effects that range from mild irritation to severe illness and sometimes death. Following are examples of some toxic compounds found in plants:

- Alkaloids are nitrogenous compounds that usually create a bitter taste. The alkaloid coniine is found in poison hemlock, atropine in deadly nightshade, hyoscyamine in henbane, and gelsemine in yellow jessamine.
- Glycosides are compounds that produce sugars (glycones) with toxic aglycones (nonsugars). These can be found in ivy. The cardiac glycoside digoxin is found in foxglove.
- Cyanogenic glycosides are nitrogenous compounds that convert to cyanide in the digestive tract. These can be found in the raw seeds and kernels of various *Prunus* species such as peach, apple, and almond.
- Furocoumarins (or furanocoumarins) are photoactive compounds that can cause a severe skin reaction when exposed to sunlight. They can be found in giant hogweed.
- Toxalbumins are highly toxic protein molecules such as ricin in the castor oil plant and abrin in rosary pea.

The degree of plant toxicity varies amongst different species ranging from minimal to extreme. In addition, toxins often run in botanical families. For example, the cultivated tomato is a member of the *Solanaceae* or Nightshade family, as is the notorious belladonna, which is also known as deadly nightshade. Members of this family contain the alkaloid solanine, which is toxic in high amounts. Most, but not all, of the fruits and vegetables in this family are safe to eat because the amount of solanine is low and decreases as the fruit ripens.

Botanical and Common Names

While botanical names may be challenging to remember, common names and folk names are a source of confusion because some of them are used for multiple plants and most plants have more than one or two common names, sometimes many names. To make matters worse, folk names are often applied incorrectly, causing even more confusion and, in some cases, perpetuating the mistake. Also, while two plants may share a folk name, it does not mean that all folk names apply to both plants. This may seem minor, but keep in mind that some plants are extremely toxic and can be dangerous even to handle or fatal to ingest. This is important because you may have a deadly plant or two in your garden.

In ancient times, plants were classified into simple intuitive categories. Eventually, classifications were based on scientific study, but for several centuries, plants were named by different botanists without any type of cohesive logical standard. Swedish naturalist Carl Linnaeus (1707–1778) stepped into the breach and changed all that by developing an identification system, which resulted in a branch of science called taxonomy. Botanical names are almost always Latin because during Linnaeus's time it was a common language amongst people engaged in scientific research. Over time, as further botanical research revealed new information, plant names were changed to reflect the new data. This is why botanical names often have synonyms. The antiquated names are not completely dropped because they often aid in identification. For example, the plant wormwood may be noted as *Artemisia absinthium* syn. *Absinthium officinale*. Occasionally, a synonym may be applied to a plant because of scientific disagreement or plain old-fashioned stubbornness.

The basic hierarchy of classification includes kingdom, phylum (sometimes called division), class, order, family, genus, and species. The full classification hierarchy in modern taxonomy has about sixteen levels, but for simplicity, the plant profiles in this book include only family, genus, and species names. Botanical families are based on the physiological characteristics of a plant's development and structure. In addition to changes in plant names due to updated information, the logical rules for naming them is periodically revised. For example, the ending *-aceae* was added to family names—with a few exceptions—to distinguish them from orders, classes, and other levels within the naming structure.

The two-word plant names that we find at garden centers are the genus and species. The genus, which is often a proper noun, is always capitalized. The species name is an adjective that usually provides something descriptive about the plant. However, to indicate multiple species, a little botanical shorthand is used by adding an abbreviation after the genus name. For example, *Datura* spp. means various species in that genus.

Helpful Botanical Words and Terms

The term *vulgare*, as in *Tanacetum vulgare* (tansy), means that it is a common plant and not that it is crude or unrefined. The terms *officinarum* and *officinale*, as in *Mandragora officinarum* (mandrake) and the previously mentioned wormwood, indicate that a plant is, or was at one time, officially recognized as a medicinal plant. The term *bane* is sometimes found in common names, such as *wolfsbane* and *henbane*. *Bane* is an Anglo-Saxon (Old English) word for poison and was incorporated into the names of plants as a warning.[1] For the same reason, folk names often include the word *devil* to indicate that the plant causes pain or is dangerous or deadly.

Certain specialized terms are used in botany for describing plants. The following table lists the terms used in the plant profiles.

Helpful Botanical Terms	
Axil	The area of a plant between a stem or branch and a leaf stem
Bract	A modified or specialized leaf situated at the base of a flower
Catkin	A thick cluster of tiny flowers; male catkins are usually larger than female catkins and pendulous; female catkins are most often upright
Lobed	A leaf with deeply indented edges, such as oak or maple tree leaves
Rhizome	An underground stem that is usually considered a type of root
Sepal	The outermost part of a flower that protects the young bud
Spathe	A large, specialized leaf that surrounds and protects a flower

1. Storl, *The Herbal Lore of Wise Women and Wortcunners*, 234.

Helpful Botanical Terms (Continued)	
Toothed	A leaf with jagged edges; also called serrated
Whorl	A circular or spiral growth pattern of leaves, needles, or flower petals

About This Book

Part 1 contains five chapters that provide a historical background of poisonous plants and fungi and how they played an integral part in the development of medicine. We will see how some of these plants became associated with witches and how Indigenous healers and shamans also used them. This part also follows the baneful path of plants used as weapons of war and traces their role in murder throughout history. As we will see, poison is an equal opportunity murder weapon and a killer doesn't have to be strong, just smart. Real or fictitious, plants have served as an interesting and convenient device in literature and art. We will also take a peek over the fence to see how some poisonous plants are grown intentionally (or unwittingly) in gardens. Last but not least, a chapter is devoted to fungi. Technically, fungi are not plants; they have their own separate kingdom in the taxonomic scheme of things, at least since 1969. However, in the minds of most, they are regarded as plants. After all, like plants, we eat them, and like plants, some are poisonous and make us sick… or worse.

Parts 2 through 6 each contain a dozen profiles of individual plants according to themes from ancient use, Classic Killers, to mushrooms, Frightful Fungi. Each profile includes the plant's common name, genus and species, folk names, and botanical family. A description of the plant is followed by information on its toxicity. While the poison used on Snow White's apple had a cure—love's first kiss—we will see that not all toxins have antidotes. The plant profile also includes its history, folklore, and medicinal uses, as well as how it may or may not be used today. While there are thousands of poisonous plants, I have included the ones that I thought have the most interesting stories.

As for the title of this book, we can be frightened yet fascinated by something dangerous, especially when we know we are safe. And so, let us journey through history to see how poisonous plants fuel this fascination.

PART 1

Poisonous Past

Once upon a time, there was a belief that the nastier the taste and its effects, the better the medicine—there was a very fine line between killing and curing. We will follow the development of medicine and medical literature and the role that poisonous plants have played. These floras also had a role in demonizing witches, and as Europeans set out to conquer the world, the same treatment was applied to shamans and Indigenous healers. With never an intent to cure, we will also see how plants were used for outright killing. The deadlier the plant, the better for warfare, and the more discreet, the better for murder. Of course, this has made great fodder for many stories and novels. The fantastical world of fungi is also explored.

CHAPTER 1
CURE OR KILL MEDICINE

While for the most part all is well and good in our relationship with plants, some are dangerous and can cause harm, and some can kill us. We can only assume that it must have been trial and error for early humans to figure out which plants were for eating and medicine, and perhaps most importantly, for avoiding. Observation most likely played a part since many domestic livestock often avoid poisonous plants such as oleander. However, this is not always the case because some plants that animals may enjoy and snarf up like there's no tomorrow are dangerous for us. The genus name for henbane, *Hyoscyamus*, means "hog's-bean" and was so named because hogs love it, but as we've already seen, the term *bane* is a warning.[2] At any rate, as cultures and civilizations developed, plant knowledge and herbal medicine were passed along generation to generation, traded with outsiders, and eventually systematized.

Ayurveda is believed to be the oldest system of healing and has its roots in oral tradition from over five thousand years ago in India. Information was eventually formalized and written down in the Sanskrit texts known as the *Vedas* (c. 1500 BCE). Traditional Chinese Medicine dates to approximately 200 BCE with a text called the *Yellow Emperor's Classic of Internal Medicine*. In Europe, Greek physician and pharmacologist Pedanius Dioscorides (c. 40–c. 90 CE) compiled the first herbal manuscript in Europe, *De Materia Medica*, meaning the "material of medicine." The forerunner of modern pharmacopeias, *De Materia Medica* was the authoritative go-to source on botanical medicine for over a thousand years. In addition, eight of the thirty-seven books compiled by Roman naturalist and historian Gaius Plinius Secundus, known simply as Pliny

2. De Cleene and Lejeune, *Compendium of Symbolic and Ritual Plants in Europe*, 252.

the Elder (23/24–79 CE), dealt with plant pharmacology and were a valuable resource for herbalists up through the seventeenth century.

The Anglo-Saxons also organized herbal information into leechbooks, which served as handbooks for doctors. The word *leech*, or *læce*, comes from the Old English *læccan*, meaning "to heal," and was an honorific that indicated a person was skilled in medicine.[3] It had nothing to do with the use of worms called leeches; that practice began in the nineteenth century. What the various traditions and medicines throughout the ages have in common is the use of poisonous plants. The record of poisonous plants is an integral part of the history of medicine with roots in ancient Egypt, India, China, and Persia, and later in Greece and Italy. Poisons and their effects were known to these ancient civilizations.

It's All in the Dose

Although "poisonous" does not always mean "deadly," medicinal doses sometimes trod a fine line between healing patients or putting them in the grave. As English physician and toxicologist Alfred Swaine Taylor (1806–1880) put it: "A poison in a small dose is a medicine, and a medicine in a larger dose is a poison."[4]

Since ancient times, the aconites (monkshood and wolfsbane) were used throughout many traditions including Ayurveda and Traditional Chinese Medicine. In addition to these, Ayurveda employed rosary pea and strychnine, and in Traditional Chinese Medicine, Chinese ephedra was used. One of the Hindu texts, the *Rigveda* (c. 1500–1200 BCE) includes medicinal and poisonous plants as well as antidotes for them. The treatise called *Sushruta Samhita* written by Hindu surgeon Sushruta (fl. c. 600 BCE) detailed hundreds of drugs from plant, animal, and mineral origins. For anesthesia, he recommended wine mixed with a species of marijuana. An early Chinese pharmacopoeia called *Shen Nong Bencao Jing* is attributed to the mythical emperor Shen Nong (fl. c. 2695 BCE), whose name is sometimes noted as Shen Nung and Shennong. Containing information on poisonous plants, the book describes their effects and provides

3. Barnhart, *The Barnhart Concise Dictionary of Etymology*, 426.

4. Grell, Cunningham, and Arrizabalaga, *It All Depends on the Dose*, 10.

antidotes. It includes aconite, opium, cannabis, and rhubarb. According to legend, Shen Nong gained knowledge by experimenting on himself.

Egyptian medicine and the knowledge of poisons was regarded as the most advanced in the ancient world. Their use of plants is documented in the sixteenth-century BCE Ebers Papyrus, named for German Egyptologist Georg Ebers (1837–1898). In addition to botanical recipes for healing and cosmetics, it also provides some formulas expressly for killing. Amongst the seven hundred or so plants are hemlock, aconite, castor oil plant, sea squill, and the opium poppy. In fact, references to the medicinal use of opium have been found in Sumerian cuneiform tablets dating to approximately 3000 BCE. Gula, the Sumerian goddess of healing and medicine, who was also known as Ninkarrak and Ninisina, is the earliest-known deity associated with poisons.

Greek physician Hippocrates (460–377 BCE), who is usually regarded as the Father of Medicine, has been noted for his approach to healing and his do-no-harm philosophy. He originated the theory of the Four Humors or fundamental fluids of the body, which consisted of yellow bile (from the liver), phlegm, black bile (from the spleen and kidneys), and blood. It was believed that when these fluids became out of balance, they could be restored through the use of enemas, laxatives, and diuretics. Other remedies were aimed at causing sweating or vomiting, which was usually achieved with botanical remedies that included plants such as hellebore and henbane. Of the over four hundred plants Hippocrates named in his work, many were poisonous and included bryony, hellebore, and hemlock. Greek philosopher and scholar Theophrastus (c. 371–c. 287 BCE) described both plant and mineral poisons as well as how to treat their effects. Perhaps it is no surprise that the word *pharmacy* comes from the Greek *phámakon*, which means "drug" or "remedy" as well as "poison."[5]

As previously mentioned, Dioscorides's *De Materia Medica* was an important source of information about the medicinal use of plants including poisonous ones. Serving as a surgeon in the Roman army, his travels took him throughout southern France, Italy, Greece, and Asia Minor, which broadened his botanical studies. Some of the poisonous plants in his text include opium poppy, black nightshade, and mandrake. Mandrake was commonly used as a surgical anesthetic in the ancient world.

---

5. Barnhart, *The Barnhart Concise Dictionary of Etymology*, 562.

An illustrated copy of Dioscorides's work was used as a medical guide in a Constantinople (now Istanbul) hospital for almost a thousand years. The book was created around 512 CE for Juliana Anicia (462–527/528), an aristocratic woman in the eastern Roman Empire. Originally entitled the *Juliana Anicia Codex*, it is now called the *Vienna Dioscorides* and is kept in the National Library in Vienna.

A Light in the Dark Ages

After the Roman Empire fell apart, Europe experienced an immense social upheaval. While there may not have been complete lawlessness in the streets, without the steady hand of Roman administrators as well as funding, towns and cities found it extremely difficult to keep the *civil* in *civilization*. Without the ancient equivalent of a police department, fire brigade, aqueduct/roadworks division, and sanitation crews, life would have been a lot less comfortable, less clean, and a great deal more challenging. Those who could afford to escape the uncertainties and discomforts took off to other lands. Many physicians and scholars relocated to the Middle East and along with them went a storehouse of information. Keen on expanding their knowledge, Arab scholars welcomed the newcomers and Baghdad became an important center of learning where European texts were eagerly translated into Arabic. The city was an intercultural crossroads for medicine and a gateway for trade with Asia and India, which were sources for plants unknown or not readily available in Europe. Research in medical botany flourished.

Building on the legacy of Greek and Roman medicine, Islamic scholars enhanced it with their own material and observations. Preeminent Persian physician Ibn Sina (980–1037), known in the West as Avicenna, compiled a five-volume encyclopedia, which came to be known in English as the *Canon of Medicine*. Avicenna organized, systematized, and summarized the work of Hippocrates, Dioscorides, and Roman physician Claudius Galenus, better known as Galen (130–200 CE), as well as others. Of course, Arabian plant knowledge and pharmaceuticals that were common in the Levant were added to European medical texts.

While the Middle East was the happening place, the early medieval period in Europe, which has been called the Dark Ages, was not completely dark because there were bright spots that kept the flame of learning and civilization burning. Monasteries and convents were repositories for medical knowledge and the forerunner of public hospitals. They were also places of botanical research. Originating in monasteries, the Physic Garden was a place where medicinal plants were grown for study and use. Basically, they were an apothecary's laboratory.

Although French philosopher and writer Voltaire, pseudonym of François-Marie Arouet (1694–1778), noted that the Holy Roman Empire was neither holy nor Roman, its first ruler Charlemagne (747–814), who had been king of the Franks, ushered in some stability as well as a cultural and intellectual revival. Charlemagne was an enthusiastic advocate of the Physic Garden for his own private estates and encouraged them throughout his domain. Some of the plants he deemed essential were also quite toxic, including opium poppy, rue, caper spurge, and various species of squill.

Of course, the term *stability* to describe life in Europe at that time is somewhat relative. People didn't gather in the streets, hold hands, and sing kumbaya. Then as now, there were wars, bickering, plagues, and pandemics, but overall, there was improvement, especially for those with means. Scholars were gradually filtering back, bringing with them a fusion of Greek, Roman, Arab, and Indian medicine along with more extensive botanical knowledge. The ancient texts that had been translated from Greek and Old Latin into Arabic were translated again into Medieval Latin. Avicenna's *Canon of Medicine* was also translated into Latin during the twelfth century and served as an important textbook for the medical schools that were emerging in Europe.

Fostered by the monastery of Monte Çassino in southern Italy, *Schola Medica Salernitana*, the Salerno School of Medicine, was founded in the late ninth century. Far ahead of its time and exceedingly rare, women were included in the student body. In fact, the school also had an outstanding woman on the faculty, Trota of Salerno (d. 1097), who was also known as Trota of Ruggerio—her name is sometimes given as Trocta, Trotula, and Trutella. She wrote at least one section of the three-part compendium on women's health that bears her name, *The Trotula*. Despite the prevailing Christian belief that women should suffer pain in childbirth, Trota promoted the use of opium during labor. Botanical experimentation was encouraged at Salerno and a general anesthetic for surgery was developed that had the jaw-dropping recipe of opium, mandrake, and henbane in equal parts. It would certainly kill the pain, if not the patient.

German abbess, writer, and mystic Hildegard von Bingen (1098–1179) is the only medieval woman whose work with botanicals and theories on healing has survived intact. Remedies with common herbs appear in her books *Physica* and *Causae et Curae* (*Causes and Cures*) as well as poisonous ones such as hellebore and tansy. She also believed that any mushroom that grew on trees could be eaten or used for medicine. A fact she got wrong and, in some cases, dead wrong.

English physician and botanist John Gerard (1545–1612) was Master of the Company of Barber-Surgeons in London. These were handy practitioners who could provide a shave and a haircut as well as remove a tooth or a limb. Drawing heavily on the work of Dioscorides, Gerard's book *The Herball or Generall Historie of Plantes* was published in 1597 and became a classic text. Amongst the plants that he studied and grew in his own garden were opium poppy, mandrake, and other toxic flora. As a remedy for bad headaches, Gerard recommended rubbing belladonna leaves on the forehead; however, he noted that using too much could result in hallucinations and intoxication.

The unorthodox Italian scholar Giambattista della Porta (1535–1615), also known as John Baptiste Porta, had a divergent range of scientific interests, including medicine and botany. One of the books in his twenty-volume *Natural Magick* consisted of his experiments with plants and medicines. Long before Snow White's evil stepmother delivered the questionable fruit, della Porta devised a sleeping apple made from opium poppy, mandrake, hemlock, and henbane rolled into a ball. He also warned that the combination of thorn apple seeds and deadly nightshade roots could cause madness.

Murky Roots of Toxicology

A discussion of kill-or-cure medicine wouldn't be complete without mentioning Swiss physician and alchemist Theophrastus Bombastus von Hohenheim (1493–1541) whose philosophy was that a little bit of something dangerous could be healing. Better known as Paracelsus, he adapted his persona from the highly acclaimed first-century Roman physician Aurelius Cornelius Celsus (c. 25 BCE–c. 50 CE), and then added the prefix *para-* so his name would mean "above Celsus."[6] He was not shy about grand self-promotion.

6. Hayes and Kobets, *Hayes' Principles and Methods of Toxicology*, 13.

Paracelsus was influential in the development of chemistry as a science and is regarded as the founder of modern toxicology. Although he is sometimes attributed with creating the Doctrine of Signatures, the concept dates back to Greek scholar Theophrastus. However, in medieval Christian Europe, the Doctrine of Signatures was based on the belief that the shape, color, or patterns of a plant was God's signature on it, which provided a hint on how it should be used. For example, because a walnut resembles the brain, it was thought to cure headaches.

Paracelsus and his later followers popularized the use of laudanum, a tincture of opium, to be used as a painkiller and sleeping aid. Strychnine arrived in Europe and Britain during the sixteenth century and was used medicinally without its cumulative effects being understood. An extract from the seed was known as strychnine and the powdered seeds were called *nux vomica* from the Latin meaning "vomiting nut," which described its prevalent use. Purges from either end of the alimentary canal were popular cures, but also dangerous. Despite the risks, there was a persistent belief that a medicine with a foul taste and nasty effects made for a better cure. By the nineteenth century, strychnine held a prominent place as a remedy and not only as a laxative. American doctors prescribed small doses of it for breathing difficulties, labor pains, and even babies' colic. But wait, it gets worse. Strychnine was also a component of many quack medicines, which usually contained a substantial amount of alcohol along with other hazardous botanicals such as opium and coca.

As scary as it seems, both quack and conventional remedies were more or less a game of botanical roulette. Nineteenth-century doctors on both sides of the pond seemed to be fascinated with poisonous plants and used them in small doses for a wide range of complaints. Aconite was popular with European and American doctors in the nineteenth century and was used for fevers, pneumonia, and laryngitis as well as a painkiller and diuretic. The use of poisonous plants, and poisonous substances in general, was an issue of debate amongst American doctors who prescribed hemlock for calming teething babies and enthusiastically promoted the use of belladonna. Belladonna was available as a bandage to dull pain and in a liniment for a range of ailments. Into the early 1920s, it was combined with aconite to treat a sore throat.

Medicine has come a long way since the early twentieth century with modern scientific techniques that aid in understanding how many toxins work.

While today's materia medica is standardized and regulated to avoid killer doses, it still employs components from poisonous plants. These include the narcotic alkaloids of morphine and codeine from the opium poppy for pain relief, digoxin from foxglove for heart strength and rate, artemisinin from sweet wormwood for malaria, and ephedrine from ephedra to treat a range of conditions.

Through the centuries, poisonous plants were stock-in-trade medicines for some, but they were evidence of witchcraft for others. While the focus of the Inquisition in Europe was to root out and punish heresy, witchcraft became associated with devil worship and trafficking evil spirits, putting it dead center in the crosshairs of the Catholic Church.

CHAPTER 2
Witches, Shamans, and Indigenous Healers

During medieval times in Europe, possessing certain plants became a stigma and was used to marginalize lower-class women in the healing arts while also bringing everyone else to heel. The field of medicine in Europe became extremely uneven terrain where only educated white men with the right connections could safely tread. Elsewhere in the world, shamans and other Indigenous healers used many of the same plants as well as others that were valued for their psychoactive properties. As Europeans ventured to other parts of the world, it didn't take long for the ugly hand of colonialism to come down like an iron fist on those with different beliefs and practices.

Scaremongering and Scapegoats

An almost surefire way to control people is to scare them, and then make them believe that only you can provide guidance and protection. It's an effective tactic used today and one that worked very well in early medieval times. The power vacuum left in the wake of the Roman Empire provided the Church with a golden opportunity to step in and expand its reach to control people's lives. From the fourteenth through eighteenth centuries, the traditional folk healers became a convenient scapegoat to help keep the masses in line.

While the early Middle Ages was a time of uncertainty for many, the monasteries and convents became centers of stability and learning. Not only did the monks and nuns who made copies of ancient manuscripts learn about medicinal plants, but they also gained valuable knowledge from local folk healers. Monasteries offered medical assistance and care, but many people continued to seek aid from the wisewomen who had always given advice and served as nurses, midwives, and pharmacists. Wisewomen were the people villagers trusted and went to for help, especially if there wasn't a monastery or convent close by. In addition, women would quite naturally feel more comfortable discussing their intimate health issues with midwives, the women they knew and who could also aid in controlling fertility and pregnancy. In addition, these wisewomen helped in matters of the heart as well as in other aspects of life.

Healing was one thing but providing advice on personal matters put them into direct competition with local parish priests. Because these women helped people who could not afford the fees of university-trained doctors, they also ran afoul of the emerging medical establishment and its associated guilds. As mentioned in the previous chapter, women studied medicine and at least one woman taught it at Salerno, but the school did not evolve into a full-fledged university and was eclipsed by the medical schools at Paris and Montpellier in France and Bologna in Italy. While women initially attended the school in Paris, by 1220 they had been marginalized and all but pushed out. Women like the eleventh-century doctor Trota of Salerno who pioneered women's medicine would never have made such achievements in the thirteenth century. In fact, Renaissance scholars doubted that *The Trotula*, a compendium of women's medicine, was even written by a woman.

In 1325, the faculty at the Paris medical school petitioned Pope John XXII (1249–1334) for the regulation of medical practice. This resulted in the bishop of Paris creating a catch-22 situation by decreeing that without attending a bona fide medical school, women could not practice medicine in the city or the surrounding areas. Specifically mentioning midwives in his decree, the bishop also hinted that women were practicing witchcraft under the guise of medicine.

As waves of bubonic plague and other diseases rampaged across Europe and the need for doctors and healers was greater than ever, the powers that be defied all logic. Instead of training and licensing women to practice medicine, these valuable healers were prosecuted as witches. The push was on by the Church, medical establishment, and professional guilds to rid the world of laypeople practicing any form of healing. To aid in this, the use and possession of certain plants, potions, and other items became a way to identify witches. The fearmongering of the witch trials and demonization of women were methods that discouraged most people from questioning authority. After all, they were being protected, right?

Witch Trials and Broomstick Flight

A great deal of witch lore comes from the transcripts of the trials, which contained testimony extracted under torture, as well as from imaginative ideas espoused in witch-hunter manuals. While the *Malleus Maleficarum* (*Hammer of Witches*), written by German Dominican monk and inquisitor Heinrich Kramer (1430–1505) and published in 1487, is the most well-known of these guides, another called the *Compendium Maleficarum* (*Compendium of Witchcraft*) listed the plants that witches were said to use. It included hemlock, nightshade, mandrake, opium poppy, castor oil plant, and darnel. The *Compendium Maleficarum* was compiled and written by Francesco Maria Guazzo (c. 1570–1640), a cleric from Milan who claimed to have had firsthand experience with bewitchment and possession.

Familiar with Greek mythology, the learned men of the Church and universities reasoned that Hecate, goddess of magic and enchantment, was the patroness of witches. They also noted that the poisonous plants Hecate was said to have consecrated were used by her alleged followers. It was conveniently overlooked by these upstanding pillars of society that the same plants appeared in the works of Pliny the Elder, Galen, Dioscorides, and others who were held in high esteem.

One of the feats that witches were said to perform was to fly on a broomstick with the aid of a magical ointment, which was made of hallucinogenic herbs and used by rubbing on the body. Although sometimes described as a paste, witches' flying ointment was most often said to consist of a combination of deadly nightshade (belladonna), datura, mandrake, henbane, aconite, and sometimes hemlock. One of the earliest books to document witchcraft and flying ointment was *The Book of All Forbidden Arts* published in 1456. It was written by German physician Johannes Hartlieb (1410–1468), who did not always practice what he preached as his earlier writing contained instructions on various types of divination, including geomancy (interpreting lines and textures found on the ground), palmistry, and lunar astrology. Forbidden arts, indeed.

Also known as sorcerer's pomade, the reputed base ingredient for witches' flying ointment ranged from bear grease and cats' brains to the fat from murdered children. Some formulas included chimney soot and bat blood to aid in flying at night. In his treatise *An Examen of Witches*, Henry Boguet (c. 1550–1619), a judge in Burgundy, France, and chief prosecutor in several witch trials, noted that after a witch applied flying ointment to her body, she left her home by traveling up the chimney.

Ironically, the clergy were known to dabble in magical practices; however, not all of them managed to stay safely under the Church's radar. Guillaume Edelin (1400–1455), the Prior of St. Germain-en-Laye near Paris, was suspected of sorcery and condemned to death after confessing (under torture) that he had flown with a broomstick. With his botanical and magical interests, Italian scholar Giambattista della Porta managed to run afoul of the Church for experimenting with flying ointment. His aim was to unlock the secrets of nature so he could understand the ointment's actual effects. In the end, della Porta got away with just a slap on the wrist: he had to disband his scientific society, *Academia Secretorum Naturae*, and his writings were suppressed for a time.

Accusations that henbane was used in spells to bewitch people was a theme in the 1538 witch trials in Pomerania, Germany. The plant was also administered to the accused to extract confessions. Along with physical torture, the use of potions and ointments for extracting confessions of sex with demons and the devil was fairly common pretrial practice. Throughout Germany, thorn apple (a type of datura) was said to be an important ingredient in a witches' salve that reputedly produced erotic sensations, vivid dreams, and hallucinations. In addition, wormwood was believed to be employed when making a pact with the devil.

Witches were also said to grow mandrake to further their vile deeds. Reputedly, it was best when harvested from beneath gallows because the evilness of criminals hanged upon them would be conferred to the plant. Married witches were said to give their husbands a sleeping apple to keep them blissfully unaware of their wives' nocturnal activities. Although honeysuckle was also known as witch-snare and used for protection against witches, it was also believed to be used by them. The plant was rumored to be a favorite of witches in Scotland and parts of Germany. During the Great Scottish Witch Hunt of 1597, which was the second of five such nationwide efforts, Janet Stewart (d. 1597) stood trial for using a healing wreath of honeysuckle. Such a wreath was used by passing it over the patient's head, and then down around the body to remove disease. Londoner Joan Peterson (d. 1652), who became known as the Witch of Wapping, was another herbalist and healer accused and hanged because of her chosen work.

While the witch craze was dying down in Europe, the United States had its most famous one, the Salem Witch Trials of 1692. Although a number of factors were involved, many historians believe the hysteria and strange behavior that occurred was caused by an ergot infestation. Ergot is a fungus that grows mainly on rye. During the Middle Ages it caused severe epidemics in Europe that killed thousands of people. In contrast, the outbreak in Massachusetts would be considered mild and illustrates Paracelsus's theory. It's all in the dose.

Indigenous Healers and Shamans

Far from the power plays and intrigues of Europe, Indigenous peoples went about their business. Like their European counterparts, the medicine men and women and shamans used poisonous plants in their healing work. These plants were also used in a variety of ceremonies. Eventually, like other traditional healers, Indigenous practitioners in the New World were demonized by the Europeans who usurped their lands.

In the early seventeenth century, the Mexican Inquisition was an extension of the one in Spain; however, rather than focus on rooting out heresy, its aim was to completely stamp out Indigenous spiritual and ceremonial practices. The use of substances such as peyote were targeted and condemned. Although Franciscan friar Bernardino de Sahagún (c. 1499–1590) was sent to collect information about the Aztec and other peoples to aid in converting them to Christianity, his work became a valuable record of the various Mesoamerican cultures and customs.

The word *shaman* comes from the Tungus language of Siberia and northern China and was previously used to describe certain healers in Siberia and Mongolia, but it has since been applied to practitioners worldwide. While a medicine man or woman uses traditional healing methods to cure disease and illness, a shaman communicates with and enters the spirit world to mediate with supernatural powers for a cure that also heals a patient's soul. The soul of the Siberian shaman is said to leave the body and travel to an upper world in the sky or a lower world underground to work with spirit helpers. This is sometimes referred to as shamanic flight. While shamanistic practices vary greatly in the Americas, spirit helpers are said to communicate with a shaman while they are in a trance.

Healers and shamans use psychoactive plants to produce a trance state for various ceremonies and to attend the sick. The fly agaric mushroom that was said to be an ingredient in European witches' flying ointment was also used by

Siberian shamans. Burning and inhaling the smoke from the marsh rosemary was another aid for achieving a trance state.

In addition to peyote, the Aztec, Maya, Olmec, and Zapotec used turbina vine, a cousin to morning glory. The Maya drank a ceremonial beverage called balché, which was a mixture of honey and peyote. The Olmec used datura, tobacco, and water lily in ceremonies. The early indigenous tobacco crops had a much higher nicotine content than today's plants. The Pima of Mexico and the Yuman of the American Southwest used it in rituals to induce hallucinations and work with spirit helpers.

Aztec priests communicated with the gods using a hallucinogenic psilocybin mushroom, which they called *teonanácatl*, meaning "flesh of the gods."[7] The Maya used mushroom stones in some rituals. Carved from rocks, these were figurines of humans or animals with a mushroomlike cap on their heads.

Throughout Amazonian and Andean cultures, coca was considered sacred and had ritual significance. It is the source of the drug cocaine. Coca should not be confused with cacao, which is used to make chocolate; however, the Maya, Aztec, and Olmec also regarded cacao as a sacred plant and used it in ritual, too. It was sometimes mixed with hallucinogenic mushrooms.

Known as the flower prince, Xochipilli was the Aztec god of music, summer, flowers, and psychoactive plants. He was usually depicted with turbina vine, tobacco, datura, and psilocybin mushrooms around him. The smoke of broom flowers was used by the Yaqui shamans of northwest Mexico to aid in achieving an altered state. In North America, various species of datura were used by the Apache and Hopi for ceremonial medicine and to induce visions. The narcotic nature of the sweet flag rhizome was used ceremonially by the Pawnee and Winnebago; the Cheyenne also used it in sweat lodges. On the other side of the world in Southeast Asia, sweet flag was used by the Dusun shamans on the island of Borneo.

While poisonous plants have had a place in healing arts and religious ceremonies, their baneful nature ensured their place as a weapon of war. In the next chapter we will see how their use for political assassination and common everyday murder became widespread.

7. Lawrence, *The Magic of Mushrooms*, 13.

CHAPTER 3

Murder Most Foul

It is well known that poison was used in ancient Greece for capital punishment usually by allowing the accused to take his own life and often with friends present. Although not a pleasant way to go, it was perhaps a little kinder and less violent than being hanged, guillotined, or drawn and quartered. Of course, the death of philosopher Socrates (469–399 BCE) with a cup of hemlock is the most famous case of judicial poisoning. He was guilty of the amorphous social charge of impiety for refusing to acknowledge Athens's deities and for corrupting the city's youth by encouraging them to question their elders. The *Phaedo* is an account of Socrates's last days written by his student Plato (c. 428–347 BCE).

Socrates wasn't the only prominent person executed with hemlock. After making too many controversial moves to suspend traditional institutions, Athenian politician and general in the Peloponnesian War, Theramenes (c. 455–404/403 BCE), was compelled to drink it. The statesman Phocion (c. 402–318 BCE) was caught between the proverbial rock and hard place during Macedon's control of Athens. After being convicted of treason, he was also given the bitter chalice.

The idea of execution by poison did not originate with the Greeks; they picked it up from the Egyptians, who had a long history of using toxic plants. The first pharaoh of a unified Egypt, Menes (fl. c. 3000 or 3100 BCE), is reported to have cultivated and studied the properties of poisonous plants. In addition, the Ebers Papyrus reveals that the Egyptians knew how to refine poisons. For example, they knew how to extract cyanide from peach kernels, which was used in a trial by ordeal known as the Penalty of the Peach. Seeming more like peach roulette, the accused was forced to consume the cyanide; death indicated guilt, and survival, innocence.

If You Can't Beat 'Em, Poison 'Em

Roman rivalries were often intense and assassination with poison became a common method for settling differences or getting ahead, especially in politics. While a few sources indicate that Roman Emperor Claudius I (10 BCE–54 CE) was murdered with a dose of aconite from monkshood, most others note that it was mushrooms. All agree that his fourth wife and niece, Julia Agrippina (15–59 CE), had a hand in expediting a regime change to advance her son Nero (37–68 CE), who was from a previous marriage. Agrippina was also suspected of hiring the professional assassin Locusta of Gaul (d. 69 CE) to carry out the deed. As the saying goes, the apple doesn't fall far from the tree, and the following year Emperor Nero made sure that he didn't have any competition to his rulership from his stepbrother Britannicus (41–55), the son of Claudius from a previous marriage. The event took place at a banquet and possibly with aconite in water used to cool a beverage that was served too hot for Britannicus to drink, and thus cleverly circumventing the food tasters.

Although the frequent spread of illnesses caused by virus or bacteria may have fanned the fear of mass poisoning, murder with poison was a widespread problem throughout the Roman Empire. The crime of poisoning was called Veneficium, and the practitioners Veneficus or Venefica.[8] These names also implied that a person could be a sorcerer or sorceress. With murder and poisonings on the rise, general and statesman Lucius Cornelius Sulla (136–78 BCE) issued a set of laws, the Lex Cornelia, which included a ban on such practices. Unfortunately, the law didn't seem to be effective. Aconite continued to be so common in murder and suicide that Roman poet Ovid (43 BCE–17 CE) called it mother-in-law's poison.[9] The use of aconite got so out of hand that Emperor Trajan (53–117 CE) outlawed its cultivation. Whether or not the number of deaths by aconite were reduced didn't matter; poisoners had many other easy-to-obtain choices in their arsenals such as autumn crocus, hellebore, white hellebore, hemlock, henbane, mandrake, opium poppy, and yew. Emperors Caligula (12–41 CE) and Caracalla (188–217 CE) stockpiled their own poisonous plant collections, just in case a political or personal assassination became

8. Ando and Rüpke, *Religion and Law in Classical and Christian Rome*, 49.

9. Hayes and Kobets, *Hayes' Principles and Methods of Toxicology*, 11.

necessary. Amidst the flourishing poison trade, Roman entrepreneurs also capitalized on the market by offering ready-to-use antidotes.

With motherly interest, Egyptian queen Cleopatra (69–30 BCE) reputedly poisoned her coruler and younger brother Ptolemy XIV (c. 59–44 BCE), using aconite to put her son on the throne. Despite a romanticized story about her committing suicide with the help of an asp over the death of Roman general Mark Antony (83–30 BCE), more recent theories suggest that it was a political assassination—sans the serpent. Cleopatra is thought to have been too strong-willed and savvy to throw away her queenship over a lover, especially one who had become a liability. Plus, Roman emperor Octavian (63 BCE–14 CE) could have easily done her in with the commonly used mixture of aconite, hemlock, and opium.[10]

Antidotes and Assassinations

Assassination with poison, as well as the fear of it, was also common in India. The *Arthashastra*, a Sanskrit text on statecraft, is attributed to the scholar and royal advisor Chanakya (c. 350–283 BCE) and includes information on how to detect poisons for protection. Chanakya reputedly aided in the establishment of the Mauryan Empire, the first pan-Indian empire, where *visha kanyas* (poison maidens) carried out political assassinations.[11]

Mithridates VI (135–63 BCE) the ruler of Pontus, a small kingdom on the Black Sea in what is now northeastern Turkey, was paranoid about being poisoned, and rightfully so. When he was a boy, his father had been poisoned either by enemies or possibly by his mother, who was believed to have done away with several relatives who could claim the throne. Perhaps more importantly, Mithridates believed that his mother was going to poison him so she could become ruler rather than regent. As a young man, he secretly experimented with poisons and antidotes on himself and, later, on condemned criminals. Over the years, he amassed an impressive medical and botanical library and regularly corresponded with physicians in Egypt.

Ingesting small amounts to become immune, Mithridates later created an antidote with a long list of ingredients that he took each day prior to downing

10. Tsoucalas and Sgantzos, "The Death of Cleopatra," *History of Toxicology*, 19.

11. McCrery, *Silent Witnesses*, 181.

a dose of poison. He continued to study toxicology not only to avert his own assassination but to know which poisons would be most effective and undetectable to use against his enemies. He also kept a bit of poison at hand for suicide in case the unthinkable became necessary. It did. He provoked the ire of Rome by usurping some of its territory, which led to confrontations. The Mithridatic Wars came to an end after his defeat by General Pompey, Gnaeus Pompeius (106–48 BCE). Because Mithridates had become immune to poison, he was unable to commit suicide and ordered a mercenary soldier to end his life.

The practice of combining poisons with antidotes became common in Europe where so-called medicines known as Mithridatium were available for purchase. From Charlemagne to King Henry VIII (1491–1547) and his daughter Queen Elizabeth I (1533–1603), many monarchs and political leaders took some form of Mithridatium mixture. Belief in its potency and wide-ranging effects was so strong that English physician John Gerard recommended it to counteract the plague.

Greek physician and poet Nicander of Colophon (185–136 BCE) is famous for the *Theriaca* and *Alexipharmaca*, two pharmacological poems about poisons and their antidotes, which were later combined into one text. His work contains information on poisons from venomous animals, minerals, and plants, including opium, henbane, poisonous fungi, autumn crocus, aconite, and hemlock, as well as their antidotes. Nicander categorized the poisons according to those that killed quickly and those that did so slowly. Based on the idea of the Mithridatium, Greco-Roman physician Galen further developed Nicander's theriaca into a universal antidote that had about seventy-five ingredients. Over time, the word *theriaca* was used to indicate an antidote against all types of poisons. The mixtures were so widely used that ornate vases and canisters, usually inscribed with the word *Theriaca*, became popular household items.

Emperor Nero had his physician Andromachus (fl. first century CE) improve on the theriaca by adding squill, opium, and other ingredients. Mixed with honey to make it sweet and thick, it became known as Theriaca Andromachi and reputedly contained about seventy ingredients. Centuries later in England, it was known as Venice Treacle and used as an all-purpose medicine until the early eighteenth century. Even though she had cleared his pathway to power, Nero's mother reputedly took antidotes regularly in case her son decided that she was no longer useful.

In Italy, assassination by poison was raised to a fine art and professional practitioners were hired throughout Europe. According to Elizabethan poet and playwright Thomas Nashe (1567–c. 1601), Italy was the "apothecary-shop of poison for all nations."[12] From the fourteenth through eighteenth centuries, the Council of Ten, a governing body in the city-state of Venice, was tasked with upholding security and averting threats against the state. Dispatching political adversaries with poison was one of their frequently used tactics. Poisoning was also a lucrative business and so common that it spawned a thriving cottage industry of protective amulets and antidotes. Arsenic, a semimetal or metalloid, was the preferred poison for generations of the prominent and infamous Borgias family, who was originally from Spain but established themselves in Italy. However, the Borgias were known to have dabbled in hemlock, monkshood, henbane, yew, and opium poppy from time to time. Dining with them was risky business.

One of the volumes in della Porta's *Natural Magick* included methods and recipes for poisoning. He noted that adding poison—usually a solution of deadly nightshade, strychnine, aconite, and hellebore—to wine was the easiest way to administer it. Della Porta also included a potion called *Venenum Lupinum* (also spelled *Veninum Lupinum*), which translates to "wolf poison," but it was not intended for four-legged creatures. It was a strong solution made of yew, caustic lime, arsenic, bitter almonds, and powdered glass, mixed into a paste with honey so it could be rolled into pill form. One had to be very serious and determined about murder to consider using Venenum Lupinum.

Jewish philosopher and physician Moses Maimonides (1135–1204) compiled a treatise on poisons (botanical and animal) along with their antidotes. His work was translated into Latin in 1305 and other European languages in subsequent centuries. Maimonides noted that the simplest method to poison someone was to add it to a highly spiced dish or, as della Porta had suggested, in a glass of wine.

Italian physician and scholar Pietro d'Abano (1257–1316) was one of many influenced by the newly translated Arabic botanical and medical texts. Classifying poisons as animal, mineral, or vegetable, he noted that they could be absorbed through the skin or from the air. The poisonous plants he grew in his garden

12. Nashe, *The Works of Thomas Nashe*, 186.

included bryony, colocynth, cherry laurel, fool's parsley, hellebore, and strychnine. Already in trouble with the Church, he defiantly protested by drawing astrological symbols on the Padua city hall, which didn't endear him to local authorities. D'Abano was put on trial twice but died in custody before sentencing.

Everyone Was Doing It

Catherine de Medici is credited—or discredited as the case may be—with having introduced Italian methods of poisoning into France. The term *Florentine malady* became a moniker for it. Deemed appropriate for the king's second son, Catherine was bundled off to France at the age of fourteen. Three years later, she and her husband were bumped up to top rung on the ladder of succession after the eldest son, as believed by many, was bumped off with poison. Catherine and her husband had the most to gain from the death. Nevertheless, although Sebastiano de Montecuccoli (d. 1536) had been a faithful servant to the prince since his arrival in France as part of the entourage that accompanied Catherine, he became the prime suspect. One reason: he was Italian. Another: a book of toxicology had been found amongst his possessions. He was executed by being drawn and quartered.

It wasn't until Catherine became the extremely powerful Queen Mother during three of her sons' reigns that her bad rep was established by employing perfumer and fellow Florentine René Bianchi (d. 1578). Also known as Maître René, he was legendary and somewhat feared for his powders and potions and readily supplied Catherine with poisoned gloves, rouge, and other fancy, seemingly innocent accouterments. Bianchi also supplied her with a scented apple that she gave as a gift to Huguenot leader Henri I de Bourbon, Prince of Condé (1552–1588). Suspicious of the present, a small piece was given to a dog that promptly dropped dead. Almost a century later, after priests at Notre Dame reported a shocking number of confessions to murder by poison, King Louis XIV (1638–1715) forbid apothecaries to sell arsenic, or anything reputedly poisonous, to any person unknown to them.

Of course, laws and decrees even from a king didn't shut down the sale of poisons. Known as La Voisin, Catherine Deshayes (c. 1638–1680) started out as a fortune teller in Paris but found that peddling aphrodisiacs and potions to attract a lover—or kill one—was a far more profitable business. Most of her clients were upper-class women who often wanted to dispose of a husband or a rival. In a scandalous criminal case known as the Affair of the Poisons, Deshayes and several prominent people were implicated, including the king's mistress. While many people were imprisoned, Deshayes was convicted and publicly burned at the stake for witchcraft; always an effective accusation when nothing else would stick.

In Naples, La Toffana or Madame Giulia Toffana (1653–1723) became notorious for her potion Aqua Toffana, also known as Aqueta, which was prepared with arsenic and belladonna. Toffana claimed it was made with a sacred liquid exuded from the tomb of St. Nicholas of Bari (270–343), who was associated with miracles and much later with the story of Santa Claus. Sent to buyers throughout Italy, the potion is said to have killed hundreds. When the authorities were too close and hot on her trail, Toffana would retreat into nunneries to hide and prop up a façade of holiness. She couldn't run forever and was eventually found and executed.

By the eighteenth century, strychnine was so widely used that it became known as Inheritance Powder. In England, the Lambeth Poisoner, Thomas Griffiths Wainwright (1794–1847), employed it to speed up the inheritance process as well as for insurance fraud to profit from the death of his in-laws. Fond of large rings, he found jewelry a convenient way to carry and dispense strychnine crystals. Wainwright had been a successful artist, moving in the same social circles as poet and painter William Blake (1757–1827) and Charles Dickens (1812–1870). He ended up as a prisoner and was shipped off to Tasmania. Obviously, his crimes didn't pay.

While poisonous plants are helpful for dispatching people, sometimes disruption is enough to achieve a goal. Approximately 590 BCE, Athens and several other city-states declared war on the city of Cirrha or Kirrha, which served as a harbor for Delphi. Not only had the Cirraeans harassed pilgrims on their way to Apollo's famous temple and oracle, but they had also appropriated some of the sanctuary's land. During the siege of the city, the water in the aqueduct from the Pleistos River was poisoned with hellebore roots. The violent purgative action weakened the Cirraeans and their ability to defend the city.

Another example of mayhem caused by a plant occurred accidentally in the American colonies with the unwitting use of the thorn apple species of datura. Experiences with this plant have been said to border on madness. One of its common names, jimsonweed, evolved from Jamestown weed in reference to an incident in 1676 at Jamestown, Virginia.[13] British soldiers were sent to put down Bacon's Rebellion, the first popular uprising against English rule. After unwittingly ingesting thorn apple in their food, a troop of British soldiers ran amuck in a wild state of delirium and confusion.

Knowledge of poisonous plants was widespread and so was their use in stories from ancient times to the present, and not just in cozy murder mysteries. The next chapter provides a survey of the poisonous plant as literary device as well as garden feature.

---

13. Dobelis, *Magic and Medicine of Plants*, 226.

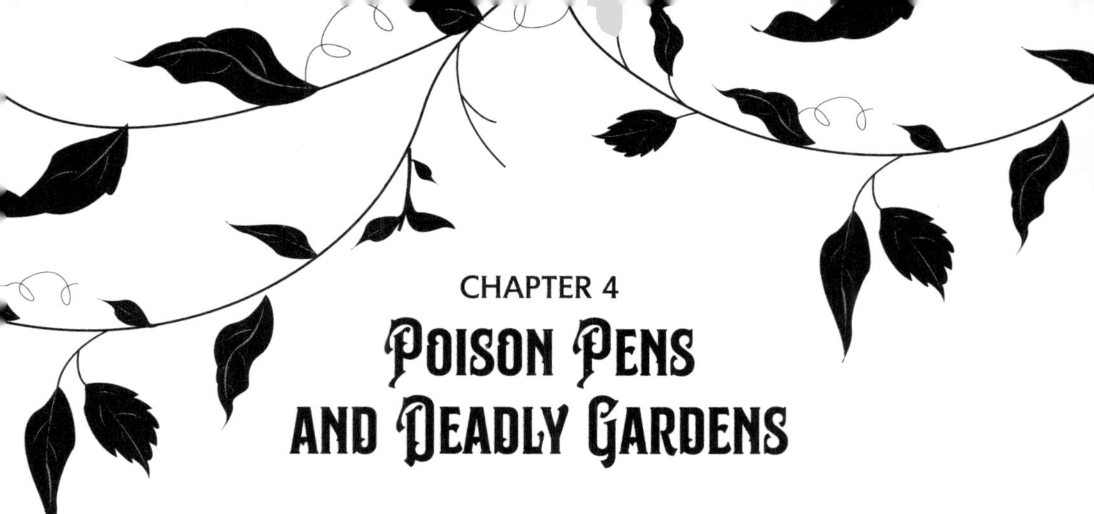

CHAPTER 4
Poison Pens and Deadly Gardens

The use of poisonous plants may be stock-in-trade in certain genres of modern fiction, but they have been cropping up, so to speak, in literature since ancient times. Deadly plants not only populate the pages of fiction, but they also occupy garden space. Sometimes they are grown intentionally and sometimes not. Do you know if there's something deadly lurking in your garden?

Poison, She Wrote

Many of us enjoy a good whodunit murder mystery, and the undisputed queen of the genre is English author Agatha Christie (1890–1976), who wrote sixty-six novels as well as short stories and plays. In over twenty of her books, the villains used poisonous plants to do away with their adversaries. Having worked as a nurse during the First World War and then as an apothecary's assistant in a hospital dispensary, Christie knew a thing or two about kill-or-cure doses of poison.

Some of Christie's deadly toxins are well known and come from a range of plants such as aconite from monkshood, which she used in her books *They Do It with Mirrors* and *4.50 from Paddington*, atropine from deadly nightshade in *The Big Four* and *The Caribbean Mystery*, datura from thorn apple in *The Cretan Bull* and *Sleeping Murder*, and ricin from the castor oil plant in *The House of Lurking Death*. She used digoxin from foxglove in *Crooked House*, hyoscyamine from henbane in *A Pocketful of Rye*, and morphine from the opium poppy appeared in *Hickory, Dickory, Dock*. Other poisons that Christie served up as devices for murder include taxine from the yew tree in *A Pocketful of Rye*, nicotine from tobacco in *Three Act Trilogy*, and gelsemine from yellow jessamine in *The Big Four*. Cyanide from the seeds of trees in the *Prunus* genus (such as plums, peaches, cherries) appeared in *The Mirror Crack'd from Side to Side*. While some of these substances require extremely large doses to be effective toxins, Miss Marple and Hercule Poirot understood what it would take to kill.

Sherlock Holmes and his sidekick, Dr. Watson, had their share of adventures with poisonous plants such as opium poppy, deadly nightshade, monkshood, and strychnine. Plus, Holmes was an avid user of cocaine, giving him an edge in understanding how toxins work. In the late nineteenth century, Austrian founder of psychoanalysis Sigmund Freud (1855–1939) helped make the use of cocaine fashionable.

Like many writers, Arthur Conan Doyle (1859–1930) took the occasional literary license with facts. In one Sherlock Holmes story, *The Adventure of the Devil's Foot*, Doyle used the fictious botanical name of *radix pedis diaboli* for the killer plant devil's foot. The symptoms described in the story caused speculation amongst readers that Doyle based his fictional devil's foot on Indian aconite and its dried roots or yellow jessamine, which the author experimented with as a medical student. In addition to his novels, Doyle was a successful physician, and during his schooling in Edinburgh, he took a course at the Royal Botanic Garden. Until the 1960s, medical students at the University of Edinburgh were required to study botany.

Set in twelfth-century Shrewsbury, England, the *Cadfael Chronicles* is a series of twenty books by British author Edith Pargeter (1913–1995) written under her pen name Ellis Peters. Benedictine Brother Cadfael is the hero and sleuth who, in one story, uncovers a poisoning by ... you guessed it, monkshood. In more recent novels by other authors, poisons are obtained from hemlock, deadly nightshade, and devil's trumpet, which is a close cousin to thorn apple.

The murder mystery isn't the only genre in which killers employ poisonous plants, nor is it a modern theme. This type of dirty work can be found throughout the work of William Shakespeare (1564–1616). Although he did not provide specific botanical details about the plants that appeared in his work, over the years, researchers have made comparisons with contemporary medical books, such as Gerard's *Herball*, and have found some clues and potential answers to the identity of various plants. For example, Hamlet's father was poisoned through the ear with the cursed hebenon (act 1, scene 5), which is believed to refer to henbane because of the close spelling. In sixteenth-century France, it was hannebane. However, the yew tree has also been a contender for killing Hamlet's father because it was called hebon and heben during Shakespeare's time and its poisonous nature was well known.[14] Although it may seem odd to try to poison someone in the manner Shakespeare suggested, in England at the time it was believed that healing remedies placed in the ear would be disseminated to other parts of the body and, thus, so would poison.

For inducing sleep and death, mandragora (mandrake) is mentioned by the character Iago in *Othello* (act 3, scene 3) and by Cleopatra in *Antony and Cleopatra* (act 1, scene 5). In *Romeo and Juliet* (act 4, scene 2), Juliet takes a potion containing deadly nightshade to make her appear dead. When Romeo finds her in the following scene, he takes his own life with aconite (monkshood). In *King Lear* (act 4, scene 4), when Cordelia told the doctor that her missing father was insane, she mentioned that he was wearing a crown of hemlock and darnel. The inference is that madness may have occurred if he had eaten some of the darnel. And in that famous scene from *Macbeth* (act 4, scene 1) the witches add "root of hemlock, digged i' the dark" as they stir their cauldron.

Involving intrigue and poison, the story of Fair Rosamund was first published in London as part of a collection of ballads in 1607. But alas, while a poisoning took place, the story was a case of mistaken identity. According to the ballad, Queen Eleanor of Aquitaine (c. 1122–1204) forced Rosamund Clifford (c. 1140–c. 1175/76), the mistress of her husband King Henry II (1133–1189), to choose between suicide by dagger or poison. While in fact Rosamund had been Henry's lover, according to contemporary accounts, she retired to a nunnery at Godstow Abbey near Oxford when their affair ended. Prior to the 1607 ballad, the earliest mention of a Queen Eleanor killing a Rosamund occurred in the fourteenth-century *French Chronicle of London*. However, it is a story about Eleanor of Provence (1223–1291), wife of King Henry III (1207–1272), and his mistress Rosamonde.

Stories about fatal poisonings are thousands of years old. Based on myths about Medea and Jason of Argonaut fame, the play *Medea* by Greek tragedian Euripides (c. 480–c. 406 BCE) tells the story of her revenge on Jason, the husband who jilted her. As a dish best served cold, she presented Jason's new bride with the beautiful gift of a gown and coronet. Jason should have known better than to mess with a goddess-sorceress, and his bride, Glauce, died an agonizing death after donning the tainted apparel. As the daughter of Aeëtes, King of Colchis, Medea's choice of poison was colchicine from the roots of the autumn crocus.

---

14. Grieve, *A Modern Herbal*, 395.

While not a murder story, Greek poet Homer (fl. eighth or ninth century BCE) mentioned the poisonous potions used by the sorceress Circe in *The Odyssey*. During his long voyage home after the Trojan War, the eponymous hero Odysseus stopped at the island of Aeaea where Circe mixed a baneful potion into the food that she served to some of his crew, which turned them into pigs. Luckily, the god Hermes happened to be around and helped Odysseus find a root to counteract the poison. Although mandrake is often associated with Circe, datura is another candidate for the active ingredient in the potion she fed the sailors because of the hallucinations and delirium it produces. The antidote plant known as moly that Hermes helped Odysseus find is the snowdrop, which is poisonous in its own right.

Morpheus, the Greco-Roman god of dreams, is associated with the opium poppy. In one myth, he gave it to Demeter to ease her grief after her daughter Persephone had been abducted to the underworld by Hades. Morpheus could shape, transform, or morph the dreams of mortals by sprinkling poppy seeds on them as they slept. The drug morphine, which is derived from the opium poppy, was named for him.[15] In addition, the Greek and Roman gods of sleep, Hypnos and Somnus, respectively, were usually depicted holding bowls of poppy seedpods.

Morticia's Garden

Part of the ghoulish fun in the 1960s Addams Family television show was Morticia's garden of poisonous plants. She grew hemlock, henbane, poison ivy, roses—for their thorns, not flowers, of course—and Cleo, a fictitious species of African strangler plant.

A real-life poison garden was kept by Attalus III of Pergamon (c. 170–133 BCE) in what is now western Turkey. Attalus was often described as an eccentric king who preferred tending his garden and tinkering with botanical experiments to overseeing the business of his country. According to Greek historian Plutarch (c. 45–120 CE), Attalus cultivated henbane, hellebore, hemlock, aconite, and datura. The legacy of Attalus was the inspiration for Mithridates, the ruler of Pontus.

---

15. Barnhart, *The Barnhart Concise Dictionary of Etymology*, 489.

Although the de Medici family, and Catherine in particular, was rumored to have kept a garden of poisonous plants, I couldn't find evidence of its existence in the past or in modern re-creations of the gardens at their villas in Italy. However, in 1543, Cosimo I de Medici (1519–1574), Grand Duke of Tuscany and cousin of Catherine, funded the establishment of the first botanical garden in the world, which was created by botanist and physician Luca Ghini (1490–1556). De Medici's request to Ghini was that it specialize in medicinal plants, and it most likely contained some poisonous plants. The garden has since been associated with the University of Pisa and moved to a different location. The Padua Botanical Gardens has a special assortment of poisonous plants situated alongside its medicinal plant collection. The garden was established in 1545 by the University of Padua on the grounds of the Benedictine monastery of St. Justinia and occupies its original site.

Located in northeastern England, Alnwick Castle was like many old estates saddled with expensive upkeep and repair. Also, like other estates, its owners the Duke and Duchess of Northumberland created extensive gardens that could be opened to the public as an added source of income. In a stroke of genius, or diabolical cunning, the duchess created and played up a special garden stocked with poisons plants. With about one hundred toxic plants, her Poison Garden is behind a tall iron fence and is only accessible via guided tour. If photographs of the castle seem familiar, you may have seen it as Brancaster Castle in the Downton Abbey films or as Hogwarts in the first two Harry Potter movies.

Inspired by Agatha Christie's crime novels, the Potent Plant Garden at Torre Abbey in Torquay, England, where Christie spent much of her life, was created in her honor. Although the garden is simply marked with Do Not Touch signs, some of the plants are poisonous, but most are benign.

Not all poison gardens have been created for literary or ghoulish delight. Near Cork, Ireland, Blarney Castle—home of the famous blarney stone—has a poison garden. Marked with signs sporting skull and crossbones, its purpose is to teach people about the poisonous plants that can be found in the wild as well as in the home garden. The Montreal Botanical Gardens in Canada has a Toxic Plants Garden that was established in the 1940s. With about forty types of plants, it is located next to the Medicinal Plants Garden but is somewhat hidden behind walls and a fence. At Cornell University in Ithaca, New York, the Weed Science Teaching Garden is home to their poisonous plant collection, which dates back to the early 1950s. Its purpose is to give students and the public an opportunity to learn about and recognize harmful plants.

While you may not have or want the infamous botanical femme fatales in your garden, you may be surprised that some quite ordinary plants rank amongst the venomous vegetation and may be hiding in full view in your garden. First of all, there's the ever-popular daffodil. By late winter and early spring, we are more than ready for sunny yellow flowers; however, daffodil petals are mildly poisonous. They won't kill you if you happen to eat them, but they can cause some unpleasant effects. All parts of the beloved foxglove are deadly toxic. While digoxin from foxglove is used in cardiac medications—carefully processed and in controlled amounts, of course—ingesting the plant can be fatal.

Another sweet garden favorite is lily of the valley. With its delightful scent, who can resist picking a handful? But be careful; its flowers, leaves, berries, and stems are toxic, and ingesting any part of it can be deadly. Rhubarb has made a comeback in the garden and can be found in supermarket produce sections, but only the stalks. The leaves and all other parts of the plant are toxic and can have very unpleasant consequences. Morning glory and its wild cousin bindweed add interest as they wind their way around and over anything in the garden, but all parts of these plants are poisonous and can be fatal if ingested.

While, yes, it is a dangerous world out there, there's no reason to hang up your trowel and call it quits. Afterall, we don't usually plant a flower garden, trees, or shrubs because we plan to eat them. We do what people have done for thousands of years—we teach our children to never pick anything and put it in their mouths. I have delightful childhood memories of playing hide-and-seek under the rhubarb in my grandmother's garden. We were warned that it was only eaten when served at the dining table. And, of course, we keep our pets away from hazardous plants.

What some people find frightening, others find fascinating. However, if you want to enjoy feeling like a lion tamer by keeping a fierce floral specimen under control in your yard, or if the history of particular poisonous plants appeals to your imagination, use common sense and take precautions. Your fascination with them doesn't have to be deadly.

Now we will leave the kingdom of plants for a visit with fungi. The world of mushrooms may seem strange or even alien, and it's every bit as fascinating as the botanicals.

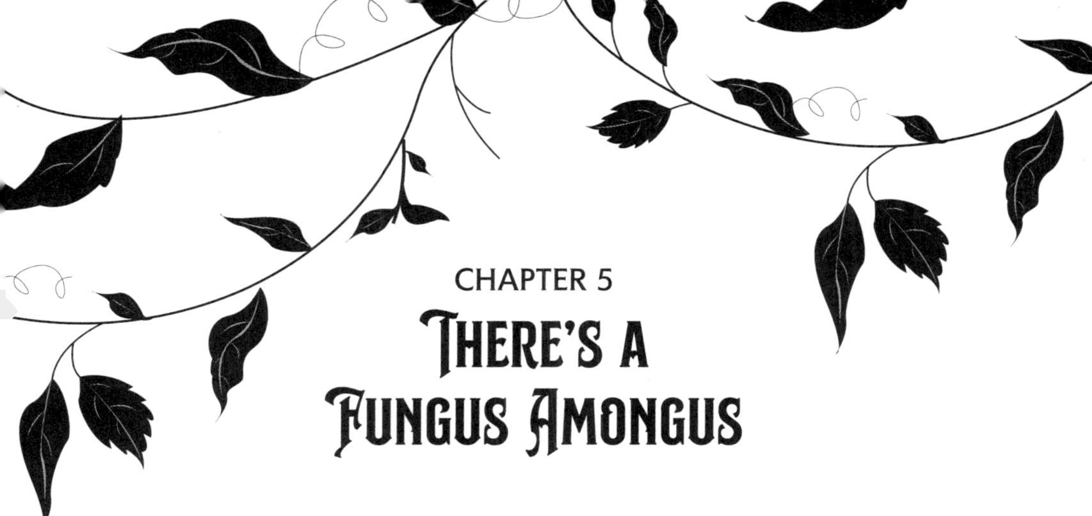

CHAPTER 5

There's a Fungus Amongus

Fungi are fascinating and sometimes frightening because of their weird shapes. However, not all fungi are mushrooms: only ones that have a, well, mushroom- or umbrellalike shape are called mushrooms. Lichen and yeasts are fungi, but they are not mushrooms. Of course, *mushroom* is also a verb.

The study of fungi is called mycology, which was derived from the Greek *mykos*, meaning "fungus," and *logon*, "discourse."[16] The term was coined by clergyman and botanist Miles Berkeley (1803–1889), who is generally regarded as the founder of British mycology. English naturalist Charles Darwin (1809–1882) donated the specimens he collected in Tierra del Fuego to Berkeley. Although his clerical colleagues believed that the Irish potato famine was the devil's doing, Berkeley caused outrage when he proposed that it was caused by a fungus. He was eventually proven right, of course.

In the world of mycology, the mushroom we see aboveground is called the fruiting body. It consists of a cap, gills that are riblike structures arranged radially underneath the cap, and a stem, which is also known as a stalk or stipe. The purpose of the gills is to disperse the spores (seeds). A membrane that covers the entire mushroom until it begins to mature is called the veil. Remnants of the veil are sometimes visible on the stem of some mushrooms. The aboveground fruiting body is a small part of a much larger fungi organism. Mycelia are white, threadlike fibers that carry water and nutrients and create a fine, cottony web throughout the soil. The mycelium grows into the soft root hairs of trees and other plants, creating a symbiotic relationship. Depending on plants for photosynthesis and nourishment, fungi return the favor by supplying nutrients from the soil. They also aid in water uptake for plants. In this

16. Millman, *Fungipedia*, x.

relationship, there is an exchange of carbohydrates for fungi and nitrogen and phosphates for plants. As weird as it may sound, the mycelium also provides a channel for communication via chemical and electrical signals. Suzanne Simard (b. 1960), a Canadian scientist and professor of forest ecology at the University of British Columbia, dubbed the mycelium network the wood-wide web. American mycologist Paul Stamets (b. 1955) called it nature's internet.

Just as plant roots grow and move, mycelium makes its way through the soil to find nutrient sources, plants to partner with, and sometimes to attack other fungi that may be competitors for resources. Most fungi are recyclers that replenish the soil with nutrients; they also sequester carbon into the ground. But it's not all *Mister Rogers' Neighborhood* with fungi. Some are parasitic, such as species from the genus *Ophiostoma* that cause Dutch elm disease and *Armillaria* species that block nutrients from tree roots. Not all these bad boys are completely bad; some parasitical fungi that make holes in trees aid cavity-nesting birds. However, when some mushrooms are bad, they are really bad and turn into cannibals. Yes, cannibals. The lentil shanklet and mushrooms in the *Asterophora* genus feast on decaying *Lactarius* and *Russula* species. Some cannibals change appearance. For example, when the shrimp of the woods parasitizes the honey mushroom, it ends up looking like popcorn or a lumpy irregular blob. This is called its aborted form; the unaborted form, or non-cannibal, looks like a normal mushroom.

Mysterious Origins

In ancient times, mushrooms were regarded as mysterious because they seemed to appear out of nowhere. In many cultures worldwide, mushrooms were associated with storms because they so frequently popped up after rain, lightning, and thunder. In Egypt, mushrooms were regarded as a gift from the storm god Set and therefore a food fit only for the pharaoh and other high-ranking individuals. The Greeks believed mushrooms were created from lightning bolts flung to earth by Zeus.

Roman naturalist Pliny the Elder and others of his time were well aware that mushrooms could be deadly, and Greek physician Hippocrates mentioned accidental poisonings in his writings. However, it was commonly believed that their poisons could be neutralized with a range of substances, including wine, vinegar, chicken manure, honey, cabbage, and nettles, to name a few. Nevertheless, wealthy Romans were especially fond of fungi and served them at feasts. They enjoyed the highly prized boleti—which is now known as the imperial agaric or Caesar's mushroom—and prepared them in special pots called boletaria.[17] Emperor Claudius I's final fungi feast is believed to have included death caps, compliments of his wife.

Pliny also noted that thunder aided the growth of mushrooms. Elsewhere from India to the Bedouin of Arabia, it was believed that thunder, more than rain, brought mushrooms. In the Philippines, fungi gathered after rainstorms were known as thunder mushrooms. Because they seemed to occur most often after storms, in Germanic and Norse areas of Europe, mushrooms were associated with the thunder and storm gods Donar and Thor. Of course, the best day to pick mushrooms was Thursday, Thor's day.

In Yorkshire, England, the vast number of little white meadow mushrooms that grew in fields well fertilized by horses was thought to have sprouted from stallion semen. In some areas of East Asia and India, mushrooms were believed to occur where a dog had urinated.

Toads, Witches, and Fairy Circles

The term *toadstool* has been used to indicate a poisonous mushroom; however, there is no scientific difference between a toadstool and a mushroom. One explanation for the origin of the word *toadstool* is that *toad* is a corruption of the German word *tot* or *todt*, meaning "dead," and *stuhl*, "chair." However, to the English, toadstools, like tadpoles, seemed to magically appear. From Middle English before 1398, they were called tadstoles: *tadde*, meaning "toad," and *stole*, "stool," which evolved into tode stole.[18] A pejorative since at least Shakespeare's time, to call someone a toad meant they were ugly.

Mushrooms in general and toadstools in particular had a negative reputation because they live in dark, dank places and often amongst decay. Of course, many types of fungi are recyclers and it's their job to break down a once-living organism and return it to earth. In *Alexipharmaca*, one of two pharmacological poems about poisons and their antidotes, Greek physician and poet Nicander called poisonous mushrooms the "evil ferment of the earth" and noted

17. Kiple and Ornelas, *The Cambridge World History of Food*, 316.

18. Barnhart, *The Barnhart Concise Dictionary of Etymology*, 818.

that vinegar was an antidote for them.[19] In Wales, poisonous mushrooms were called *bwyd ellyllon*, meaning "meat of the goblins."[20]

As scapegoats for anything bad, witches were said to cause evil mushrooms to grow. Witches were also believed responsible for their shape, which was regarded as obscene by good Christians. In Austria and Germany, fly agaric was known as *hexenpils*, "witches' mushroom," and said to be an ingredient in their famous flying ointment. During the inquisition in France, puffballs were associated with the dark arts because they release their spores in what looks like a brown puff of smoke. In Germany, puffballs were said to grow where witches danced at night. Up until the 1930s in Germany and Denmark, it was believed that the spores from puffballs could cause blindness.

Mushroom folklore flourished everywhere. During the nineteenth century in France, a person who found a lot of morel mushrooms was suspected of frequent lying. In Germany, France, and Italy, a sudden plethora of mushrooms was a warning of a rise in child mortality or other negative events. It was quite the opposite in China for the lingzhi or reishi mushroom. Regarded as the mushroom of immortality, it was used as a talisman and hung above home entrances to ward off evil spirits.

Mushrooms and fairies seem to go hand in hand, especially when the fungi appear to be intentionally placed in a circle. Over one hundred species form rings, but the most common is the fairy ring champignon. In England, fairy rings were said to mark a place where the fae danced in the moonlight. According to some stories, running around a fairy ring on the first night of a full moon makes the subterranean revels of fairies and elves audible. In Shakespeare's play *The Tempest* (act 5, scene 1), Prospero notes that a pastime of elves is to make midnight mushrooms. In many stories, mushrooms were noted as small seats or tables for the wee folk. In Scandinavia, mushroom rings are known as elfdans and said to be caused by dancing elves. On the Isle of Man, they indicated the location of an underground fairy village.

There was a darker side to fairy circles, at least so legends go. In the Netherlands, rings of white mushrooms were said to mark where milk had spilled from the devil's milk churn. Called *hexenringe*, "witches' ring," in Germany,

---

19. Blyth, *Poisons, Their Effects and Detection*, 4.

20. Folkard, *Plant Lore, Legends, and Lyrics*, 451.

they were believed to have been created by witchcraft. The circles were also said to mark where witches had danced. In Scots Gaelic, the word for mushroom, *bocán*, also means "hobgoblin" or "sprite."[21]

The Elephant in the Room

Or more to the point, the penis in the room, because there's no ignoring the fact that many mushrooms at some point in their development have a very phallic shape. None more so than the stinkhorn, which was named for its strong, feces-like smell. Although given its odor, it's hard to believe that in some parts of Europe the stinkhorn was regarded as an aphrodisiac; however, in other areas, it was attributed to a witch's curse. During its early ovoid form of growth, it was known as a witch egg. In parts of Germany, this mushroom was thought to grow where a stag had rutted.

The father of modern taxonomy, Carl Linnaeus, didn't mince words when he named the genus and gave the common stinkhorn the scientific name of *Phallus impudicus*, which translates as "shamelessly phallic." It has a thick white stem with a dark cap that is slightly bell-shaped, close fitting, and covered with a sticky gel-like substance. Sixteenth-century English herbalist John Gerard noted it as "*fungus virilis penis effigie*" and "the pricke mushrome."[22] According to family lore, Charles Darwin's daughter Henrietta Darwin Litchfield (1843–1927) ran a one-woman campaign to rid their property of stinkhorns. She collected and burned them as soon as they appeared lest curious children ask awkward questions or excitable servants become distracted from their work. American naturalist and poet Henry David Thoreau (1817–1862) noted in his journal: "Pray what was nature thinking of when she made this? She almost puts herself on a level with those who draw in privies."[23]

Go Ask Alice

Mushrooms are scattered throughout fairy tales, and a very memorable one is the seat for a hookah-smoking caterpillar who gives advice to Alice. He tells her that eating from one side of his mushroom would make her tall, but partaking of the other side would make her small. Better known as Lewis Carroll,

---

21. Mac Coitir, *Ireland's Wild Plants*, 293.

22. Gerard, *The Herball*, 1582.

23. Thoreau, *I to Myself*, 287.

English author Charles Dodgson (1832–1898) may have gotten his inspiration from the book *The Seven Sisters of Sleep*. The fly agaric mushroom is included in the book as one of the sisters. Written by English botanist and mycologist Mordecai Cubitt Cooke (1825–1914), who was interested in psychoactive and narcotic plants, the book is still in print and considered a psychedelic classic. Cooke has been referred to as a Victorian hippy.

Shamans worldwide have been using hallucinogenic plants and mushrooms for hundreds, if not thousands of years. American author and former banker R. Gordon Wasson (1898–1986) and his wife, Valentina Pavlovna Guercken Wasson (1901–1958), let the genie out of the bottle and brought psychoactive mushrooms to world attention in 1957 with articles in *Life* and *This Week* magazines, respectively. A Russian scientist and physician, Tina stoked her husband's interest in mushrooms while they were on honeymoon. Several years later, Gordon and a friend visited the Mazatec people of Oaxaca, Mexico, and are believed to have been the first non-Indigenous people to experience the effects of *Psilocybe* mushrooms used in traditional rituals.

The Wassons were instrumental in the new discipline of ethnomycology, which is a blend of ethnography and mycology that explores the folklore, beliefs, and use of fungi by different cultures. The Wassons, and especially Tina, set the stage for clinical psychologist Timothy Leary (1920–1996) and his Psilocybin Project at Harvard University in the early 1960s where he experimented with mushrooms and LSD. Tina had suggested the therapeutic use of psilocybin mushrooms in her article, which was as controversial as Leary's work at the time. Today psilocybin is used in certain mental health treatments and is being further researched.

Inspired by Fungi

Fungi's place in the arts could fill several volumes and is beyond the scope of this book, but I would be remiss to not mention a few classic examples. First there's French novelist Jules Verne (1828–1905) in whose 1864 book, *Journey to the Center of the Earth*, has a group of ardent explorers to inner earth encountering a forest of giant mushrooms. In the 1898 short story "The Purple Pileus" by English writer H. G. Wells (1866–1947), an unassuming shopkeeper who is struggling in his business and marriage improves his life with the help of magic mushrooms. The 1914 novel *The Mystery of the Poisoned Dish of Mushrooms* by

English author Ernest Bramah (1868–1942) features a fictional mushroom with the scientific name *Amanita bhuroides* that could kill within half an hour of consuming. At the time, Bramah's character, detective Max Carrados, was as popular as Sherlock Holmes. Fatal fungi have shown up in murder mystery novels ever since.

In the Victorian sentimental fantasy world of fairies and idealized children, mushrooms were an integral part of the enchanting spectacle and appear throughout the genre of fairy paintings. Best known for Peter Rabbit, the beloved English author and illustrator Beatrix Potter (1866–1940) was also a naturalist and mycologist. She produced over 350 illustrations of fungi that are every bit as beguiling as Flopsy, Mopsy, and Cottontail, and of course, scientifically accurate.

In the highly detailed surreal worlds depicted by Dutch painter Hieronymus Bosch (c. 1450–1516), some of his subjects appear to be under the psychoactive influence of fungi. Throughout the Renaissance, mushrooms appear in landscapes and still lifes. The 1662 *Still Life with Insects and Amphibians* by Dutch painter Otto Marseus van Schrieck (1613–1678) presents a dark scene with mushrooms amongst snakes, a toad, and a dead tulip. It's a picture Morticia would appreciate.

PART 2
Classic Killers

Many of the following plants could easily fit under the next section, Baneful Backyard, because they are grown (and many adored) as garden ornamentals. But the ones featured in this section are the notorious poisons that were used by people throughout the ancient world. While it's common knowledge that the Greeks used hemlock to poison philosopher Socrates as judicial punishment, the Romans' use of aconite to execute criminals is less known. Harry Potter fans may know some of the folklore about screaming mandrake, but medieval Arab herbalists had their own take on this peculiar attribute. Let's journey to the past to see how datura was one of the most important ceremonial plants in South America and how hellebore was a popular murder weapon from ancient Rome to medieval England.

Aconite

THE QUEEN OF POISONS

Monkshood (*Aconitum napellus*); also known as Adam and Eve, bear's-foot, blue rocket, cuckoo's cap, friar's cap, helmetflower, mousebane, wolf root, wolfsbane

Wolfsbane (*A. lycoctonum*); also known as badger's bane, monkshood, northern wolfsbane, white-bane, yellow monkshood, yellow wolfsbane

Botanical Family: Ranunculaceae / Buttercup

These plants are known for their distinctive elongated flowers that grow in clusters atop graceful stems. The leaves of both plants are deeply lobed and their flowering spires range from two to six feet tall. Wolfsbane flowers are yellow or whitish yellow, but sometimes purple, and its leaves are light green. Monkshood flowers are dark blue-violet and its leaves are dark green with a feathery appearance. These botanical cousins cause a lot of confusion because they look so similar and their names have been used interchangeably for centuries. Monkshood is native to central and western Europe; wolfsbane to much of Europe and northern Asia.

Toxicity and Cautions

All parts of these plants are extremely toxic, especially the roots, seeds, and pre-flowering leaves. They contain aconitine, one of the deadliest plant poisons, and other related alkaloids that are potent cardiotoxins and neurotoxins. Ingestion can cause confusion, nausea, vomiting, hallucinations, and heart palpitations. Aconitine can slow or increase the heart rate, cause shortness of breath and death from cardiac or respiratory failure. Even a small amount can be fatal. Toxins can be absorbed through contact with broken skin when handling the plant. Accidental poisonings have occurred when the root has been mistaken for wild horseradish (*Armoracia rusticana*).

History and Lore

During the Middle Ages, these plants acquired the name *monkshood* because the shape of the flower resembled the head covering worn by monastics. The genus name, *Aconitum*, is thought to have been derived from the Greek *akos*, meaning "dart," referring to its use as arrow poison.[24] Originating in ancient China, the practice of poisoning arrows with aconite spread to India and eventually to Europe.

Greek scholar and the Father of Botany, Theophrastus used the name *akoniton* as a general term for poisonous plants. In Latin, *aconitum* also meant "a poisonous plant."[25] According to Greek historian Theopompus of Chios (d. 320 BCE), the plant was named for Aconae, a ridge on the Heraclea Pontica in present-day Turkey, where the plant grew in great abundance. Same location, but the legend about its origin is more colorful. According to Greco-Roman myth, aconite sprouted from the spittle of Cerberus, the triple-headed hound of hell, when Hercules dragged him out of the underworld at Heraclea Pontica. Reputedly, this also accounted for the plant's toxicity.

The Greeks used aconite for medical euthanasia; the Romans, to execute criminals. Both used it medicinally as an anesthetic. Pliny the Elder noted that when taken in warm wine, aconite could cure scorpion stings. Although it was known to have the power to kill, for centuries it was believed that when aconite was exposed to another poison, they would cancel each other out, making it useful as an antidote for venomous stings.

Following the lead of the Greeks and Romans, the Anglo-Saxons used one name, *thung*, for aconite and poisonous plants in general. Aconite was used to poison bait and kill wolves, which still roamed England at that time. Through

---

24. Foster and Johnson, *National Geographic Desk Reference to Nature's Medicine*, 252.

25. Quattrocchi, *CRC World Dictionary of Plant Names*, 33.

the seventeenth century, it was used to get rid of rats and foxes. Not only was it good for dispatching unwanted creatures, in Europe it was commonly believed that a piece of aconite root carried in a pocket, or somewhere in one's clothing, would keep all types of vermin at bay.

According to eleventh-century Persian scholar Avicenna, a certain species of field mouse that fed on the roots of aconite could be used as an antidote to the poison. Intrigued by the theory, and because poisoning by aconite was so common in his day, Italian physician Guido da Vigevano (c. 1280–c. 1349) went looking for the mouse. While he didn't track down the rodent, he found snails that fed on monkshood. Vigevano boiled them with the all-purpose antidote theriac and experimented on himself. He lived to tell the tale, but the snails didn't become a popular antidote.

Although aconite was used for a range of ailments, Flemish herbalist Rembert Dodoens (1517–1585) sounded the alarm about its dangers. Nevertheless, certain beliefs persisted. According to English physician and botanist John Gerard, aconite provided protection from venomous beasts and the plague. Referring to yellow wolfsbane (*A. anthora*) as Mitridate (perhaps as in Mithridatium), Gerard noted that it could counteract the poisons of the other aconites. Throughout the nineteenth century, aconite was popular with European and American doctors. Listed in European pharmacopoeias for laryngitis, influenza, bronchitis, and colds, it was used until the mid-twentieth century when it was finally deemed too unsafe.

Like many poisonous plants, aconite was regarded as a witches' magical plant in medieval Europe and said to be an ingredient in their legendary flying ointment. Witches were also believed to be able to eat aconite without dire consequences or death, although why they would want to do so is unknown. In Scandinavia, aconite was associated with trolls, and an Old Norse name for the plants was *Trollhat*.

From the time of the Romans through the Renaissance and beyond, aconite was a favored poison for murder and became known as the Queen of Poisons. In county Monaghan, Ireland, Mary Anna McConkey (d. 1841) was executed after being found guilty of poisoning her husband by mixing monkshood leaves in his bacon and greens. Although the husband was said to have mentioned the sharp taste, he ate it anyway. Scottish doctor Edward William Pritchard (1825–1865) murdered his wife and mother-in-law with aconite. As their attending physician, he almost got away with it by declaring autopsies unnecessary. Pritchard was the last person to be publicly hanged in Glasgow. Known as the Wimbledon Poisoner, Dr. George Henry Lamson (1852–1882) had served in the Franco-Prussian war and, like many soldiers, had become addicted to morphine. Increasingly in debt, he poisoned his brother-in-law to expedite and increase his wife's inheritance. Lamson was convicted and executed. Poisoning with aconite isn't a thing of the past. In 2009 London, Lakhvir Kaur Singh (b. 1969) became known as the Curry Killer after murdering her former lover with it. She was sentenced to life in prison.

Miscellany

Despite the risks, aconite is used in Ayurvedic and Traditional Chinese Medicine as well as homeopathy. Monkshood, wolfsbane, and other related species are popular garden plants.

Autumn Crocus

MEDEA'S FAVORITE

Autumn Crocus (*Colchicum autumnale*); also known as meadow saffron, naked ladies, wild saffron

Botanical Family: Liliaceae / Lily

Native to northern Africa, Europe, and the British Isles, this flower is not a true crocus; those are in the genus *Crocus*. True crocus plants produce their flowers and leaves at the same time; the autumn crocus does not. Sprouting up in the spring, the broad, lance-shaped leaves of autumn crocus are dark green and envelope a round seedpod from the previous year. The flowers don't appear until the autumn on leafless stalks, which is the source of the folk name *naked ladies*. The flowers can be pink, white, or purple. The corm (similar to a bulb) has a dark brown outer layer. The interior is white with a bitter, milky juice.

Toxicity and Cautions

All parts of the plant, especially the seeds and corms, contain the highly toxic alkaloid colchicine, which is one of the most powerful plant poisons. It can be deadly whether ingested, inhaled, or absorbed through the skin. Handling the plant can cause dermatitis. Ingestion can cause a burning mouth, nausea, vomiting, severe cramps, muscle weakness, kidney failure, and respiratory failure. Death can take several days. Those who survive colchicine poisoning sometimes experience symptoms for years.

Autumn crocus leaves have been mistaken for wild garlic (*Allium ursinum*), which has resulted in accidental deaths. Autumn crocus flowers are very similar to the saffron crocus (*Crocus sativus*), which is also known as autumn crocus because it appears in the autumn, although its leaves do too. The spice called saffron is the dried flower stamens, which are the filament strands inside the flower. The saffron crocus has three stamens, the autumn crocus has six.

History and Lore

The genus of this plant was named for Colchis, a region in Greco-Roman geography that is now present-day Georgia on the Black Sea. In Greek myth, it was the destination for the adventurers Jason and the Argonauts to find the golden fleece and where the Titan god Prometheus was punished for giving humans the gift and power of fire. Like many poisonous plant origin stories, autumn crocus flowers were said to have sprung up where blood—in this case from Prometheus—touched the ground. As the daughter of the king of Colchis, the sorceress Medea's favorite poison was, quite naturally, colchicine.

Whether fiction follows fact or the other way around, throughout the ancient Mediterranean world the corm of this plant was ground into powder to produce a convenient murder weapon. For poisoners in ancient Rome, autumn crocus ranked high on the list along with aconite, henbane, and opium poppy.

Medicinally, the Greeks and Romans used colchicine to treat gout, as did the Egyptians before them. The autumn crocus was described in the Ebers Papyrus where it was also noted as a treatment for rheumatism and inflammation. Greek physicians called the plant *Hermodactyl*, meaning "finger of Hermes," in reference to the corm because it was used to ease joint pain.[26] Greek botanist Theophrastus recognized its toxicity, as did physician Nicander, who included it in his universal antidote, theriaca. Dioscorides compared its potency as a poison to the *Amanita* species of mushroom.

Fifth-century physicians in the Byzantine Empire and Arab doctors throughout the Middle East prescribed colchicine for gout and arthritis. It also became known in Latin as *anima articulorum*, meaning "life of the limbs," because it was believed to aid the restoration of physical movement.[27] Centuries later, English botanist and physician Nicholas Culpeper (1616–1664) referred to it by the botanical name *Colchicum vulgare*, *vulgare* meaning "common." He noted that while it was deadly, it was safe when prepared properly

26. Holblyn, *A Dictionary of Terms Used in Medicine*, 287.

27. Holblyn, *A Dictionary of Terms Used in Medicine*, 43.

and prescribed it as an expectorant. Modern scholars believe that Culpeper may have confused it with the saffron crocus.

The autumn crocus was used on and off medicinally in Europe and the British Isles throughout the Middle Ages and Renaissance. During the seventeenth and eighteenth centuries, it was listed in the London Pharmacopoeia, dropped, and then reinstated. In Italy, the corm prepared with sherry was called *vinum colchici*, meaning "wine of colchicum," and *tinctura colchici* was a tincture made with the seeds. Throughout much of Europe, colchicine was used as a remedy for inflammatory afflictions as well as dropsy and liver problems. While Benjamin Franklin (1706–1790) is often noted as having used colchicine for his gout and said to have introduced it into America, not all scholars agree on either point. There is no mention in his prolific writing or personal correspondence that he even tried it.[28]

Colchicine was used for murder in ancient times and Victorian England. In a case notorious at the time, Lincolnshire nurse Catherine Wilson (1842–1862) was put on trial for poisoning her employer. While she was tried for only one murder, she had killed at least seven previous patients, people who had employed her as a live-in nurse and then conveniently died after changing their wills. The soothing draughts she gave them were anything but, as throughout her poisoning career she often used a combination of colchicine, arsenic, and sulfuric acid. In addition, she may have also murdered her lover. Found guilty, Wilson was hanged in front of a crowd numbering in the thousands. She was the last woman publicly hanged in London.

Like aconite, murder with colchicine is not a thing of the past. In 1992, Debra Rogers (b. 1954) of Louisville, Kentucky, used it to kill her husband for life insurance money. She was sentenced to twenty-eight years in prison. Kaitlyn Conley (b. 1993) of Oneida County, New York, used it, too, and in 2015 was charged with killing her employer, who was her ex-boyfriend's mother. She was convicted of first-degree manslaughter and sentenced to twenty-three years in prison.

---

28. Finger, *Doctor Franklin's Medicine*, 293.

Miscellany

Colchicine is an effective painkiller with anti-inflammatory properties. As in the past, extracts from the autumn crocus are used to treat acute cases of gout. The plant is the source of modern drugs because it cannot be economically synthesized in a laboratory. Colchicine's cell division–inhibiting properties were hoped to fight leukemia, but the side effects were too severe. It is being used in cancer research.

The plant is popular for gardens in Europe and across North America to add a splash of color that is slightly different from most autumn hues. Enjoy the plant, but don't let it seduce you into thinking it's saffron.

Bryony

FAKE MANDRAKE

White Bryony, Red Bryony (*Bryonia dioica* syn. *B. cretica* subsp. *dioica*); also known as dead creepers, devil's turnip, hedge grape, red-berried white bryony, English mandrake, wild hop, wild nep, womandrake

Botanical Family: Cucurbitaceae / Cucumber

Black Bryony (*Tamus communis* syn. *Dioscorea communis*); also known as black bindweed, blackeye root, devil's berries, devil's cherry, lady's seal, mandrake, wound root

Botanical Family: Dioscoreaceae / Yam

The common name *bryony* is also spelled *briony*.

Frequently found in scrublands and hedgerows, these plants are fast-growing, scrambling vines that have long, divided parsnip-like taproots. Native to central and southern Europe, white bryony has light-colored roots, coiling tendrils that help it climb, and leaves with five lobes. The middle lobe is longer and larger than the others. Its five-petaled flowers are yellow-green and its berries are red. Black bryony has black roots and heart-shaped leaves that turn yellow or purple in the autumn. It does not have tendrils. Its five-petaled flowers are yellow or greenish yellow and its berries are also red. Black bryony is native from Britain through Europe to northern Africa and the eastern Mediterranean and western Asia. These plants are not botanically related.

Toxicity and Cautions

All parts of these plants are poisonous. The roots of white bryony are particularly toxic and the plant sap can cause severe skin irritation. White bryony contains the alkaloid bryonicine and the glycoside bryonidin, which is an extremely strong purgative. Ingestion causes a decrease in heart rate, severe headache, nausea, vomiting, severe diarrhea, and convulsions. Death often occurs in a few hours. Surviving a poisoning leaves the kidneys and liver damaged. White bryony is also an abortifacient. Another species that is known as white bryony and black-berried white bryony (*B. alba*) is equally toxic.

Black bryony contains saponins and calcium oxalate crystals. Ingestion can cause severe irritation of the stomach and intestines, seizures, kidney failure, and dangerously slow breathing. Externally, it can cause severe skin irritation, rashes, swelling, and welts. Black bryony was so named because of its similarity to white bryony as well as its toxic effects.

History and Lore

White bryony was treasured by medieval gardeners and artists for its dainty flowers and delicate, curling tendrils. Ornamentally draping over arbors and other garden structures, it was pleasing even in autumn with bright red berries dangling amongst a lacework of brown stems. Although poisonous, it was used medicinally by the Anglo-Saxons who called it hymele, the same name they used for hops (*Humulus lupulus*). In a medieval book of herbal remedies known as the *Old English Herbarium*, white bryony was given the scientific name of *Hymele brionia*, meaning "hops briony." Some scholars believe that bryony may have been confused with hops or it was possibly used in a remedy that resembled beer or was added to beer.

Throughout England, white bryony was used by women to stimulate fertility and in East Anglia they drank a beverage known as mandrake tea to aid conception. In Dorset, it was used as a substitute for castor oil. Also used as a laxative in Sweden and Germany, a bryony root was hollowed out and filled with beer, which was then consumed slowly. The women of Salerno, Italy had another use for the plant: dabbing a little juice from the roots on their faces gave their skin a pink, glowing appearance, no doubt because it was irritated by the toxins.

While white bryony was used as a topical treatment for leprosy in fourteenth-century England, sixteenth-century herbalist John Gerard recommended it for tanning leather. Beads made from the dried roots were strung together and worn as a necklace to ward off the evil eye or placed on babies to aid with teething, a practice that could have upped the infant mortality rate. In East Anglia, Cambridgeshire, and Buckinghamshire, the roots were given in horse feed to make their coats sleek. In addition to taking care of their horses, people of the Fens hung white bryony leaves in privies to freshen the air during the hot summer.

In England and Europe, it was considered unlucky to take white bryony indoors because of the belief that witches used the roots as black magic charms or made poppets for spells with them. In England, black bryony also had a magical use: a piece of root was fashioned into a bullet to kill a hare that was suspected of being a witch. It was long believed that witches often shapeshifted into hares.

In addition to bullets, black bryony roots had a few medicinal applications. They could be boiled and applied like a plaster to ease rheumatism and gout or made into a syrup to treat asthma. According to John Gerard, black bryony roots were effective for easing bruises. A French name for both white and black bryony was *herbe aux femmes battues*, meaning "herb of beaten wives."[29]

Like mandrake, the roots of both white and black bryony often divide and grow arms and legs, which—with some imagination—resemble the human form. In England, white bryony was credited with many of the same powers as the very magical mandrake. Believed to have supernatural powers of its own, black bryony also became associated with mandrake. While a mandrake root takes about three years to develop, a white bryony root matures in just one summer. This made it popular and profitable for herbalists through the sixteenth and seventeenth centuries to substitute bryony for mandrake, which commanded a much higher price. Bryony roots were sometimes doctored by growing them in special molds to guide their development into the desired humanlike shape. Another method was to simply cut them to form and then temporarily return them to the soil to dirty them up and give them a more authentic look.

Throughout England, white bryony was regarded as female and black bryony as male. In Lincolnshire and Yorkshire, white bryony was known as womandrake and black bryony as mandrake. The theory of pairing plants and designating them as male and female dates to ancient Greece and is found in

---

29. Watts, *Elsevier's Dictionary of Plant Lore*, 35.

the work of physician and botanist Dioscorides. Rather than denoting gender per se, the terms were meant to indicate the robustness or delicacy of a plant. In the sixth-century *Vienna Dioscorides*, the terms were taken literally and the anthropomorphic drawings of the two mandrakes Dioscorides described were undeniably female and male. Ever since, herbalists have used the distinction, which was carried over to bryony.

Miscellany

Despite serious safety concerns, white bryony is used in some homeopathic remedies. Both white and black bryony are used in herbal medicine.

Datura

DELIRIUM AND DEITIES

Thorn Apple, Jimsonweed (*Datura stramonium*); also known as datura, devil's apple, devil's trumpet, Jamestown weed, locoweed, mad apple, moonflower

Purple Datura, Devil's Trumpet (*D. metel* syn. *D. fastuosa*); also known as black datura, garden datura, Hindu datura, jimsonweed, purple moonflower, purple thorn apple

Botanical Family: Solanaceae / Nightshade

These two species are shrubby, sprawling plants. Thorn apple generally grows three to four feet tall; purple datura tends to grow in two-to-three-foot mounds. The leaves of both plants are coarse, unevenly toothed, and foul smelling. Thorn apple's leaves are more deeply lobed. The cigar-shaped flower buds unwind after dark, releasing their honeysuckle-like fragrance. The striking, trumpet-shaped flowers have pointed petals and sit upright from the stem. They remain open until around noon the following day before fading. The round, walnut-sized seedpod is spiny (thorn apple) or knobby (purple datura). Thorn apple is native to North America but has become naturalized in Europe; purple datura is native to India and southeast Asia.

Toxicity and Cautions

All parts of these plants are extremely poisonous and contain the tropane alkaloids atropine, hyoscyamine, and scopolamine. Ingestion can cause dry mouth, dilated pupils, nausea, headache, convulsions, coma, and death. Other symptoms are similar to schizophrenia. The sap can cause skin rashes.

History and Lore

Datura is most famously known for the incident in Jamestown, Virginia, when British troops were sent to put down an uprising in 1676. After accidentally ingesting datura in their food, the soldiers ran amuck in a wild state of delirium that lasted eleven days. The British weren't the only army to have a run-in with datura. Before hooking up with Cleopatra, Mark Antony led a campaign into Parthia, a kingdom located in what is now northeast Iran. Short on supplies and in retreat, the Roman soldiers ate what they could find, which included datura. It resulted in a great deal of confusion in the ranks and many fatalities.

Throughout history, datura has been associated with insanity. Although the species name *stramonium* is Latin, it was derived from the Greek, *strychnos*, meaning "nightshade," and *manikos*, "mad."[30] According to scholars, the sorceress Circe in Homer's *Odyssey* most likely laced the food she served Odysseus's crew with datura because of the hallucinations and delirium described in the aftermath of their meal. In sixteenth-century Italy, scholar and polymath Giambattista della Porta noted that the combination of datura seeds and deadly nightshade roots could cause madness. In Mexico, one species, *D. ceratocaula*, is called *Torna Loco*, meaning the "maddening plant."[31] Oddly enough, in nineteenth-century France and Austria, thorn apple was used to treat insanity. While the plant was said to be used by witches, throughout Europe it was administered to those suspected of witchcraft along with physical torture to extract confessions.

Although it has some medicinal properties, datura has been more readily used for its psychoactive and hallucinogenic qualities and was mentioned in early Sanskrit, Tibetan, and Chinese writings. The genus name was derived from the ancient Sanskrit name for the plant, *Dhattūra*. In India it is regarded as a sacred hallucinogen and associated with the worship of the Hindu god Shiva. The fruits are left in temples as offerings to him. It is mentioned in the *Vāmana Purāṇa*, a sacred text dedicated to Vishnu that was written during early medieval times. Purple datura is one of the psychoactive plants used in Indo-Tibetan Tantric Buddhism. Although the oracle at Delphi in Greece was noted as chewing a sacred laurel leaf, or eating some type of mint, a few scholars have noted

30. Husen, *Exploring Poisonous Plants*, 309.

31. Pratt, *An Encyclopedia of Shamanism*, 134.

that she may have also consumed datura or the vapors said to rise from the ground in the temple may have been from burning the plant.[32]

Anthropologists and ethnobotanists recognize other species of datura, such as downy thorn apple (*D. inoxia*), as important ceremonial plants in South America and the southwestern United States. In Mexico, it is used as a sacred hallucinogen in shamanic rituals and ceremonies. The Aztec were known to have used it. For the Navajo, it aids prophecy and visions as well as the mundane locating of lost property. The Zuni use it for prophecy, second sight, and to communicate with ancestors. For the Yokuts of California, datura was part of the initiation ceremonies and puberty rites for boys and girls. The Tarahumara of northern Mexico still use the seeds in a ceremonial drink of fermented maize.

Avicenna and other Arab physicians noted the plant's medicinal qualities but classified it as a narcotic and noted its potentially fatal effect. By the middle of the sixteenth century, thorn apple and purple datura appeared in English and European herbals for pain relief as a poultice or ointment. English physician John Gerard prescribed the juice of thorn apple boiled with hog grease as an unguent for burns and inflammation. His recipe was used as a cure in East Anglia well into the twentieth century. The Germans called the plant *rauch öppfelkraut*, meaning "smoke apple herb," in reference to its use as an inhalant for treating asthma.[33]

Datura also figured in twentieth-century entertainment. Agatha Christie used it as a murder weapon in *The Cretan Bull* and *Sleeping Murder*. *Devil's Trumpet* was the title of the first book in the Rachel O'Connor Gardening Mysteries series by American author Mary Rosenblum (1952–2018). The name *datura* and images of its flowers continue to crop up in a range of noir-style fiction and artwork to symbolize something exotic and sinister. However, the plant's dangerous and deadly effects were overlooked or unknown to the singing cowboy actor, musician Gene Autry (1907–1998). His 1939 song "Back in the Saddle Again" includes a line about cattle eating jimsonweed. Imagine a herd of longhorns going berserk across the prairies.

32. Hanson, Venturelli, and Fleckenstein, *Drugs and Society*, 368.

33. Janick, *Horticultural Reviews*, 50.

Miscellany

Today datura is used for a range of ailments in Ayurvedic, Traditional Chinese Medicine, and homeopathic remedies. In conventional medicine, it is used in the treatment of Parkinson's and epilepsy and is being studied in cancer research. Purple datura and downy thorn apple are commonly used as garden ornamentals; thorn apple less so because it has a weedy appearance.

Although recreational use by teenagers and young adults sometimes occurs, it is a pursuit done only once. If an overdose doesn't kill, the experience tends to cure people from wanting to do it again.

Deadly Nightshade
BEAUTY AND A BEAST

Deadly Nightshade, Belladonna (*Atropa belladonna*); also known as banewort, devil's cherry, mad berry, sorcerer's berry, witches' berry

Botanical Family: Solanaceae / Nightshade

Reaching three to five feet tall, deadly nightshade is a medium-sized branching shrub with oval, dark-green leaves. The distinctive, bell-shaped flowers are reddish purple or brownish purple and grow singly from the leaf axils. The glossy black berries are about the size of cherries. Deadly nightshade is native to Europe, the Mediterranean, and western Asia, but has now naturalized in many parts of the world, including North America.

Toxicity and Cautions

Deadly nightshade lives up to its name; all parts of the plant are extremely poisonous, especially the berries. It contains the alkaloids atropine, hyoscyamine, scopolamine, and belladonnine. These compounds can block neurotransmitters that handle normal functions throughout the body. Ingestion can cause dilated pupils, delirium, confusion, hallucinations, rapid heartbeat, coma, and death. Handling the plant can cause contact dermatitis. Atropine can be absorbed through skin.

History and Lore

In Greek mythology, deadly nightshade was associated with the cult of Dionysus and, along with an abundance of wine, may have helped fuel the Roman Bacchanalian orgies. Given this lore, it was believed to be an aphrodisiac and used as such in medieval Europe.

Despite the 82 BCE Roman law intended to crack down on widespread poisonings, it had little effect. The poet Juvenal (c. 55 CE–c. 130 CE) wrote satires about Roman life and noted how deadly nightshade was popular with wives who wanted to get rid of their husbands. Possibly even one who was emperor. Emperor Augustus, also known as Octavian, had a whirlwind romance with Livia Drusilla (59 BCE–29 CE), divorced his wife on the day she gave birth to their daughter, and then married Livia three days later. According to rumors, Livia poisoned Octavian and possibly others with belladonna. According to Roman historians Publius Cornelius Tacitus (c. 56–c. 120) and Lucius Cassius Dio, known as Dio Cassius (c. 150–235), several young men in Octavian's family, who had stronger claims to succession, died prematurely. This paved the way for Livia's son Tiberius (42 BCE–37 CE) to become emperor.

Throughout medieval Europe, belladonna was believed to be a plant of witches and sorcerers. In legend, Hecate, goddess of magic and witchcraft, grew belladonna in her garden. It was alleged that witches used it to avoid detection and as an aid for scrying and clairvoyance. The plant was noted in the writings of Italian scholar and occultist Giambattista della Porta and in the *Compendium Maleficarum* it was listed as an ingredient in the famous witches' flying ointment. Spanish doctor Andrés Laguna (1499–1559), who served as a physician to several kings and a pope, claimed to have obtained a jar of flying ointment and found it to contain deadly nightshade, hemlock, mandragora, and henbane. After experimenting on several subjects, he concluded that the ointment provided a sensation of flying and produced vivid hallucinations about sexual encounters as well as memories as real as any others. Laguna also noted that a little belladonna could provide a pleasant experience, but a little too much could cause insanity. According to folklore in Normandy, walking barefoot on deadly nightshade was believed to cause madness.

Italian physician Andrea Mattioli (1501–1577) noted that Venetian women used a decoction of deadly nightshade to dilate their pupils. While this gave them a doe-eyed look of sexual arousal, they were unwittingly poisoning themselves. Spanish majas, belles of the lower class, were also said to have used belladonna in their eyes. Because of this practice, the plant was called *herba bella donna*, meaning "herb of the fair lady."[34] The name *belladonna* is a sharp con-

34. Foster and Johnson, *National Geographic Desk Reference to Nature's Medicine*, 37.

trast with its doom-and-gloom name of *deadly nightshade*. But of course, it is deadly, which is why Linnaeus derived its genus name from Atropos, one of the three Fates in Greek mythology who had the power of life and death.

Dilating the pupils to look sexy is one thing, but using it to disguise murder is another, which was the ploy used by Robert Buchanan (1860–1892). A respectable physician in New York City, Buchanan married brothel proprietress Anna Sutherland (d. 1892) apparently to inherit her fifty thousand dollars. Although his toxin of choice was morphine, pinpoint-sized pupils were a telltale sign of its poisoning. To solve the problem, he put atropine drops in her eyes. After his ruse was discovered, he was tried, convicted, and executed in 1895 at Sing Sing prison. In more recent years, English serial killer Graham Young (1947–1990), who became known as the Teacup Poisoner, began experimenting when he was fourteen years old by putting atropine drops in his sister's morning tea. He went on to use other poisons for killing.

Because of its sedative effects, in early medieval England, belladonna was called dwale, based on the Scandinavian word *dvale*, meaning "stupor."[35] A narcotic drink that contained a combination of hemlock, henbane, belladonna, and opium was also called dwale and used as a surgical anesthetic. The Anglo-Saxons used belladonna leaves medicinally as a poultice for swelling and inflammation and an extract as drops for earache. To cure a toothache, a flower or two were placed in the mouth; the effects would probably leave a person oblivious to any dental pain.

Sixteenth-century English herbalist John Gerard warned of its dangers, giving it the botanical name *Solanum lethale* and calling it sleepy nightshade.[36] Seventeenth-century apothecaries knew it as *Solatrum mortale*. By the nineteenth century, doctors on both sides of the pond seemed to have been fascinated with deadly nightshade. In England, it was used for whooping cough until the 1940s; in America, belladonna plasters were used for topical pain relief. While most products were honestly produced, quackery and the chance to make a quick buck resulted in some plasters with no atropine and others with dangerously high levels. Although belladonna became a marketing buzzword, many of the ointments, salves, and liniments labeled with it didn't contain any. American physicians were so enthusiastic about belladonna that,

35. Pollington, *Leechcraft*, 143.

36. Gerard, *The Herball*, 340.

in addition to external application, it was an ingredient in suppositories and sometimes administered by injection. Cincinnati physician and author of *Eclectic Materia Medica*, Harvey Wickes Felter (1865–1927), prescribed belladonna in combination with aconite for certain ailments. It's a wonder that there were any patients left.

Miscellany

Despite the risks, deadly nightshade is used in homeopathic and herbal remedies, and belladonna plasters for pain relief are widely available. Ophthalmologists use drops containing atropine to dilate patients' pupils for examinations and surgery. Deadly nightshade plants and seeds are available for the garden.

Hellebore

MADNESS AND ALCHEMY

Black Hellebore (*Helleborus niger*); also known as Christmas rose, snow rose, winter rose

Botanical Family: Ranunculaceae / Buttercup

White Hellebore (*Veratrum album*); also known as false helleborine, false hellebore, white veratrum

Botanical Family: Melanthiaceae / Bunchflower

Winter-blooming black hellebore is a bushy, clump-forming plant with lance-shaped leaves that are dark green and deeply lobed. The white, cup-shaped flowers have overlapping petals. While it may seem odd that a plant with white flowers is called black, it was so named because of the color of its roots. White hellebore has pleated, oblong base leaves. The erect, branching flower stem carries dense clusters of white, star-shaped flowers. Black hellebore is native to southern and central Europe, white hellebore to Europe and parts of western Asia.

Toxicity and Cautions

All parts of black hellebore are toxic, especially the roots and sap. The plant contains the cardiac glycoside hellebrin and the cardioactive steroid hellebrigenin. It also contains helleborin, a potent narcotic. Like other plants in the buttercup family, the glycoside ranunculin is present. Ingestion can cause irritation of the gastrointestinal system, nausea, vomiting, diarrhea, irregular heartbeat and respiration, and death. It is also an abortifacient. The sap is a skin irritant that can cause blistering and severe dermatitis.

All parts of white hellebore are also toxic, especially the roots. It contains the steroidal alkaloids protoveratrine and veratramine. Ingestion can cause nausea, vomiting, abdominal pain, headache, slowed heart rate, a drop in blood pressure, seizures, and death. The sap is a dermal irritant and the plant's toxins can be absorbed through the skin.

History and Lore

Although these plants are not related, they are presented together because of their common name *hellebore* and because history does not always distinguish between them. Hellebore is one of the four classical poisons along with aconite, hemlock, and deadly nightshade. When Roman emperor Trajan outlawed the cultivation of aconite, hellebore was plentiful enough for poisoners to continue plying their trade without interruption. In medieval England, hellebore and aconite were the plants most commonly used for murder. In a prank gone terribly wrong, hellebore may have been what Richard Roose (d. 1531), the cook for the Bishop of Rochester, added to the soup to make the dinner guests evacuate their bowels suddenly and without warning. Instead, all who ate the tainted broth became severely ill and two died. The reason for Roose's prank is unknown but it resulted in his gruesome execution by being boiled alive. Apparently, some believed it was a fitting end for a murderous cook.

Hellebore's use as a remedy for madness dates to the ancient Greeks and Romans. The Greeks knew the plant as melampode. It was named for Melampus, the legendary seer and healer in Greek mythology who was most known for his ability to understand the language of animals. In one legend, Melampus cured the daughters of Proetus, king of the city-state Argos, of madness. The remedy he gave them was the milk of goats that had eaten hellebore. Interestingly in the mid-seventeenth century, English botanist Nicholas Culpeper recommended goat's milk as an antidote for hellebore. Perhaps Melampus's mixture was the forerunner of Mithridatium, a formula containing both poison and remedy.

First-century Roman physician Aurelius Cornelius Celsus recommended black hellebore for melancholy and depression, and white hellebore for hysterics. When the medicinal approach failed, the good doctor Celsus condoned flogging and chains. Purging was believed to rid the body of disease and hellebore was believed to have the added feature of cleansing the brain. Purging the intellectual faculties with hellebore was even mentioned by first-century poets. In a satire, Roman poet Persius (34–62 CE) suggested that Emperor Nero use it.

The Anglo-Saxons associated hellebore with insanity and sometimes referred to both species as *wedeberge*, meaning "madness berries."[37] In the Middle Ages, black hellebore was used for epilepsy, which was believed to be related to insanity. Like Celsus, seventeenth-century English herbalist John Gerard noted black hellebore for melancholy, nervous disorders, and hysteria but also included skin disorders. Physicians William Babington (1756–1833) and James Curry (1763–1819) of Guy's Hospital Medical School in London recommended hellebore, nightshade, and wolfsbane as a cure for insanity. The association with insanity continued in the fourth edition of the *Encyclopaedia Britannica* of 1810, which noted that the phrase "to have need of hellebore" meant that a person was out of their senses.[38]

Hellebore had other medicinal applications. Medieval abbess Hildegard von Bingen noted it for gout and jaundice. For gout, she recommended adding the plant juice to wine and drinking it on an empty stomach. In the folk medicine of England and Europe, dried hellebore was used as a sneezing powder. Sneezing was believed to be a form of purging that helped rid the body of illness.

In the early sixteenth century, Swiss physician and alchemist Paracelsus noted that his elixir for long life was made from the dried leaves of black hellebore. He also mentioned that the roots were effective to cure leprosy, dropsy, and stroke as well as to guard against infection. In late eighteenth-century Paris, *Eau Medicinale d'Husson* was a remedy for gout and other diseases. The concoction contained white hellebore tempered with laudanum.

During the Middle Ages throughout Europe, hellebore was regarded as highly magical and strewn on floors to banish evil spirits. It was believed

37. Pollington, *Leechcraft*, 160.

38. Millar, *Encyclopaedia Britannica*, 195.

in France that sorcerers scattered powdered root in the air around them to become invisible. Although both species of hellebore were used to ward off witches, they reputedly used black hellebore for hexes.

When it came to transmuting base metals into something more valuable, alchemists favored white hellebore. It was listed in formulas to change silver into gold, but if an alchemist didn't have silver, they could take one step at a time and change the cheaper, more accessible iron into silver. The formula called for white hellebore and any type of asphodel (*Asphodeline* spp. or *Asphodelus* spp.) to be pounded together with several poisonous toads. The resulting icky substance was then mixed with vinegar, white sulfur, and iron. With the appropriate amount of ingredients, correct procedures, and proper incantations, *voilà*, silver!

Miscellany

Both black and white hellebore are used as garden plants. In addition, black hellebore is often grown as a houseplant and is a popular cut flower. Both plants are used in homeopathic remedies.

Hemlock
EXECUTION AND MURDER

Poison Hemlock, Spotted Hemlock (*Conium maculatum*); also known as deadman's oatmeal, devil's flower, herb bennet, kexies, lace flower, madwort, mother-die, poison parsley

Botanical Family: Apiaceae, formerly Umbelliferae / Carrot, Parsley

Hemlock leaves are delicate and parsley- or fernlike with toothed edges and have an unpleasant, musty odor when crushed. The plant has a white, fleshy taproot. The stems are hollow and marked with purple blotches. Small white flowers grow in umbrellalike clusters atop branching stems. The green seedpods are deeply ridged and turn grayish brown when mature. Hemlock is native to Europe and the Mediterranean and has become naturalized in North America, Asia, and Australia.

Toxicity and Cautions

All parts of hemlock are poisonous, especially the seeds, and fatal if ingested. The leaves are particularly potent in the spring before flowering; however, even when dried, they remain dangerous. Hemlock contains the alkaloid coniine, which is a neurotoxin that disrupts the peripheral nervous system. Handling the plant can cause dermatitis, plus the toxins can enter the bloodstream through a cut or through the mucous membranes of the nose. Ingestion can cause a burning mouth and throat, drowsiness, nausea, vomiting, diarrhea, abdominal pain, trembling, paralysis, and death. Hemlock is easily mistaken for Queen Anne's lace (*Daucus carota*) and parsley (*Petroselinum crispum*).

History and Lore

Hemlock is perhaps one of the most well-known poisons and, as previously mentioned, its most famous victim was the philosopher Socrates. The poison was used by the ancient Greeks and Romans for judicial punishment, usually allowing the accused to take their own life, often at home in the company of friends and family. Caught in a plot to murder Roman emperor Nero, philosopher and statesman Seneca (c. 4 BCE–65 CE) was sentenced to kill himself, which he did at his villa in a dramatic way by drinking hemlock and cutting his veins. The toxins kill slowly through paralysis, which begins in the extremities, followed by loss of speech, and ultimately death by suffocation when the lungs become paralyzed. During the entire process, the mind is said to be clear and functioning.

A rather sad, accidental death by hemlock occurred in Scotland in 1845. Edinburgh tailor Duncan Gow (d. 1845) was struggling to make ends meet, often economizing on food for himself so his family could eat. One day, he was delighted when his children delivered a sandwich to him in his shop that contained his favorite greens, parsley. Unfortunately, the greens that the children foraged weren't parsley and Gow collapsed and died later that day when he tried to walk home. Such mistaken identity isn't a thing of the past or only made by children. In 2010, a fifty-five-year-old woman in Tacoma, Washington, died after putting hemlock, which she had gathered from her yard, in a salad.

Hemlock is documented as a known poison in the Ebers Papyrus from ancient Egypt and was identified by Greek physician Hippocrates, who was interested in clinical toxicology. Like other poisonous plants, hemlock has a narrow therapeutic margin of curing or killing. In early medieval Italy, it was used medicinally along with several herbs to treat the bite of a mad dog. Greek and Arabian doctors prescribed it for cancerous tumors and scrofula, an infection of the lymph nodes in the neck. Called hemlic by the Anglo-Saxons, hemlock was used as a treatment for lice. Added to ale, along with wormwood, the patient was to drink it after fasting for a night. If it didn't kill the patient, they would probably be unaware of any lingering parasites.

During the Middle Ages and Renaissance in Europe and Britain, hemlock was used as a treatment for St. Anthony's Fire, ergot poisoning. Seventeenth-century English physician Nicholas Culpeper echoed Pliny's recommendation to drink it in the best and strongest wine available. In the Fenlands of Cambridgeshire, women who wanted to terminate a pregnancy could obtain pills containing hemlock, pennyroyal, and rue made by Granny Gray (d. 1898) of Littleport. Gray also offered pills for anemia made from iron filings swept from the floor of a local smithy. Also in Cambridgeshire, a method of controlling an unruly horse was to rub powdered hemlock on its nose. The plant continued to be used medicinally in nineteenth-century England for epilepsy, coughs, and asthma. For a brief time, American doctors prescribed it to calm teething babies.

As Shakespeare told us in *Macbeth*, hemlock was an herb of witches, who stirred it into their cauldron. Likewise, the late sixteenth-century witch-hunter manual, the *Compendium Maleficarum*, listed it as one of the plants witches used in their legendary flying ointment. In German folklore, hemlock was associated with toads that were believed to absorb poison from the plant. Despite the perils, hemlock was used as a love charm in Ireland. Mixing ten dried, powdered leaves into the food or drink of the desired individual was said to result in gaining their affection. Of course, if the person died, it couldn't have been true love.

Ever since the queen of crime fiction, Agatha Christie, killed off a victim with hemlock via a glass of beer in *Five Little Pigs*, it served as a murder weapon in countless other books. Murder with hemlock is nothing new; it was a tool of homicide thousands of years ago. The common cocktail of poisons for getting rid of someone in ancient Rome was aconite, hemlock, and opium. Assassination was a thriving industry with professionals for hire, and a trio of women in first-century Rome—Locusta, Martina, and Canidia—was notorious. Canidia was said to be especially frightening because of her cold efficiency. Hemlock in honey was her preferred method, but not to entice or soothe the victim. Acting as a preservative, honey prevented the plant material from drying out, which kept it at its highest potency. In several poems, Roman satirist Horace (65–8 BCE) represented Canidia as a sinister woman and hideous witch.

The folk name *kexies* comes from the Middle English word *kex*, which was a term for the standing, dry hollow stems of plants in the *Apiaceae* family.[39] In autumn, the dried stalks of hemlock are often draped with the brittle remnants

39. Skeat, *The Concise Dictionary of English Etymology*, 231.

of seedpods that make a rattling noise in the wind like a botanical rattlesnake sounding its warning.

Miscellany

Despite its dangers, hemlock is used in homeopathic remedies for various ailments. It was introduced into North America in the nineteenth century as a garden plant and marketed as winter fern. Hemlock has become naturalized in many areas and is classified as an invasive or noxious weed.

Henbane

WITCHES, MAGIC, AND BEER

Black Henbane (*Hyoscyamus niger*); also known as common henbane, black nightshade, devil's eye, hen-bell, henpenny, hog's-bean, insane root, stinking nightshade

White Henbane (*H. albus*); also known as yellow henbane

Botanical Family: Solanaceae / Nightshade

Sprouting from woody stalks that reach up to three feet tall, henbane's leaves are dull green and lance shaped with wavy edges. Growing at the base of the upper leaves, the funnel-shaped flowers of black henbane are brownish yellow with purple veins and centers. The fruit is a spherical capsule containing several hundred seeds that are kidney shaped and brownish. White henbane flowers are less funnel shaped and do not show veining on the petals. Both plants are native to parts of Europe and northern Africa, and white henbane also in western Asia; both have been naturalized in many areas throughout the world.

Toxicity and Cautions

All parts of these plants are poisonous and contain tropane alkaloids, including the psychoactive scopolamine and hyoscyamine. Ingestion of henbane can cause heart palpitations, hallucinations, delirium, convulsions, coma, and death from heart or respiratory failure.

History and Lore

The common name *henbane* comes from the Anglo-Saxons, who called the plant *hanibane* and *hennbana*, meaning "hen killer," because it was especially lethal to poultry.[40] They also knew it as belene and hennebelle and used it medicinally for a few ailments as well as to ward off evil. Although both black and white henbane were commonly used by the ancient Greeks and Romans, Egyptian henbane (*H. muticus*), which is just as poisonous, was also in their herb cabinets. While he suggested the use of white henbane, first-century Greek physician Dioscorides noted that the black and Egyptian species should be avoided as they could too easily produce insanity. Because they were known to be extremely toxic, the henbanes were used medicinally in small amounts, mostly to alleviate pain.

Henbane is one of the oldest-recorded narcotics used as a surgical anesthetic from Roman times to the nineteenth century, sometimes in combination with mandrake and opium. During an archaeological dig in 2010, henbane and poppy seeds were found at the site of a medieval hospital near Edinburgh, Scotland. Dioscorides mentioned that burning white henbane root produced a foul-smelling smoke but suggested it as a general analgesic. This was a practice that continued through later centuries in India and Europe, particularly France and Germany, for curing toothache. The method involved burning henbane seeds and then wafting the smoke into the mouth. Although it may not have stopped the tooth pain, the psychoactive effects of henbane may have made the patient oblivious to it. The technique was also used in England during the seventeenth century and in Yorkshire until the nineteenth century. While herbalist John Gerard gave the practice of using smoke little credence, he noted that washing the feet with a decoction of henbane or smelling the flowers would cause sleep. English botanist and physician Nicholas Culpeper noted its topical use for some ailments but warned against its internal use.

Henbane seeds have been found at various archaeological sites in Denmark, including the tenth-century grave of a woman at the Viking farmstead and ring fortress of Fyrkat near Hobro in the northern region. Grave goods indicate that she was wealthy, important, and may have been a seer. Hundreds of henbane seeds were found in a small purse that had been buried with her. While it is a topic of debate, henbane is often cited as a candidate for the substance that the Vikings used to produce the wild, berserker mental state of battle fury.

40. Pauwels and Christoffels, *Herbs*, 138.

Noted as an ingredient in the notorious witches' flying ointment, the psychoactive compounds in henbane actually can produce a sensation of flying. In Germany, the plant was informally known as *Hexenkraut*, meaning "witches' herb," and *Totenblume*, "flower of death."[41] In the 1538 witch trials in Pomerania, women were accused of using henbane in spells to bewitch people as well as to sexually arouse men. It was purported elsewhere that witches used the plant to summon spirits and to change the weather. Like other plants, henbane was used against alleged witches and administered to the accused to extract confessions. In Hertfordshire, England, Jane Wenham (d. 1730), known as the Witch of Walkern, had been subjected to the abusive use of henbane. However, her 1712 trial was presided over by Justice John Powell (1645–1713), who was skeptical of what he deemed superstitious evidence and unreliable witnesses. During the course of the trial when Wenham was accused of flying, Powell countered that there was no law against it. Even though Wenham was condemned, she was later acquitted.

Despite it being a so-called witches' herb, during the eleventh century, henbane was used for rain magic in public rituals throughout the German state of Hesse and other areas along the Rhine River. The practice lasted well into the nineteenth century.

Called Bilse, Bilsenkraut, and Pilsekraut, henbane was often an ingredient in beer throughout medieval Europe prior to the use of hops. Later it was included in beer to add flavor and increase inebriation. Although the 1516 Bavarian Purity Law destroyed the future of Bilsnenbier, henbane's association with beer lingers in the Czech Republic city of Plzen, which is more widely known by its German name Pilsen and famous for its pale lager called Pilsner.

A famous murder case that involved henbane occurred in England in 1910. American homeopathic physician Hawley Harvey Crippen (1862–1910) was living in London with his wife Cora Turner Crippen (1873–1910), who was a music hall entertainer known as Belle Elmore. Although Crippen was having an affair with a younger woman, it was a different matter when Cora cavorted with someone else, which he suspected she had done a number of times. Whatever the tipping point was that set Crippen off, he poisoned his wife and dismembered her body to hide it under the basement floor of their

41. De Cleene and Lejeune, *Compendium of Symbolic and Ritual Plants in Europe*, 258.

house. People became suspicious when Crippen's lover moved in with him and Cora was nowhere to be seen. When the situation got too hot, Crippen and his new love headed for Canada. Winston Churchill (1874–1965), home secretary of Britain at the time, authorized a £250 reward for his capture. The story made headlines around the world during a chase across the Atlantic with London police arriving in Canada on a faster ship ahead of Crippen. The doctor was convicted and executed for his crime.

Miscellany

In modern medicine, henbane is used to treat stomach issues, respiratory disorders, and motion sickness. In Ayurveda, it is used for Parkinson's disease. Despite its unpleasant odor, henbane is grown as an ornamental garden plant.

Mandrake

SCREAMS, DOGS, AND FAKES

Common Mandrake (*Mandragora officinarum* syn. *Atropa mandragora*); also known as banewort, deadly dwale, death's herb, devil's apple, devil's cherries, love apple, mayapple, mandragora, sorcerer's root

Botanical Family: Solanaceae / Nightshade

Mandrake has a base rosette of pointed, wrinkled leaves that are dark green and resemble Swiss chard. The flowers have five petals and are purplish to yellowish green. They grow in a cluster at the center of the plant. Initially green, the round fruit ripens to dark yellow or orangish red and looks like a little apple. The large parsnip-like root can be about two feet long and is often divided. The plant is native to southern Europe and the Mediterranean.

Toxicity and Cautions

All parts of mandrake are toxic and contain the tropane alkaloids scopolamine, hyoscyamine, atropine, and mandragorine. Ingestion can cause dizziness, vomiting, confusion, rapid heart rate, hallucinations, paralysis of the central nervous system, and death.

History and Lore

Harry Potter books and films introduced some of mandrake's folklore, mainly that it screamed loudly when pulled from the ground. According to widespread belief, hearing the sound would drive a person insane or even kill them. A method for avoiding such consequences involved hitching up a dog to the plant, and then from a safe distance, coaxing it to run. Man's best friend died in the effort, of course. German author and folklorist Jacob Grimm (1785–1863), of Grimm Brothers fame, noted that any canine used in the process had to be completely black and that the deed had to be performed on a Friday. Reasons for these details are unknown.

Contrary to European beliefs, Arab herbalist and writer Ibn-el-Beither (fl. thirteenth century) noted that the scream did not kill whoever dug it up; instead, a demon in the root took possession of the person. Ibn-el-Beither also put the record straight concerning the ancient story of the plant glowing at night by noting that glowworms were attracted to and congregated on the leaves. This resulted in the Arab folk name *devil's candles*. At any rate, like irises and other tuberous plants, a faint squeak-like noise often accompanies pulling mandrake from the ground.

Whether or not it screamed, digging up a mandrake root was a complicated process. An early description comes from third-century BCE Greek philosopher Theophrastus. He explained that three circles had to be drawn with a sword in the dirt around the plant and the person doing the digging had to face west while another person danced around in a circle reciting a specific incantation. While the use of elaborate ceremonies declined after the Middle Ages, watered-down versions of it lingered into the nineteenth century in rural Italy and the Czech Republic.

Greek philosopher Pythagoras (c. 570–c. 500 BCE) was the first to describe the root as a miniature person. In the first century CE, physician Dioscorides claimed that there were separate male and female roots. In later centuries, the plants were sometimes distinguished with common mandrake being called mandrake, and the autumn mandrake (*M. autumnalis*), womandrake. It didn't take long for imagination to take over, and a humanlike form of the root was often depicted in medieval and Renaissance art in great detail, including genitalia.

Of course, if a plant was poisonous, witches had to be involved. They reputedly harvested the root from beneath gallows because the malevolence of the criminals was believed to seep into the plant, which in turn would fuel evil spells. Arab ideas about a demon connected with the plant filtered into medieval European belief: owning a root was cited as witchcraft because it meant that a person had a mandrake goblin to do their bidding. During her trial, Joan of Arc (d. 1431) was accused of possessing a mandrake root. In 1603 a woman in Romorantin, France, and in 1630 three women in Hamburg, Germany, were executed for possessing roots. The medieval Germans called mandrake *Hexen-*

männchen, meaning "witches' manikin" or "small man," and in England they were called hag's manikin.

Attitudes gradually changed. In Germany it was eventually believed that the root held a somewhat devilish but usually benevolent spirit called Alraun, which took human form. This spirit was said to have the power to double a person's money and get rid of enemies. This idea spread throughout Europe, Scandinavia, and Britain. Possession of a mandrake was said to bring luck and wealth to a family and sometimes predict the future.

Mandrake was not common in the wild or easy to cultivate, which added to its mystique and value. The root became so prized that it was often passed on like a family heirloom. To work its magic and keep its potency, it had to be kept in a secret place and cared for properly. Information varies, but generally it had to be bathed in milk or washed with red wine on Fridays. In addition, it had to be dressed or wrapped in red or white silk and served food and drink. According to some sources, a mandrake would kill its owner if it wasn't appropriately pampered.

While the craze for mandrake reached a high point during the sixteenth and seventeenth centuries, the decline was slow, and amulets were kept well into the twentieth century. During the height of the frenzy, mandrake was so sought after that it was a widespread cottage industry to alter other types of roots, such as bryony, to look like mandrake. With an interest in the occult, Holy Roman Emperor Rudolf II (1576–1612) kept two mandrake roots, which are now in the Austrian National Library Museum in Vienna. He also had an amulet medallion containing a piece of mandrake that turned out to be alpine leek (*Allium victorialis*). Even the high and mighty were duped by the fervor.

The medicinal use of mandrake dates to the ninth century BCE and was described on Assyrian tablets as a painkiller and sleep aid. In early medieval Europe, steeping the root or boiling it in wine was a simple anesthetic for surgery. However, belief in mandrake's aphrodisiac power accounted for its most widespread use. In Greece, the plant was dedicated to Aphrodite, who was also called *Dios Mandragoritis*, meaning "goddess of the mandrake." The Egyptians and Arabs associated the mandrake with sex, referring to the plant as phallus of the field and devil's testicles, respectively.[42] The Persians called it love-root.

42. Watts, *Elsevier's Dictionary of Plant Lore*, 340.

Miscellany

Despite its dangers, mandrake is used as a homeopathic remedy and in some herbal medicine; however, the North American mayapple (*Podophyllum peltatum*), which is also known as mandrake, is sometimes used in its place. While mandrake plants are not widely available, the seeds can be purchased online for the adventurous gardener.

Poppy

NOTHING BUT TROUBLE

Opium Poppy, White Poppy (*Papaver somniferum*); also known as bale-wort, blue poppy, carnation poppy, drowsy poppy, garden poppy, Hungarian poppy, opium plant, white poppy

Botanical Family: Papaveraceae / Poppy

Poppy plants reach three to four feet tall and have deeply lobed, toothed leaves. The cup-shaped flowers range from white to deep mauve with a purple spot at the base of each petal. Its seedpod is spherical and topped with a disc that formed from the stigma, the little knob at the top of a tubelike structure in the center of the flower. Poppy seeds are called khus khus. The poppy is native to southeastern Europe and western Asia but has become naturalized in a wider area.

Toxicity and Cautions

All parts of the plant are toxic and contain the alkaloids codeine, morphine, and thebaine. Opium is produced from the latex sap of the poppy pods. Heroin and oxycodone are derivatives of morphine. Ingestion can cause confusion, delirium, decreased awareness, breathing difficulty, nausea, vomiting, constipation, extreme sleepiness, and death. Only processed, food-grade poppy seeds are edible.

History and Lore

The opium poppy may be the world's oldest medicinal plant, but it seems to have brought nothing but trouble. Or, more accurately, the inappropriate use, profiteering, and greed have caused trouble. Originating in the Mediterranean region, the poppy was domesticated from a wild ancestor, *P. somniferum* subsp. *setigerum*. Pods and the remnants of poppy-seed bread have been found in a Neolithic settlement in Switzerland dating to 5500 BCE. The Sumerians were cultivating poppies by 3000 BCE. According to clay tablets, they called it *gil hul*, meaning the "joy plant."[43] Its euphoric effects were apparently known. Cultivated in extensive fields near Thebes, poppies were noted in the Egyptian Ebers Papyrus as an anesthetic and an ingredient in several remedies. It was also used to calm crying children. The poppies that the Egyptians hybridized at Thebes were later known by the Latin name *Opium thebaicum*, which is the source of the modern name of the alkaloid thebaine.

The Greeks were well aware of opium's power and dedicated the plant to Hypnos, the god of sleep, and his son Morpheus, the god of dreams. Greek physicians prescribed it as a sedative for physical and spiritual pain. Arab physicians prescribed opium extensively, especially as a sedative and an anesthetic for surgery. Eleventh-century physician and philosopher Avicenna wrote a treatise about opium and may have used it as a recreational drug himself, which was common at the time. Partaking of alcohol was prohibited under Islam, but not the use of hashish or opium.

Sixteenth-century Flemish herbalist Rembert Dodoens regarded opium as dangerous and evil but noted that it was sometimes necessary to use. Quite the opposite and with his usual full-steam-ahead enthusiasm, Swiss physician and alchemist Paracelsus created little black pills of opium that he called the stones of immortality. Using information from ancient texts, he came up with laudanum. His recipe called for opium, brandy, crushed pearls, a tincture of henbane, and frogspawn. Not a remedy for vegans. A century later, English physician Thomas Sydenham (1624–1689) threw out the frogspawn and pearls and standardized the laudanum formula using opium, saffron, cinnamon, and cloves dissolved in Spanish wine. It became very popular.

Opium was readily available in England as Queen Elizabeth I had instructed merchants to import the best from India. By the early nineteenth century, apothecaries and grocers in England carried laudanum and opium. In addition, most British gardens had a patch of poppies. The seeds were boiled and the liquid used as a remedy for fever, general aches and pains, and other

43. Cumo, *Encyclopedia of Cultivated Plants*, 834.

complaints. In English and French literary and artistic circles, it was stylish to smoke opium, and the universal tranquillizer, laudanum, served as a source of inspiration for poets and writers, many of them famous. The morphine alkaloid was isolated in 1803, and its widespread medicinal use led to addictions; however, it was generally regarded as a fashionable habit and not illicit. In the late nineteenth century, the ordinary morphine addict tended to be a wealthy person and not someone who would become a social problem. About seventy years later, a derivative of morphine, heroin, was discovered and regarded medicinally as miraculous. Morphine users gravitated to the new substance.

As the Egyptians had done, Europeans used opium on children. It was customary in England and parts of Europe to give babies and toddlers a decoction of seed capsules or laudanum to help them settle down and not cry. Sadly, but not surprisingly, it was sometimes fatal. Teething babies in England were given poppy tea or a few seeds tied into a linen pouch to suck on. From the working poor to the wealthy, this was standard practice.

In the 1890s, American tabloid publisher William Randolph Hearst (1863–1951) used the racist label Yellow Peril to describe Chinese men and their opium as a danger to the Western world. Tragically ironic, it was the other way around. Although opium had been spreading eastward along the Silk Road, Arab traders introduced Egyptian opium into China. Initially used for medicinal purposes, as elsewhere, the recreational use caught on. It was consumed as a drink until the seventeenth century when the Dutch introduced tobacco and pipes. Even though opium was a luxury only affordable by the wealthy, there was a market for old smoking pipes that were cleaned out and the scrapings of opium sold to the poor.

The Chinese consumed more than they could produce, and the obliging Portuguese stepped in to supply the market. In the mid-eighteenth century, China tried to save itself by banning imports, but smuggling was extremely profitable. While the British East India Company dominated the opium trade, there was so much money involved that some Americans couldn't resist getting in on the act. Thomas H. Perkins (1764–1854) of Boston, who was already engaged in the despicable slave trade, was one of them. Another was New York businessman John Jacob Astor (1763–1848), who made millions in opium smuggling behind the façade of upper-class respectability.

It wasn't until the early twentieth century, as England was struggling to reduce opium use on its own shores, that it finally entered into a treaty with China to restrict the opium trade. But it was too late—Pandora's box had been opened, and the whole world is still dealing with the scourge of opiates.

Miscellany

Processed, food-grade poppy seeds are used in many baked goods and other foods. Even though they are not harmful, they contain traces of opiates that remain in the blood for about forty-eight hours. My daughter-in-law unexpectedly discovered this during routine medical tests.

Poppy seed oil is used in cooking, Western herbal remedies, Ayurveda, and Traditional Chinese Medicine. Opium poppy is available as a garden plant and can be grown for seed production, but, as you may expect, it is illegal to produce opium.

Strychnine Tree

OF MICE AND MEN

Strychnine Tree (***Strychnos nux-vomica***)*;* also known as dog button, nux vomica tree, poison nut tree, semen strychnos, quaker buttons

Botanical Family: Loganiaceae / Logan

Native to Southeast Asia and India, the strychnine tree grows about forty feet tall and resembles a pear tree with its shiny oval leaves that curl slightly inward. The small pale green flowers are funnel shaped and have an unpleasant odor. The fruit looks like a small orange and contains up to five seeds surrounded by white pulp. The disc-shaped seeds are hard and gray.

Toxicity and Cautions

All parts of the tree are toxic, especially the bark and nuts, and contain the alkaloids strychnine and brucine. Strychnine affects the central nervous system. Ingestion may cause restlessness, jaw tightness, difficulty breathing, painful muscle spasms, and violent convulsions. Poisoning often leads to a rigid arched back, a position that only long-term yoga practitioners can achieve. Death is usually from asphyxiation and can occur in less than an hour if exposed to a high dose. Victims are usually conscious of the effects.

Parasitic plants that attach to the tree absorb the toxins and become equally deadly. Bush rope (*S. toxifera*), strychnine's South American cousin, was one of the sources of curare that Indigenous people used to poison arrows.

History and Lore

One of the more famous poisons, strychnine, is a killer of mice and men, or rather a killer of pests and people. It was known in Europe and Britain in the sixteenth century and widely used to kill rodents because it was cheap and available from the local apothecary. Rats, mice, moles, magpies, and crows were common targets, but it was also used to dispose of unwanted cats and dogs, and sometimes people. An extract from the seed was known as strychnine and the powdered seeds were called *nux vomica*, which in Latin means "vomiting nut." Before the cumulative effects of strychnine were understood, it was used medicinally as a purge. During severe plague years, it was anything goes, and strychnine was often offered as a cure.

In eighteenth-century England, India Pale Ales (IPAs) became a popular beverage. Brewed with more hops than other ales, IPAs tended to be bitter. By the nineteenth century, it had become somewhat common for pub owners to water down beer to boost profits. However, when it came to IPAs, they could use more water and add a little strychnine to hold the hop-like bitterness as well as give the customers an extra buzz.

In early nineteenth-century France, professor of medicine Pierre Fouquier (1776–1850) came up with the theory that strychnine could provide a jolt of energy that would help patients with paralytic limbs regain normal movement. Mixing strychnine extract with alcohol, he experimented on hospital patients and, sometimes, it seemed to work. We can only hope that Fouquier's intent was to improve the process; however, one unfortunate patient who had strychnine administered via enema might not have agreed. As if that wasn't bad enough, the same patient was also accidentally given strychnine in pill form. Although he didn't die, he didn't improve, either. Fouquier removed the man from his list of patients, most likely to keep up his success ratio.

Eventually, the risks of strychnine became clear and outweighed its potential medicinal value. As least in hospitals. Apothecaries found that it was popular with customers. In the late nineteenth and early twentieth centuries, strychnine was used as a stimulant and tonic. Even Emily Inglethorp in Agatha Christie's *The Mysterious Affair at Styles* took strychnine tonics for her nerves.

Because strychnine can cause the sense organs to become more sensitive, French scientists experimented on its potential sexual applications. Although nothing came of it, so to speak, rumors lingered from the Victorian era of its Viagra-like use. In fact, the idea persisted into the 1960s when a Miami-based company, All Products Unlimited, discovered the Victorian aphrodisiac and cashed in on the changing mores. In 1966, their product Jems was marketed as a natural pep pill for strength and, according to their advertisement, night pep (wink wink). These little gems were pep pills with a small dose of strychnine. Ironically, the company was taken to court and indicted for making false claims about the product's sexual benefits but not for its strychnine content.

Of course, strychnine is the stuff of murder. In Staffordshire, Dr. William Palmer (1824–1856), who became known as the Rugeley Poisoner, was convicted and executed for murdering his friend John Parsons Cook (d. 1855) with strychnine. Palmer was also suspected of poisoning his brother, mother-in-law, and sister-in-law with prussic acid. In Leeds, William Dove (1824–1856) killed his wife with strychnine so he could marry the woman next door. At his trial he pleaded insanity using his past record, which showed that as a child he'd chased his sister with a hot poker, set his bedroom curtains on fire, and tormented cats. He also claimed that a local wizard had incited him to murder. His oddball defense strategy didn't work and he was executed. Scottish-Canadian doctor Thomas Neill Cream (1850–1892), who had been a medical student with Arthur Conan Doyle in Edinburgh, became known as the Lambeth Poisoner. After murdering several people in Canada and Chicago and serving ten years in jail, he moved to London where he continued his practice, medical and otherwise. In the end he had murdered eight women, one of whom was his wife, and one man with strychnine.

Perhaps the most bizarre episode of strychnine use took place at the 1904 Olympics in St. Louis. Although the marathon race began and ended in the stadium, it was mostly run on deserted country roads, and American runner Thomas Hicks (1876–1952) took the lead in the first mile. When he was about halfway through the course, he begged for water from his trainers, who had followed in a car. Instead, they gave him an energy drink of egg whites with a little strychnine. At that time, the medical establishment still believed strychnine to be a short-term stimulant, plus performance-enhancing drugs were not outlawed in athletic competitions. Further along the course, Hicks was dosed again with strychnine and brandy. He won the race with his trainers holding him upright, his legs moving mechanically in the air as they carried him over the finish line. Hicks was hallucinating as he was declared the winner and amazingly lived to tell the tale.

Miscellany

Nux vomica is used in homeopathy and in Ayurveda, where it is known as Kupilu. Strychnine is still used to dispatch rodents. Because it is a white, odorless, crystalline powder, it is sometimes an adulterant in street drugs.

Yew

MEMENTO MORI

English Yew (*Taxus baccata*); also known as common yew, European yew
Botanical Family: Taxaceae / Yew

The yew is an evergreen bush or spreading tree that often has multiple trunks with reddish-brown, peeling bark. When the trees get old and gnarled, their twisted trunks look as though they had been liquid at one time. The yew has dark green needlelike leaves that are glossy on top with two yellowish or grayish green bands underneath. The flowers are small, scaly, and conelike. The red, cup-shaped aril or berry holds a stone (seed) in the middle. It is not uncommon for yews to live several thousand years. Yew is native to Europe, western Asia, and northern Africa.

Toxicity and Cautions

Except for the red fleshy aril, all parts of the yew are poisonous and contain taxine alkaloids, which are cardiotoxins. Ingestion can cause nausea, vomiting, diarrhea, headache, dizziness, tremors, shortness of breath, abnormal heartbeat, cardiac or respiratory failure, and death. Symptoms can occur within an hour, and death, within twenty-four. The aril is said to have a sweet taste, but it is not worth the risk to find out.

History and Lore

The yew's association with death and the dead is at least several thousand years old. The Greeks and Romans dedicated the tree to Hecate, goddess of the underworld, possibly because it is dark and poisonous. For the Greeks, a yew in a cemetery was a symbol of mourning. In medieval France, mourners carried yew branches at funerals. As Shakespeare noted in *Twelfth Night* (act 2, scene

4), the English custom was to tuck sprigs of yew into burial shrouds. Although associated with death, because it is a long-living evergreen, it was also a symbol of immortality and the afterlife.

According to Greek mythology, the goddess Artemis dipped her arrows into yew poison to murder the daughters of Niobe as a punishment for her pride. Roman poet Ovid noted that yew trees grew in the underworld along the River Styx. Although British anthropologist and folklorist James George Frazer (1854–1941) asserted that mistletoe was the golden bough carried by Trojan hero Aeneas to gain access to the underworld, more recent scholarship points to the yew. A yew branch fits the description of the golden bough being used like a staff, which is something impossible with a clump of mistletoe. Plus, on rare occasion, a single branch on a yew tree can turn a golden-yellow hue. A very old yew in Defynnog, Wales, has been producing golden boughs for about twenty years.

Yew is the most ancient type of wood known for making weapons with samples dating to the Paleolithic. A spear with a fire-hardened tip was found at Clacton-on-Sea in Essex, England, and a spear at Lehringen in Lower Saxony, Germany, was found amongst the bones of an extinct species of elephant. The Latin genus name, *Taxus*, may have been derived from the Greek *toxon*, meaning "bow," or toxicon, the poison used on arrows, which was most often from the yew in Europe.[44] The tree was highly revered by the Gauls, who used it for both arrow poison and bows. The ancient Irish poisoned their weapons with a combination of yewberries, hellebore, and devil's bit (probably *Succisa pratensis*). For thousands of years from Homer to Shakespeare, bows of yew wood had a reputation for being the best. In the *Iliad*, the archers besieging the city of Troy used them, and in *Richard II* (act 3, scene 2), the yew is noted as "double-fatal," killing through the power of a bow or its poison. The English and Welsh favored yew wood for longbows because of its strength and flexibility.

Because of its poisonous nature, the yew found little use as a medicinal plant. First-century Greek physician Dioscorides warned that it caused diarrhea and death. Roman naturalist Pliny the Elder noted that even drinking wine from a cask made of yew wood could cause death. Similarly, it was considered dangerous to place beehives near a yew tree because it was believed that the

---

44. Watts, *Elsevier's Dictionary of Plant Lore*, 445.

bees would pick up the poison and taint the honey. However, Pliny also noted that hammering a copper nail into a yew would render it harmless.

Greek physician Nicander and historian Plutarch were a little more extreme in noting that it was dangerous for a person to be near a yew and even seeking relief from the sun underneath one could cause death. This belief existed well into the sixteenth century and was echoed by Flemish herbalist Rembert Dodoens. English herbalist and astrologer Robert Turner (fl. 1640–1664) also acknowledged the dangers but noted that a yew planted in a churchyard was useful because it absorbed the poisonous vapors exhaled from the graves, thus protecting the living. Reputedly, it also prevented the appearance of ghosts. According to folklore in Brittany, roots of a churchyard yew grew through the mouth of each corpse. Perhaps to keep them in place or to free their souls.

Throughout Britain, yews often marked places of public assembly as well as meeting places for official courts and moots. A yew in the churchyard of Berkhamsted, England, was the spot where New Year's Eve revelers gathered. The great Ankerwycke Yew at Runnymede along the River Thames was the place where the Magna Carta was signed in 1215 and, according to legend, where Henry VIII proposed to Anne Boleyn (c. 1507–1536).

Despite its many associations with death, medieval German abbess and herbalist Hildegard von Bingen called the yew *laetitiam signat*, meaning a "symbol of joy."[45] Through the centuries, the yew served as a memento mori, a reminder of death, and certainly in medieval times death was a thing greatly feared and often at the forefront of many people's minds. Yet, I get the feeling that Hildegard may have been harkening back to the more ancient reminder of death and the yew's duality of symbolizing death and the continuity life. Yes, memento mori—remember you will die, but in the meantime, live and enjoy life.

Miscellany

The chemical constituents taxotere and taxol have been isolated from the European yew and the Pacific yew (*T. brevifolia*) and are used in chemotherapy drugs for certain malignant tumors. Because of its dense foliage, the yew became popular in formal Tudor and classic French gardens for a crisp, clipped appearance and topiary. It is still popular as an ornamental tree.

45. De Cleene and Lejeune, *Compendium of Symbolic and Ritual Plants in Europe*, 745.

PART 3
Baneful Backyard

Just as some plants listed under Classic Killers are widely used in gardens today, some of the plants in this category had their place in antiquity. Cherry laurel served as a botanical murder weapon for the Romans, and pennyroyal appeared in Greek mythology. Although rhubarb may seem like a common garden vegetable (or fruit depending on your point of view), who would have thought that it had a journey along the exotic Silk Road from China? While tansy and oleander have been associated with death and used as funeral plants for many centuries, the beloved lily of the valley has enjoyed a sweet reputation even though it can be lethal. Let's have a look at what delightfully deadly menace might be growing in your backyard.

Arnica

MISTAKEN IDENTITY

Mountain Arnica (*Arnica montana*); also known as fallkraut, leopard's bane, mountain daisy, mountain snuff, mountain tobacco, sneezewort, wolf's bane, wolfsblume

Botanical Family: Asteraceae, formerly Compositae / Aster, Daisy

Indigenous to the mountains of Europe, Siberia, and Asia, arnica grows up to three feet tall and has round, hairy stems. The bright green upper leaves are toothed and sometimes have a wooly texture; the lower leaves have rounded ends. Their scent can cause sneezing. The daisylike flowers are bright yellow with a center disc that is yellowish orange. Of the approximately forty species of arnica, at least twenty-six are native to North America.

Toxicity and Cautions

The flowers and aerial parts of this plant contain the toxic terpene helenalin. The roots and rhizomes contain thymol, which is a registered pesticide in the United States. Ingesting arnica can cause painful irritation to the gastrointestinal tract, vomiting, liver failure, damage to the heart, and possibly death. Although it is generally regarded as safe externally, prolonged use can cause skin irritation, eczema, and dermatitis. Arnica should never be used on broken skin as the toxins can be absorbed. This plant is also an abortifacient.

History and Lore

It is somewhat incongruous that a plant with a genus name that may have been derived from the Greek *arnikos*, meaning "lamb's skin," in reference to the texture of the leaves, has folk names that associate it with wolves and leopards.[46] This is possibly due to arnica's misidentification, which lasted for centuries. During the Middle Ages in German-speaking areas of Europe, it had the names *wolverly* and *wohlverleih*, meaning "to bestow well-being," which is ironic because of its poisonous nature.[47] At any rate, the words seem to have been misunderstood by non-German speakers, and arnica was given a range of names linking it with wolves. Although the plant has potentially deadly properties, they are probably not enough to dispatch a large canine. However, it may be that the bitter, pungent taste of the leaves and fetid smell of the flowers were enough to link the plant with danger and a propensity for killing.

Calling it Wolfesgelegena, twelfth-century German mystic and herbalist Hildegard von Bingen may have also associated arnica with wolves. The exact meaning of the name she gave it is unclear; however, she was known for inventing words that have puzzled scholars for centuries. That said, Hildegard prescribed arnica for the treatment of skin ulcers, plus the Latin *lupus*, meaning "wolf," was a colloquial word used during medieval times for a wide range of skin disorders. Perhaps it doesn't take a great leap of the imagination to see a logical point to the name *Wolfesgelegena*. On the other hand, in her medical treatise *Physica*, she made quite a big jump from arnica's healing properties to noting that it was an overwhelmingly powerful aphrodisiac used in love magic. This is one of those things that makes you go *hmmm*.

Concerning the folk name *leopard's bane*, arnica looks very similar to the plant known as great leopard's bane (*Doronicum pardalianches*), which was believed to have enough poisonous power to bring down a leopard, or at least keep it away from the house where the plant grew. Although great leopard's bane and arnica are native to the mountainous regions of Europe, it seems curious that people would concern themselves with leopards since there haven't been any in the wild there for over ten thousand years. Be that as it may,

46. Foster and Johnson, *Desk Reference to Nature's Medicine*, 20.

47. Drysdale, Dudgeon, and Hughes, *The British Journal of Homeopathy*, 299.

Italian physician and naturalist Andrea Mattioli experimented with arnica on a dog, which died. Perhaps as a warning, the name *leopard's bane* has more of a dramatic ring to it than *dog's bane*.

Like many plants, and especially poisonous ones, arnica was believed to have magical properties. In Bavaria, it was placed under the rafters of a home or barn or hung on the walls to protect the structure against lightning and hail. In addition, in the Tyrol region of Austria, it was believed that hanging arnica on the front door would make a house fireproof.

Despite its toxicity, arnica has a long tradition of use in German-speaking areas of Europe for the treatment of bruises and sprains. It was also used as an abortifacient. Since at least the sixteenth century, arnica was used throughout Europe and for a wider range of ailments, including muscle pain, falls, traumatic injuries, insect bites, and heart failure. Physicians readily prescribed it as a stimulant for the heart and circulatory system. In his later years, German poet Johann Wolfgang von Goethe (1749–1832) drank arnica tea to ease the pain of angina. Arnica was also used as a tobacco substitute in France and Spain where it was known as tobacco of the mountains in their respective languages.[48]

Swiss naturalist and physician Conrad Gesner, also known as Konrad von Gessner, (1516–1565), was regarded as the German Pliny because of his wide range of interests. He wrote a number of books, but two, one on medicine and the other a comprehensive book on botany, were never completed. Although he is often said to have died of the plague, Gesner experimented on himself with arnica and sent a letter to a friend, saying that he'd had no ill effects from it. He died later that same day.

Several North American species of arnica were used medicinally by Indigenous people. Heartleaf arnica (*A. cordifolia*) and broadleaf arnica (*A. latifolia*) were used for cuts and bruises by the Colville, Shuswap, and Thompson tribes in the northwestern United States and in British Columbia. The Catawba of South Carolina used common leopardbane (*A. acaulis* syn. *D. acaule*) as a liniment. Many settlers to the New World adapted local plants to the uses of similar species they left behind in Europe. In New England, during the eighteenth and nineteenth centuries, arnica was used in a topical remedy for sprains, rheumatism, and

48. Stephenson and Churchill, *Medical Botany*, 124.

backache. Called toad ointment, the recipe called for two ounces of arnica tincture, unsalted butter, and, yes, toads. Four good-sized ones to be exact.

Miscellany

Today, arnica is used in homeopathic treatments and herbal remedies as well as cosmetic and hair products. Various species, including mountain arnica, are grown as garden plants.

Brugmansia

PSYCHEDELIC BREWS

Brugmansia, Angel's Trumpet (*Brugmansia suaveolens* syn. *Datura suaveolens*); also known as angel's tears, night bells, snowy angel's trumpet, tree datura, trumpet flower, white angel's trumpet

Botanical Family: Solanaceae / Nightshade

Native to the tropics of South America, where it is now extinct in the wild, brugmansia has become naturalized in other parts of the world. It grows as a woody shrub or small tree that can reach over twenty feet tall. The large oblong leaves are coarsely toothed and slightly hairy. Its white, pendulous, trumpet-shaped flowers are sometimes yellow and can grow up to a foot long. Partly closed during the day, the flowers open at night, and their alluring fragrance becomes even stronger. There are seven species of brugmansia and thousands of cultivated hybrids.

Toxicity and Cautions

All parts of the plant are toxic, with the seeds, roots, and leaves containing the highest concentrations of the tropane alkaloids atropine, scopolamine, and hyoscyamine. These toxins can be absorbed by handling plant material. The pollen is also toxic. Ingesting brugmansia can cause increased heart rate, confusion, convulsions, hallucinations, coma, and death from respiratory failure. Hallucinations produced by the plant have been reported as hellish and terrifying.

History and Lore

Originally classified in the genus *Datura*, the flowers are an easy way to tell the difference between the two genera: *Datura* flowers sit upright, *Brugmansia* are pendulous. Nevertheless, both plants are toxic. With the scent a hallmark of brugmansia, the Latin species name *suaveolens*, which means "with a sweet fragrance," is apropos.[49]

Brugmansia has had a few medicinal applications by Indigenous people throughout South America. However, because of the powerful psychoactive effects, it was mostly used by shamans, who drank it as tea or smoked it to generate visions for initiation rituals and healing ceremonies. Although the trance state is generally peaceful, in the process of getting there, a person may become violent and require physical restraint. Reputedly, consuming brugmansia is an ordeal with aftereffects that can be quite sickening and can cause temporary insanity.

The earliest recorded use of its psychoactive properties was made by mid-seventeenth century Spanish explorers who gave the plant the name *el borrachero*, meaning "the inebriator."[50] Brugmansia was later described more fully and documented in the late eighteenth century from samples taken back to Europe by German and French explorers and naturalists. In 1935, yellow angel's trumpet (*B. candida*) was first collected by Colombian ethnobotanist Hernando Garcia-Barriga (1913–2005) in the Sibundoy Valley of southwestern Colombia. Because of its long thin leaves, it was locally known as snake inebriator. According to the people of the area, giant snakes were often encountered in the visions produced after consuming the plant.

In the Putumayo region, an area that straddles Ecuador and Colombia, the Siona people used two species of white flowered angel's trumpet (*B. Suaveolens* and *B. insignis*) to increase the psychoactive power of a drink called yage, which is also known as ayahuasca. Brugmansia was added to other similar drinks. For festivals and religious ceremonies, the seeds of various species were added to chicha, a common drink made from fermented cassava root (*Manihot esculenta*) or maize (*Zea mays*). Brugmansia seeds may have been combined with coca leaves and used medicinally as an anesthetic.

Some species of brugmansia were grown for their high psychoactive content. Golden angel's trumpet (*B. Aurea*), also known as culebra borrachero, was cultivated by the Camsá (or Kamentsá) and the Inga (or Ingano) tribes of

---

49. Harrison, *Latin for Gardeners*, 196.

50. Rätsch, *The Encyclopedia of Psychoactive Plants*, 356.

Colombia. Made into a beverage used by shamans, it was believed that during trance, the brugmansia plant spirits would speak to them. The Camsá and Inga also used it for divination, healing, and prophecy. Medicinally, brugmansia served as a remedy for arthritis. In other areas of the region, the plant was used as a purgative and as a treatment for infections. In Ecuador, the shamans of the Canelo people used brugmansia to aid in contacting and working with various spirit helpers and animal spirits as well as for prophetic dreams.

In the Andes of Colombia, red angel's trumpet (*B. sanguinea*) is regarded as sacred to the Muisca (or Chibcha) people. It is used in rituals at their Temple of the Sun located in Sogamoso. In Peru, the plant is known as *huacacachu*, meaning "plant of the tomb," because shamans use it to communicate with ancestors.[51] This name is also said to have come from its alleged use to produce visions that lead to buried treasure in ancient tombs.

In Peru, a person unwittingly intoxicated by someone else is called *chamicado*, meaning "touched by the angel's trumpet."[52] In the United States from Los Angeles to Louisiana and Florida, adventure-seeking teenagers have quite wittingly sought the hallucinogenic effects of the plant. To their dismay, instead of a recreational high, they experienced the extremely unpleasant results of brugmansia poisoning. It's an oft-repeated situation with each generation; after all, did we always heed our parents' warnings?

Angel's trumpet was introduced into Europe in the eighteenth century as an ornamental plant, and by the early nineteenth century it appeared in English magazines and gardening books. Brugmansia became popular for the garden and fulfilled the Victorians' love of hefty-sized houseplants. During the art nouveau movement in Mexico in the early twentieth century, the flowing shape of the flowers was a frequent motif for glass lampshades as well as patterns in cloth designs. Because of its dangers, brugmansia didn't figure in European medicine, except as a component in Doctor Andreu's cigarettes. Invented by Barcelona pharmacist Salvador Andreu Grau (1841–1928), they were marketed as an anti-asthmatic.

---

51. Pratt, *Encyclopedia of Shamanism*, 68.

52. Bastien, *Healers of the Andes*, 114.

Miscellany

Brugmansia is a popular ornamental plant in the garden and in containers. In Mexico, Central and South America, and parts of Florida, brugmansia has escaped the garden and invaded residential areas. If you have one in your garden, planted or uninvited, treat it with care and don't sit under it holding a beverage or its falling pollen could make you a chamicado.

Castor Oil Plant

DEADLIEST IN THE WORLD

Castor Oil Plant (*Ricinus communis*); also known as castor bean, Mexico seed, mole-bean plant, palma Christi

Botanical Family: Euphorbiaceae / Spurge

Depending on its location, this fast-growing shrub reaches six to thirty feet tall. The star-shaped leaves are deeply lobed, heavily veined, and have toothed edges. The flower stalks have both male (pale green or white) and female (red) flowers. Covered with soft bristles, the round fruit capsule holds three bean-like seeds, which are oval and mottled brown. Native to the Mediterranean, north and eastern Africa, and western Asia, the castor oil plant has become naturalized in many warm areas around the world.

Toxicity and Cautions

This plant contains the toxalbumin (toxic protein) ricin, which causes damage by interfering with cell function. While the seeds have the highest concentration and can be deadly, other parts of the plant can cause serious allergic reaction and should be regarded as poisonous. The toxin can be ingested, inhaled, or absorbed through a cut or open sore on the skin. The hull that covers the seed is extremely poisonous. Symptoms of ricin poisoning are similar to severe food poisoning and include nausea, vomiting, bloody diarrhea, and seizures. It results in tissue damage and multiple organ failure. There is no antidote. Castor oil plant is also an abortifacient.

History and Lore

The name *castor* was mistakenly used by English traders who thought the oil came from the chasteberry plant (*Vitex agnus-castus*), which the Spanish and

Portuguese called agno-casto. The name evolved into *castor*. Carl Linnaeus named the genus *Ricinus*, Latin for tick, because the bean resembles that arachnid.[53] In the sixteenth century, the plant became known as *palma Christi* or "Christ's hand," in reference to the shape of its leaves and because of its use in healing. Although it is one of the most poisonous plants in the world, the oil obtained by pressing the seeds does not contain the toxin. In sixteenth-century England, the oil was called oleum cicinum, which later became oleum ricini, and finally castor oil. It was commonly used as a laxative into the early 1960s.

The plant was cultivated by the ancient Egyptians and important enough to have been included in burials; the seeds have been found scattered in tombs. Its many medicinal uses were listed in the Ebers Papyrus and other texts of the period. The seeds were a common purge taken in beer. Other parts of the plant were used for treating wounds and to induce childbirth. The oil was used in cosmetics and as an emollient to protect skin and hair from the harsh desert environment. The Egyptians also used it as lamp oil for lighting. The Mano people of Liberia made an infusion from the leaves to bathe the temples as a cure for headaches. Similarly in the American South, wrapping the head with castor leaves was a treatment for headaches and fever.

While Hippocrates prescribed the oil as a laxative, first-century herbalist and physician Dioscorides noted that different parts of the plant could be put to wider medicinal uses. By the Middle Ages in Europe, the oil was mainly used externally as a lubricant and liniment. The roots and leaves were made into poultices in folk remedies for wounds, boils, and sores. Coming full circle, its use as a laxative became most prevalent in the eighteenth and nineteenth centuries. Regarded as a quick but gentle purge, it was regularly used to keep regular.

From at least the sixteenth century, castor was a popular ornamental plant in English gardens and graced many London neighborhoods with its tropical, exotic appearance. Plus, it was a gardener's dream. It has no pests—insects that feed on it die—and it could be used to kill moles.

However, there is a dark side to the use of castor oil. Although it is widely known that Italian dictator Benito Mussolini (1883–1945) and his fascist mob used it as an instrument of torture, the oil has been used as such before and after World War II for political control. In addition to the horror of being force-

53. Cumo, *Encyclopedia of Cultivated Plants*, 232.

fed castor oil and the resulting diarrhea, victims can die from dehydration. It is a torture that leaves no telltale marks on a prisoner's body.

Like other poisons, the castor oil plant has been used outright for murder. The Bulgarian dissident writer Georgi Markov (1929–1978) was assassinated by ricin poisoning. While walking across Waterloo Bridge in London, he was stabbed in the leg with an umbrella tip that had been outfitted with a poison pellet. In 2019, a Belgian man murdered his partner by putting castor beans in her food, and in 2020, envelopes containing ricin were sent to the White House and several Texas state law enforcement officials.

Art imitates life, or is it the other way around? Ricin is the instrument of murder in popular whodunit novels by Agatha Christie in *The House of Lurking Death*, American author Douglas Clark (1919–1993) in *Premedicated Murder*, and Canadian American author Charlotte MacLeod (1922–2005) in *Trouble in the Brasses*.

Poisoning has also been accidental in an innocent way via jewelry. The attractive markings on the seeds seem to beg to be made into necklaces. If the hard seed coat is not damaged, the bean can pass through the body intact, leaving a person unharmed. However, as is common, especially with children, a bead necklace is something to chew on, thus releasing ricin into the mouth. So how much does it take for it to be fatal? Chewing on one bean can kill a child, while it might take eight to ten to kill an adult. Put another way, ricin weighing about the same as a grain of table salt can kill a 160-pound person.[54]

Miscellany

The roots, seeds, and leaves are used in modern Ayurvedic and Traditional Chinese Medicine for a range of ailments. In Western herbal and conventional medicine, castor oil is sometimes used as a laxative and in preparations for several ailments. The plant is being researched for its possible use in cancer therapy. The oil also has industrial applications such as commercial lubricants and in the manufacture of soaps, paint, varnish, and perfumes.

Popular with Victorians, the plant's striking appearance has made it fashionable in the garden again. Some varieties have dark purplish, bronze-red, or blue-green foliage. Others have pinkish stems and seedpods.

---

54. Foster and Johnson, *Desk Reference to Nature's Medicine*, 79.

Cherry Laurel

SUBTLE AND QUICK

Cherry Laurel, English Laurel (*Prunus laurocerasus*); also known as common laurel, laurel cherry, Versailles laurel

Botanical Family: Rosaceae / Rose

Native to southeastern Europe and southwestern Asia, the cherry laurel is an evergreen shrub or small tree with dense branches. Its oblong leaves are dark green and shiny on the upper side and have a mild, bitter almond scent when bruised. The fragrant, creamy-white flowers have five petals and grow in upright cylindrical clusters that resemble a bottle brush. The flowers are followed by red cherrylike fruit that are purplish to black when ripe.

Toxicity and Cautions

All parts of the plant contain the glycoside prulaurasin, which decomposes into hydrocyanic acid or prussic acid. The highest amounts are in the leaves and seeds. Ingesting cherry laurel can cause convulsions, coma, and death by respiratory failure. Pruned waste from this shrub should not be burned or done so with extreme care, as the fumes are toxic.

History and Lore

Cherry laurel has been a botanical murder weapon since ancient times. In addition to his infamous personal debaucheries and watching Rome burn, Emperor Nero used *aqua laurocerasi* (cherry laurel water) to do away with family members and others he found unfavorable. It was also a weapon of state and used by the Romans in an execution method called the cherry death.

The plant was introduced into the British Isles during the sixteenth century and was used as a flavoring in liqueurs, sweetmeats, creams, and puddings.

Through the centuries, accidental poisonings have occurred when cherry laurel leaves were mistaken for bay leaves (*Laurus nobilis*). In 1731, Thomas Maddern (d. c. 1737), a lecturer in anatomy and surgery at Trinity College Dublin, brought cherry laurel poisonings to the attention of the Royal Society of London when he published an investigation into the deaths of two Dublin women who drank brandy flavored with cherry laurel. More on this later.

Aqua laurocerasi, also known simply as laurel water in eighteenth-century Britain, was sold by apothecaries as a general sedative and to treat spasmodic coughs and heart palpitations. To prevent it from being mistaken for plain water, spirit of lavender was sometimes added to give it color. Cherry laurel remained in the Edinburgh and Dublin Pharmacopoeia into the mid-nineteenth century.

As in ancient Rome, laurel water was convenient for murder because it was subtle and quick. One case occurred in Warwickshire, England, where Sir Theodosius Boughton (1760–1780) was living the high life of a twenty-year-old aristocrat. He occasionally took a dose of laurel water for a venereal complaint. According to murder trial testimony, his brother-in-law, John Donellan (d. 1781), a former army captain, was said to have prepared a draught of it for him. Boughton's mother testified that the medication had smelled of bitter almonds when she took it to her son. The motive was believed to have been money since Boughton was just coming of age to receive his inheritance, which in the event of his death would go to his sister. Donellan was convicted and hanged.

In Berkshire, John Tawell (1784–1845) became known as the Quaker Poisoner because of his manner of dress and speech, although he and his wife had been expelled from the Society of Friends. Years earlier he had been deported to Australia as a petty criminal but studied and became a druggist. He returned to England and built a respectable life, or at least the façade of one. Even though he was giving his mistress Sarah Hart (1815–1845) money to support her and the two children she'd had by him, she wanted a more official arrangement through the courts. After purchasing two drams of Scheele's Prussic Acid, which was widely used for varicose veins, Tawell visited Sarah on New Year's Day and slipped it into her beer. Seen leaving her house, he was apprehended, tried, convicted, and executed.

Scheele's Prussic Acid was named for Swedish chemist Carl Wilhelm Scheele (1742–1786), who was the first to isolate hydrogen cyanide, prussic acid. An outstanding research scientist, he discovered oxygen and was the first to produce chlorine gas. Scheele's premature death is believed to have been caused by frequent exposure to chemicals, such as hydrogen cyanide and arsenic, without proper ventilation. He is also said to have had a habit of tasting the chemicals he worked with.

Although the Rugeley Poisoner, Dr. William Palmer of Staffordshire, England, was tried and executed for the murder of his friend John Parsons Cook with strychnine, he was suspected of poisoning his brother, mother-in-law, and sister-in-law with prussic acid. In 1857, a year after Palmer was hanged, the first trial in Scotland for poisoning with prussic acid was held. The accused was John Thomson (c. 1830–1858), who sometimes went by the alias Peter Walker. He murdered Agnes Montgomery (d. 1857) because she had spurned his advances. Initially, she was believed to have died of natural causes until Thomson was caught attempting to murder two other people he intended to rob. Montgomery's body was exhumed and the poison detected. Thomson was convicted and executed.

In the book *The Female's Friend and General Domestic Adviser* published in 1827, an article relates a story about cherry laurel, the case that Thomas Maddern brought to the attention of the medical establishment. A woman in Dublin, who was a servant for a person who sold brandy flavored with cherry laurel, gave a bottle of it to her mother, Ann Boyse (d. 1728). At that time, cherry laurel was used to flavor baked goods and liqueurs. Ann passed it along to her shopkeeper sister to sell as refreshment for her customers. Incredulous when a customer died an hour after drinking the cordial, Ann didn't believe the brandy was the cause and drank some herself. She died fairly quickly. In *The Female's Friend* book, the story was laid out in two columns like a magazine, and I found it darkly amusing that it was followed immediately on the next line with instructions for making cherry brandy.

Despite the deaths, accidental or otherwise, Victorian gardeners loved cherry laurel. Well aware of its powers, laurel water was frequently used around the garden as an herbicide. In fact, Edwardian insect collectors dispatched their specimens by placing them in jars with a few crushed leaves.

During the 1892 trial of Lizzie Borden (1860–1927), the local druggist gave evidence that she had attempted to purchase prussic acid the day before the murders, telling him she wanted it to keep moths from damaging a fur cape.

If she had murdered her father and stepmother, perhaps she may have tried to find a kinder way to do away with them.

Miscellany

Because of its dense evergreen foliage, the cherry laurel is still popular in gardens, especially for privacy hedges and topiary. Research is ongoing to determine if it has any pharmaceutical benefits.

Daffodil

FLOWER OF HELL

Common Daffodil, Wild Daffodil (*Narcissus pseudonarcissus*); also known as bastard narcissus, daff-a-down-dilly, gold bells, Lent lily, narcissus, wild jonquil

Poet's Daffodil, Pheasant's Eye Daffodil (*N. poeticus*); also known as butter-and-eggs, Easter flowers, findern flower, sweet Nancy, white dillies

Botanical Family: Amaryllidaceae / Amaryllis

Forming clumps and often carpeting the ground, daffodils grow up to fourteen inches tall with strap-like leaves that sprout from the base of the stem. The common daffodil has narrow, gray-green leaves. The flower consists of pale-yellow petals that create a corona around the darker yellow trumpet. Its two shades of yellow are an easy way to distinguish this wild daffodil from its garden relatives. Poet's daffodil has blue-green leaves. The flower has six white, overlapping petals with a yellow corona at the center that has a narrow band of red along the edge. Common daffodil is native to western Europe, poet's daffodil to central and southern Europe. Both have been naturalized in many areas around the world.

Toxicity and Cautions

All parts of these plants are toxic, especially the bulbs, containing the alkaloids lycorine and galantamine, which are specific to the *Amaryllidaceae* botanical family. The bulbs and sap contain tiny, sharp calcium oxalate crystals that cause a burning sensation and swelling. Ingesting any part of the plant can cause nausea, vomiting, diarrhea, confusion, convulsions, and sometimes death. The sap can cause an itchy rash known as daffodil dermatitis.

Before blooming, daffodils can be mistaken for garlic chives (*Allium tuberosum*). While the two species of daffodil included here are mentioned in ancient texts and medieval literature, the information on their toxins applies to all plants in the genus *Narcissus*.

History and Lore

The daffodil is a cheery harbinger of spring beloved by everyone, but it has a dark past. Appearing throughout Greek literature, the most famous story concerns the youth Narcissus, who was the son of the nymph Liriope and river god Cephissus. A prediction made when he was born stated that when he came to know himself, he would die. As he grew up, Narcissus was indifferent to the many women who fell in love with him and instead was enamored and spellbound by his own reflection in a pool of water. Variations on the story have him wasting away from unrequited love, committing suicide, or accidentally drowning after falling into the water as he tried to touch his own image. At any rate, after his sad demise, daffodils reputedly grew where he had sat beside the water. Although Roman writer Ovid described the poet's daffodil in his version, other writers who told the story described the common daffodil.

In several other ancient myths, picking daffodils seems to have been a dangerous pastime that led to abduction. It was the flower being gathered by Phoenician princess Europa and her maidens just before she was carried off by Zeus, who was disguised as a bull. The daffodil also figures in the story of Persephone, who was taken to the underworld by Hades. According to that story, the scent of the flowers was said to surround Persephone as she picked them. Like other ancient myths, there are variations. Zeus or Gaia was said to have created daffodils and placed them in a spot to entice and attract Persephone so Hades could easily snatch her away. Daffodils were also said to have grown along the River Acheron where they had dropped from his wagon when Hades arrived in the underworld with Persephone. Whichever way it happened, the daffodil was established as a flower of the underworld associated with death and cults, such as the Eleusinian Mysteries of Demeter and Persephone.

Daffodils were said to have carpeted the legendary Elysian Fields, the Greek land of the dead, which is why they were often placed on graves. The flowers were also said to have covered the plain of Marathon, site of a battle between the Greeks and Persians in 490 BCE. The association with death continued for centuries. The Anglo-Saxons had a tradition of planting them on graves, and in medieval England, a daffodil flower bending toward a person was an omen that they were going to die soon. In the Shetland Islands, the paperwhite narcissus (*N. papyraceus*) was considered unlucky to take indoors because it was a grave flower.

The ever-practical Pliny the Elder threw a monkey wrench into the sadly romantic stories about the flower's name. Rather than the youth of legend, he noted that the plant was named for its painkilling and delirium-producing properties. Like the name *Narcissus*, or *Nárkissos* in Greek, the English word *narcotic* was derived from *nárke*, meaning "numbness," or *narkoûn*, "to make numb or unconscious."[55] Pliny also noted that mixing the crushed bulb with honey was a remedy to treat burns, wounds, and sprains. Greek physician and botanist Dioscorides followed suit and prescribed the bulb for burns, abscesses, and dislocations. He was the first to describe the emetic (nauseant) effect of the bulb and noted that it was generally unwise to consume it. Daffodil was called halswort and healswyrt by the Anglo-Saxons who used the bulbs to make a poultice for wounds and adder bites.

English physician and botanist William Turner (1509/10–1568) echoed Pliny by recommending the bulb with honey for healing wounds and joint pain. His contemporary, Flemish herbalist Rembert Dodoens, prescribed it for wounds and facial blemishes. In addition to those applications, English herbalist John Gerard recommended combining the bulb with honey and nettle seed for sunburn. A treatment that continued to be recommended into the mid-eighteenth century.

Another thing that Pliny noted was that the scent of daffodils could produce headaches. While the common daffodil has very little odor, the poet's daffodil and several others have powerful scents and can cause headaches for some people. In Victorian England, the scent was believed to sometimes cause madness. Moroccans believed that the scent of daffodils could either prevent syphilis or cure it.

---

55. Barnhart, *The Barnhart Concise Dictionary of Etymology*, 499.

Miscellany

Grown in English and European gardens since at least the Middle Ages, daffodils are as popular as ever outside or as potted houseplants. With at least thirty-six to fifty species and twenty-six thousand cultivars to choose from, there's one to suit everyone's taste. In medical research, lycorine is being studied for anticancer drugs and galantamine for the treatment of Alzheimer's.

Foxglove

FAIRY TRICKERY

Purple Foxglove, Common Foxglove (*Digitalis purpurea*); also known as dead man's bells, elf gloves, fairy caps, folk's glove, fox bells, goblin's gloves, lady's thimble, witches' bells

Botanical Family: Plantaginaceae / Plantain

Foxglove is a woodland plant that has become a beloved addition to the garden. The plant has a base rosette of leaves and spectacular flower spires that can reach three to five feet tall. Its tubular flowers point downward and are usually purplish pink or mauve. The interior of the flower has a lacelike pattern of dark purple spots. Foxglove is native to western Europe and northern Africa; it has become naturalized in other parts of the world, including North America.

Toxicity and Cautions

All parts of the plant contain the cardiac glycosides digoxin, digitoxin, and gitoxin, with the leaves and seeds containing the highest amounts. Handling the plant can cause dermatitis. Ingesting foxglove can cause nausea, vomiting, blurred vision, dizziness, severe headache, irregular pulse, hallucinations, convulsions, and death by heart failure.

History and Lore

While there are many theories for the word *fox* in the name of this plant, the most agreed-upon one is that it is a corruption of the name *folk's glove*. This is a reference to the fairy folk wearing the flowers as gloves. The genus name *Digitalis* comes from the New Latin *digitus*, meaning "finger," or Medieval Latin *digitale*, "thimble," and refer to the shape of the flowers.[56]

Foxglove was cultivated as a medicinal plant as early as 1000 in Britain. Even before that, the Anglo-Saxons used the leaves as a poultice for sores, wounds, and bruises. While foxglove was mentioned for its healing properties in a twelfth-century medical text from Bury St. Edmunds, its dangers were also noted. During the Middle Ages, foxglove was regarded as a cure-all and by 1650 it was listed in the London Pharmacopoeia. However, its most powerful use, the treatment of congestive heart failure commonly known as dropsy, wasn't discovered for another century.

Physician and botanist William Withering (1741–1799) was one of the founders of Birmingham General Hospital. After one of his patients—whom he expected would die—recovered, he sought out the folk healer who had also treated her and obtained the woman's family recipe for dropsy. Withering narrowed down the effective component in the recipe to the ingredient foxglove and for ten years diligently experimented with various extracts from the plant. He wasn't the only one exploring the possible benefits of foxglove. Also working with the plant was physician John Coakley Lettsom (1744–1815), one of the founders of the prestigious Medical Society of London, although he was said to be less ethical with his poorer patients when it came to experimentation.

As one might expect, such a wonderfully deadly plant was good for murder. French physician Edmond Couty de la Pommerais (1836–1864) used it to advance a couple of his insurance schemes. First, he did away with his mistress who was getting in the way of his plans, and then after getting married, he poisoned his mother-in-law to expedite his wife's inheritance. Pommerais was eventually discovered, tried, and executed by guillotine. Digoxin was also used for murder in the United States by serial killer Charles Cullen (b. 1960), who as a nurse may have been responsible for hundreds of deaths. He was caught in 2003 and is serving life in prison. He is also the subject of a documentary film and movie.

Of course, foxglove is often the murder weapon of choice for authors. Agatha Christie used it in *Herb of Death* and *Postern of Fate* as did English author

56. Barnhart, *The Barnhart Concise Dictionary of Etymology*, 205.

Dorothy L. Sayers (1893–1957) in *The Unpleasantness at the Bellona Club*. It continues to be the device in twenty-first century novels such as *Murder in a Teacup* by Canadian author Vicki Delany (b. 1951) and *The Mahjong Murder Mysteries* by American writer Dale A. Johnson (1936–2014).

Although risky, the side effects of digitalis were sometimes sought out. During the early nineteenth century in Derbyshire and other areas of England, foxglove tea was a cheap means of intoxication. Dutch painter Vincent van Gogh (1853–1890) is suspected of suffering from digitalis intoxication because of his heavy use of yellow during the last four years of his life, dubbed his yellow period. Digitalis-induced xanthopsia, also known as yellow vision, is a condition that effects color perception. Used as a treatment for mental disorders in the late nineteenth century, van Gogh may have discovered it during his stay at Saint-Paul Asylum in 1889. In addition, the portrait he painted of his physician shows a glass with two sprigs of foxglove on the table in front him. Perhaps a salute to the plant?

Throughout folklore, foxglove has been regarded as *the* fairy plant. However, while it was said to be a favorite of the fairies, it was also used against them and their trickery. The Irish name for foxglove, *lus mór*, means "great herb," and it was used to cure sickly children who were believed to be under the influence of fairy enchantment.[57] It was also used in Scotland to break fairy spells. In addition, the plant was said to be instrumental in detecting a changeling, a sickly fairy baby that was substituted for a human child. One way to find out was to bathe the suspected infant in the juice of foxglove. An alternative was to place a few drops of the juice under the tongue and in the ears of the infant, place it on a shovel, and then swing the baby out the door three times. These acts were believed to either force the fairies to return the human child or the changeling would die. It was thought that a human child would heal and become strong from the ordeal. In 1857 a case was documented in Caernarvonshire, Wales, where the suspected changeling died. Sadly, one wonders if destroying a suspected fairy changeling may have been infanticide.

57. Mac Coitir, *Ireland's Wild Plants*, 97.

Miscellany

Foxglove continues to be a much-loved garden plant. In addition to the quintessential purple, other species have yellow flowers (*D. lutea*) and white (*D. purpurea* f. *albiflora*). Plus, there are a variety of cultivars in a range from pinks and purples to shades of salmon.

Although some plant compounds can be synthesized or lead to a laboratory-created drug, digoxin has eluded science. It is extracted from purple foxglove and the Grecian or woolly foxglove (*D. lanata*). Perhaps foxglove is, indeed, a fairy plant that they share with humans, but through trickery don't allow us to master its secrets.

Lily of the Valley

GOOD LUCK, BAD LUCK

Lily of the Valley (*Convallaria majalis*); also known as dangle-bell, fairy cups, fairy ladder, ladder to heaven, May bells, May lily, muguet, Our Lady's tears

Botanical Family: Asparagaceae / Asparagus

This low-growing plant produces small flowers that are famous and beloved for their powerful scent. Two broad, lance-shaped leaves grow from the root; one is usually larger than the other. Small, white, bell-shaped flowers are suspended in a row from one side of an arching stem and develop into red berries in the autumn. Lily of the valley is native to Europe and Asia and has become naturalized in many areas of North America.

Toxicity and Cautions

All parts of the plant are toxic and can be fatal if ingested. Lily of the valley contains over thirty cardiac glycosides; the primary three are convallatoxin, convallarin, and convallamarin. Ingestion can cause blurred vision, halos around objects, headache, drowsiness, diarrhea, nausea, vomiting, stomach pain, irregular or slow heartbeat, and death.

History and Lore

Unlike many poisonous plants, lily of the valley does not have a dark history. It was not used as a weapon of war or by assassins, most likely because there were other more potent plants available. In fact, through the ages, it was often associated with the Virgin Mary. Lily of the valley is just a sweet little garden plant that can kill you.

The only thing that could be construed as remotely sinister in this plant's past is its association with Walpurgis or Witches' Night, April 30. According to lore, that was when witches met for a big celebration and spell-casting extravaganza in the Harz Mountains of northern Germany. Lily of the valley may have been linked with Walpurgis because of its strong association with May Day. At any rate, in modern Europe and Scandinavia, Walpurgis has more or less merged with the traditional Celtic festival of Beltane (May 1), a celebration of fertility, renewal of the land, and the start of summer.

In France and Belgium, it was customary to wish people luck on May Day and give them a sprig of lily of the valley. During the sixteenth and seventeenth centuries in France, wearing the flowers at other times was said to bring happiness and love. In some areas of England, lily of the valley was used in love potions to encourage faithfulness and sometimes placed in bridal bouquets.

Although lily of the valley was regarded as lucky in France and Belgium, in many parts of Great Britain it often had the same stigma as other white flowers and was considered unlucky. In Ireland the flowers were believed unlucky to take indoors or to give to a friend. In Devonshire and Scotland, a person who planted them risked dying within a year. In Somerset if the flowers were taken indoors, a girl child would die. On the other hand, the plant was given the folk name *ladder to heaven* because it was believed that the plant growing on a grave indicated the deceased had gone there.

As for origin stories, in Sussex the flowers were said to have been created from the drops of dragon blood that spilled on the ground as it was slain by St. Leonard (496–545) when he encountered the beast in a forest on the south coast of England. In France, the flowers were known as *goblets des fées*, meaning "fairy cups." According to legend, when the fae were gathering dew, they hung their white cups on blades of grass while they danced, but having tarried too long, the cups became stuck to the grass.

The earliest mention of the plant in a book occurs in the *Hortus Sanitatis* (or *Ortus Sanitatis*), meaning "garden of health," compiled by Jacob Meydenbach (fl. fifteenth century) and published in Germany in 1485. The *Hortus Sanitatis* started as an illustrated herbal that provided a full description of plants, their medicinal uses, and remedy recipes. It was expanded into an encyclopedia of natural history and was one of the first to be printed with moveable type.

By the sixteenth century, Flemish herbalist Rembert Dodoens was recommending lily of the valley to strengthen memory and comfort the heart. English herbalist John Gerard noted that the flowers distilled in wine could restore speech following an episode of palsy or a stroke. In Wiltshire, an infusion of the leaves or a decoction of the root was given in small doses as a nerve tonic. Italian physician and naturalist Andrea Mattioli created a remedy called *Aqua aurea*, meaning "golden water," by distilling the flowers several times or macerating them with dew and combining with wine.[58] Used as a treatment for headaches, nervous afflictions, hysterics, and fainting, it was also highly esteemed as a general preventative against most illnesses. Considered a precious remedy, many people were said to keep it in small gold or silver bottles.

Echoing Dodoens, English physician Nicholas Culpeper noted that lily of the valley strengthened the brain and memory. He also prescribed it for gout and recommended that it be prepared by putting some flowers in a glass vial and placing it in an anthill for a month. The resulting liquid was to be applied to the afflicted area. Perhaps it could have been used to soothe any bites acquired when retrieving it from the anthill, too.

Renaissance herbals prescribed lily of the valley for stroke and often as a substitute for the digoxin in foxglove. It was also used as treatment for melancholia, narcolepsy, epilepsy, and even impotence. Rarely mentioned after the eighteenth century, the plant was rediscovered in the late nineteenth century but not widely used except in England where applying the leaves to cuts was a remedy used as late as the 1970s. Of course, flowers have served purposes beyond medicinal and decorative uses. Because of its strong fragrance, lily of the valley was often used in Elizabethan England for nosegays, which were more than fashion accessories—they helped block the unpleasant odors of a smelly world.

Miscellany

Despite its dangers, lily of the valley is used in homeopathic and herbal medicine. The flower scent is extremely popular as a fragrance and the plant remains a garden favorite; however, it can be invasive and needs to be kept in check. For a little changeup, a pink variety (*C. majalis* var. *rosea*) is available.

---

58. Phillips, *Flora Historica*, 172.

Morning Glory

XOCHIQUETZAL AND THE VIRGIN MARY

Christmas Vine (*Ipomoea corymbosa* syn. *Rivea corymbosa, Turbina corymbosa*); also known as shaman's morning glory, snake plant, turbina flower

Mexican Morning Glory (*I. tricolor* syn. *I. rubro-coerulea*); also known as grannyvine, flying saucers

Botanical Family: Convolvulaceae / Bindweed, Morning Glory

Morning glories are climbing, twining vines with heart-shaped leaves and trumpet-shaped flowers. Lasting only a day, the flowers open in the morning and close if it becomes cloudy or rainy. The flowers develop into round seedpods. The Christmas vine has a creamy white flower with a yellow throat. The plant was so named because it blooms during the winter months. Mexican morning glory flowers can be white, pink, or blue with a white throat. Christmas vine is native to Mexico and Central and South America, the Mexican morning glory to Mexico. Both are widely naturalized.

Toxicity and Cautions

All parts of these plants are poisonous, especially the seeds. Morning glories contain the psychoactive alkaloids ergometrine and ergine, which is also known as lysergic acid amide (LSA) and similar to LSD. Most species in the *Ipomoea* genus contain these alkaloids in varying amounts. Ingestion can cause nausea, vomiting, diarrhea, visual and auditory hallucinations, rapid heartbeat, and psychosis.

According to a study by Tulane University, the alkaloids that produce the psychedelic effects come from a symbiotic fungus from the genus *Periglandula*. The plant darnel has a similar story.

History and Lore

With over a thousand species, these delicate climbing vines are a common sight in many gardens. Although names such as *flying saucers* and *heavenly blue* may have been intended as whimsical, they belie the plants' shamanic history and out-of-this-world effects.

Called ololiuqui by the Aztec and other Indigenous peoples of Mexico, Christmas vine was revered and used as a hallucinogen in ritual to induce a trance state for divination. Another type of morning glory was called tlililtzin by the Aztec and is believed to be the species *I. violacea*.[59] However, there are conflicting details about this species with some sources noting that its flowers vary from white, blue, red, or purple; other sources indicate that it is a white moonflower (beach moonflower) that only opens at night. Because *I. violacea* is so often confused with *I. tricolor*, perhaps the Mexican morning glory was also known as tlililtzin.

In addition to the Aztec, morning glories were used in the visionary and medicinal practices of the Maya, Zapotec, and Mazatec peoples. Ololiuqui was used medicinally as a diuretic and to treat bruises, external wounds, and tumors. In Mexican folk medicine, ololiuqui served as an antiflatulent, a sedative, pain reliever, and treatment for wounds and bruises. It was also a remedy for syphilis. The Mazatec used ololiuqui for divinatory and medicinal purposes into the late 1930s.

One of the early chroniclers in Mexico was Spanish naturalist and physician Francisco Hernández de Toledo (1515–1587), who was the first to describe the morning glory to a European audience. He also noted that ololiuqui was sometimes called *coaxihuitl*, meaning "snake-plant."[60] Another chronicler was Spanish Franciscan Bernardino de Sahagún, whose main purpose was to convert the locals to Christianity. While he may have spiritually swayed some, he spent thirty years compiling an encyclopedic manuscript called *The General His-*

59. Pratt, *An Encyclopedia of Shamanism*, 49.

60. Stuart, *Dangerous Garden*, 187.

tory of the Things of New Spain. His work is regarded as one of the most reliable sources of information about Mesoamerican pre-Hispanic culture. Written in both Spanish and Nahuatl—the language of the Aztec—and with the aid of local people, it describes the use of many plants, including morning glories. Not long after the manuscript arrived in Europe, the de Medici family came into possession of it. Today, it is housed in the Medici Laurentian Library in Florence, which is why it is now called the *Florentine Codex*.

The spiritual importance of the morning glory was also depicted in artwork by the Aztec. A temple frieze in the ancient city complex at Teotihuacán, about thirty miles northeast of Mexico City, shows a mother goddess and her priests under a stylized morning glory vine. The goddess Xochiquetzal was also portrayed with a morning glory sprouting from a flowerpot in a pictograph contained in the *Codex Fejérváry-Mayer*, a pre-Colombian manuscript from central Mexico containing almanacs and details on divination and rituals. This codex was named for two of its previous owners and is now in the World Museum in Liverpool, England.

Of course, the Spanish did their best to stamp out Pagan customs, especially the beliefs that visions were induced by sacred plant spirits. Communicating with the spirits of the morning glory seed was viewed as devil worship and missionaries punished people caught using or even possessing morning glories. However, apparently with the "if you can't beat 'em, join 'em" attitude, colonial-era friars at the Augustinian monastery in Malinalco, Mexico, employed Indigenous people to paint murals on the walls and ceiling of the arcade that surrounds the San Miguel cloister. The result was a mélange of Catholic iconography and a hallucinatory botanical landscape that, quite naturally, includes morning glories. In addition, the seeds of ololiuqui are also called *semilla de la Virgen*, meaning "seeds of the Virgin Mary."

Before American writer Carlos Castaneda (1925–1998) and his Yaqui Indian sorcerer made the scene, many young psychonauts of the early 1960s beat a path to local shops because they'd heard about the effects of morning glory seeds. Not only were the seeds accessible, but they were also cheap compared to marijuana and other illegal substances of the day. The seeds had to be prepared properly and many people were disappointed at not achieving a mind-expanding LSD type of experience. The practice of coating seeds with methylmercury as an antifungal agent was discontinued because of the high incidence of human and wildlife poisoning.

Miscellany

The Japanese may have been the first to grow the Asian species (*I. nil*) as an ornamental in the ninth century. Species from the New World were introduced into Europe and Great Britain via Spain in the early seventeenth century. Morning glories are as popular as ever in gardens around the world; however, certain species are considered invasive and banned in some areas.

OLEANDER

URBAN LEGENDS AND A PIRATE

Common Oleander (*Nerium oleander* syn. *N. odorum*); also known as dogbane, rosebay, laurel rose, nerium, true oleander, white oleander

Botanical Family: Apocynaceae / Dogbane

Oleander is an evergreen shrub that can grow almost twenty feet tall and five feet wide. Its narrow, lance-shaped leaves have a prominent center vein and produce a thick sap. Growing in clusters at the ends of branches, the five-petaled, funnel-shaped flowers are white or pink and very fragrant. The seedpods are long and narrow and the seeds resemble those of milkweed. Oleander is native from the Mediterranean to Asia.

Toxicity and Cautions

All parts of the plant are poisonous and contain the cardiac glycosides oleandrin, neriin, digitoxigenin, and oleandrigenin. Ingestion can cause nausea, vomiting, abdominal pain, muscle spasms, slowed heartbeat, delirium, coma, and death. Symptoms usually occur within two hours and death can occur in about five. Oleander is also an abortifacient. The sap can cause contact dermatitis. Toxins can be absorbed by inhaling smoke from the burning plant.

History and Lore

In ancient Greece, Italy, and India, oleander was a funeral plant. Although the flowers were used to decorate temples in India, they were also used to crown the dead. In Tuscany and Sicily, oleander flowers were scattered over the dead. Because livestock commonly ate the plant and died, the Hindus called it horse-killer and the Italians ass-bane. Greek physician Dioscorides and Pliny the Elder noted that sheep and goats often died after drinking water where oleander leaves had fallen.

Despite livestock dropping like flies, Dioscorides went on to say that a person could drink oleander in wine to cure a snakebite and that the remedy was even more effective if rue were added. Greco-Roman physician Galen was a little more levelheaded and recommended restricting oleander to external use. Nonetheless, seventeenth-century English physician John Gerard echoed Dioscorides remedy of oleander in wine. Gerard also noted that he had white and pink oleander plants in his garden. In fact, from the early seventeenth century the shrub became popular as a conservatory plant in England. Although for a time it was believed that the flowers in a closed room could kill a person, that soon changed. By Victorian times it was fashionable to keep one in the front hall at the foot of the stairs so the fragrance could waft through the entire house.

Throughout the centuries, oleander has had a place in the arts. Often depicted in ancient Roman wall paintings, it was featured in the famous murals of the Villa of Livia just north of Rome. Later artists also found the shrub of interest, including Dutch painter Vincent van Gogh with his work *Oleanders*, a still life of flowers in a jug, and Austrian painter Gustav Klimt (1862–1918) with his work entitled *Two Girls with an Oleander*. Modern mystery writers couldn't pass up such a beautiful and deadly plant. It was used as a murder weapon in the novels *White Oleander* by American author Janet Fitch (b. 1955) and *A Twist of Oleander* by Canadian author Theresa Wallace-Pregent (pen name Raven McKray).

Although it may make a good plot device, oleander was not often used for real murder; however, there was a case in 2000 in Los Angeles County, California. Angelina Rodriguez (b. 1968) tried to kill her husband by serving him tea made with oleander leaves from a neighbor's shrub so she could collect on the life insurance policy that she had taken out two months previously. After that failed, as her husband was recovering from the tea episode, she served him antifreeze-tainted Gatorade, which finished him off. She is in prison on death row. While oleander has been used for suicide for centuries, most deaths are accidental and occur from consuming folk medicine containing oleander or by children eating the leaves.

A much-repeated story with different settings and eras involving oleander branches used as skewers has reached the status of urban legend. The earliest version is about Macedonian king and military strategist Alexander the Great (356–323 BCE). As the story goes, during his Persian campaign he lost horses that fed on the shrub and soldiers who roasted meat on skewers of oleander. In the early nineteenth century during the war to control the Iberian Peninsula, Spain, Portugal, and Britain were pitted against the French. In this scenario, Arthur Wellesley (1769–1852), better known as the Duke of Wellington, was said to have lost soldiers to the same culinary application of the branches. In the same war during the occupation of Madrid, French troops under Napoleon Bonaparte (1769–1821) were said to have perished by using those ever-popular oleander skewers. Fast-forward to twenty-first century America, there are stories of camping families and Boy Scout troops being found dead after roasting hot dogs on ... you guessed it, oleander branches.

To put the legends to rest, in 2020 two scientists at the University of California, Irvine, carried out an experiment cooking hot dogs with oleander branches and found that there was a negligible amount of toxins in the food. They also found that fresh oleander branches bent too easily and could not support the weight of a hot dog, making them useless as skewers.

The species and common name, *oleander*, was bestowed by the father of modern taxonomy Carl Linnaeus from the Italian name for the plant, *oleandra*, which came from the Latin *olea*, meaning "olive tree," in reference to the leaves.[61] However, like many plants, there are myths concerning the origin of its name. In Greek mythology, the story was about the star-crossed lovers Hero, a priestess of Aphrodite, and Leander, who swam across the Hellespont (now the Dardanelles) every night to see her. After a stormy night when he didn't show up, she found his body on the shore with an oleander flower clutched in his hand. Another and very different legend involved the French pirate Jean Lafitte (1780–1826). He was said to have raided a Norwegian schooner killing everyone except one man who was clinging to an oleander shrub, which he apparently had with him. According to this story, the pirate had the man, allegedly named Ole Anderson, plant the shrub at his compound on Galveston Island. Lafitte is said to have named the plant Olea Ander in the man's honor.

61. Coombes, *Dictionary of Plant Names*, 137; Morwood, *Oxford Latin Desk Dictionary*, 128.

Miscellany

Oleander is a popular garden and hedge shrub and, with a number of cultivars available, there are a variety of flower colors to choose from. In some areas of the United States, the plant is regarded as an invasive noxious weed.

Pennyroyal

FLEAS AND CONTRACEPTION

European Pennyroyal (*Mentha pulegium*); also known as creeping Jenny, fleabane, pudding grass, pudding herb, pudding mint, whirl-mint

Botanical Family: Lamiaceae, formerly Labiatae / Mint, Deadnettle, Sage

The lance-shaped leaves of pennyroyal are grayish green, heavily veined, and toothed. Its small, reddish-purple to lilac-blue flowers grow in round, whirled clusters at the leaf axils. Both foliage and flowers have a strong minty and somewhat camphoraceous scent. There are two varieties of pennyroyal: low-growing and spreading (*M. pulegium procumbens*) and upright and lanky (*M. pulegium erecta*). Pennyroyal is native to Europe, the Middle East, and northern Africa. It was introduced into the Americas and Australia.

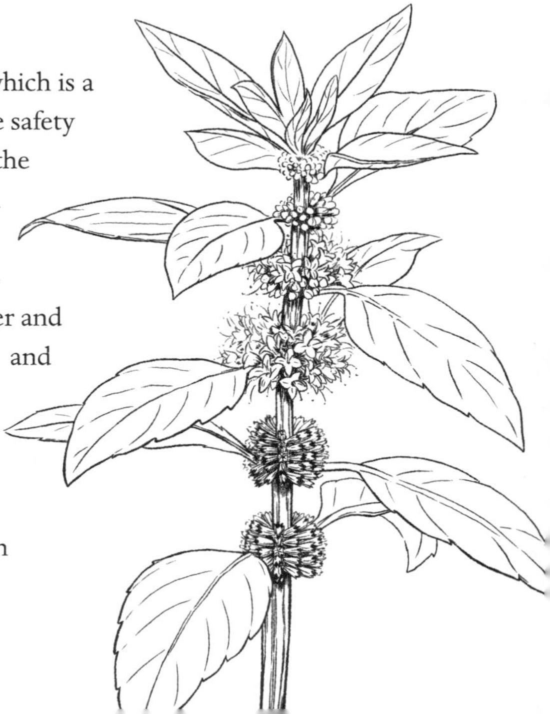

Toxicity and Cautions

All parts of the plant contain pulegone, which is a carcinogen. While sources differ about the safety of dried plant material, all agree that the plant's oil is highly toxic and can be fatal if ingested. Pennyroyal is also an abortifacient. Ingestion can cause nausea, vomiting, and abdominal pain. It can lead to liver and kidney damage, multiple organ failure, and death.

History and Lore

The name *pennyroyal* is a corruption of *pulial royal*, which came from the Latin *puleium regium*; *pulex*, meaning "flea."[62] This shows that no place, not even royal residences, was immune to invading vermin. In addition to a bug repellant, pennyroyal also had culinary and many medicinal uses. It was a popular flavoring for sausages and meats that fell under the umbrella term *pudding*, which was a source for a number of its folk names. In Yorkshire, pennyroyal was used to make stuffing for black pudding; in Cornwall and Devon, it was an ingredient in hog's pudding.

According to mythology, pennyroyal was the mint called blechon in ancient Greece. It was said to have been an ingredient in a drink or a gruel made with barley and water that was consumed by participants in the Eleusinian Mysteries, the secret rites in the veneration of Demeter and Persephone. In medieval Italy, pennyroyal was said to provide protection against the evil eye. In Sicily, sprigs were hung on fig trees with the belief that the fruit would not fall to the ground before they ripened. Pliny the Elder noted that it could purify water, and for many centuries, pennyroyal was placed in casks of brackish water on sailing ships for that purpose.

Pliny also mentioned the plant's medicinal uses for coughs and, like other mints, as a digestive aid. When hung in a sickroom, the fragrance was believed to foster healing. Another ancient use was to wear a sprig behind each ear to prevent sunstroke; however, it is not known how exactly that was supposed to work. A wreath of pennyroyal worn on the head was said to relieve headaches. This cure was echoed over a thousand years later by English herbalist John Gerard. Somewhat in the same vein, German abbess and herbalist Hildegard von Bingen suggested warming stems of pennyroyal in wine and then securing them with a cloth around the head to suppress madness. She also recommended the plant for fever as well as dabbing the juice around the eyes to relieve fogginess in the head. Alternatively, a salve could be made with pennyroyal along with chicken bile and wine.

In Scotland, pennyroyal was taken as tea for chills, coughs, bronchitis, and asthma. In Wiltshire, an infusion was used for chest and lung complaints. Gerard recommended it in honey to clear the lungs. For whooping cough, the plant juice was taken with sugar twice a day. On the Isle of Man, the leaves

---

62. Skeat, *The Concise Dictionary of English Etymology*, 342; Kowalchik and Hylton, *Rodale's Illustrated Encyclopedia of Herbs*, 412.

were made into a poultice for burns. Elsewhere, just the scent of the leaves was believed to aid in recovery from fever, and the scent of the seeds was said to help recover from speech loss.

During the eighteenth century its popularity waned and in the nineteenth century pennyroyal fell out of use in official medicine; however, one ancient use remained as a home remedy. First-century physicians Greek Dioscorides and Greco-Roman Galen noted pennyroyal as an abortifacient. It was known long before these doctors mentioned it as evidenced in the play *Lysistrata*, which was first performed in 411 BCE. Greek playwright and comedy writer Aristophanes (446–386 BCE) punned about the plant's use in a love potion that would ensure no pregnancy. He also used pennyroyal as a metaphor for a woman's pubic hair and illicit sexuality.

Throughout folk medicine from Anglo-Saxon times to the early eighteenth century, pennyroyal was not only used as an abortifacient, but also to induce labor and expel the afterbirth or a stillborn. English physician and medical author William Salmon (1644–1713) recommended this usage in his *Botanologia: The English Herbal*. Through the nineteenth century, pennyroyal tea was a common means of contraception to control family size. In Cornwall, it was called organ tea or organdy. While the name may seem strange, in some areas of England pennyroyal was known as organ, orgin, and organy from the Anglo-Saxon *organe*, which was actually the name they used for marjoram. There may have been some confusion about the plants since they have similar leaves. At any rate, up until World War I, a syrup of pennyroyal was used as an abortifacient in northern England. A bottle was often kept as a stand-by for missed periods.

In addition to contraception, *The Trotula*, a compendium of women's medicine from eleventh-century Italy, also recommended pennyroyal to restore the appearance of virginity before marriage. The procedure involved cooking a blend of sugar, egg white, rainwater, and pennyroyal. After using it as a douche, a clean linen cloth was to be dipped in the mixture, and then placed in the vagina two or three times a day. While it was risky to use pennyroyal, it offered women control of their bodies and a way around double standards of the day.

Miscellany

Pennyroyal tea and the highly toxic essential oil are widely available; however, most suppliers offer a caution about their use. The plant is used in Ayurvedic medicine.

Although the upright variety of pennyroyal is a little weedy, it is often included in cottage garden–style plantings. The low-growing variety is used in rock gardens. In some regions, pennyroyal is regarded as an invasive species.

Rhubarb

WHAT'S OLD IS NEW AGAIN

Chinese Rhubarb (*Rheum palmatum*); also known as East Indian rhubarb, Turkey rhubarb

Garden Rhubarb (*R. rhabarbarum* syn. *R. undulatum*); also known as pieplant

Botanical Family: Polygonaceae / Buckwheat

Rhubarb's large leaves are heavily veined and triangular- to heart-shaped with wavy edges. The stalks look like oversized celery. The flowers are small and grow in dense clusters on tall, statuesque spires. Garden rhubarb has white, yellow, or pinkish-green flowers and red leaf stalks. It reaches up to four feet tall. The leaves of Chinese rhubarb are deeply lobed and coarsely toothed. Its loose clusters of yellow or white flowers turn red. It can grow from six to ten feet tall. There are about sixty species of rhubarb.

Toxicity and Cautions

All parts of the plant contain oxalic acid, calcium oxalate, and cyanidin-3-glucoside with the highest amounts in the leaves, flowers, and roots. Ingestion can cause burning in the mouth and throat, nausea, vomiting, abdominal pain, diarrhea, difficulty breathing, eye pain, convulsions, coma, and death. While a person would have to eat a great deal of rhubarb for it to be fatal, ingesting any amount can produce very unpleasant consequences. Only the leaf stalks are safe to consume.

History and Lore

The exact origin of the common garden plant is unknown but generally believed to be a hybrid of Chinese rhubarb, which is native to northwestern China and parts of Siberia. The funky species name *rhabarbarum* and the shortened *rhubarb* were derived from the combination of *Rha*, the Greek name for the Volga River—an area where rhubarb grew abundantly—and the Latin *barbarum*, meaning "foreign," which is also the source of the word *barbarian*.[63] The earliest description of the plant appeared in the herbal text called *Pen-ts'ao Ching*, which is believed to have been written in the second century CE, although it is sometimes attributed to the mythological emperor Shen Nong. Known as da huang in China, the root was first used as a purgative and later as a treatment for fever and edema.

Like many unique trade commodities, rhubarb was transported along the Silk Road into India and Persia, and eventually made its way into Europe. Even though it is not known which species of rhubarb the ancient Greeks and Romans acquired, they used it for a range of ailments including colds, wounds, and kidney or liver problems. Pliny the Elder called the plant rhacoma. Thirteenth-century Arab herbalist and writer Ibn el-Beither mentioned four types of rhubarb and praised one—most likely the species from China—as being superior.

For a time, Chinese rhubarb was more expensive than many highly prized spices, such as cinnamon and saffron, because it was extremely difficult to grow outside of its native range. Despite Arabian texts touting the superiority of it, the garden species and Siberian or wild rhubarb (*R. rhaponticum*), which were cultivated along the Volga River, gained in popularity because of their wider availability and lower cost. Known by the name *rhapontic* in medieval Europe, apothecaries sold rhubarb as a preventative for the plague.

Prior to the seventeenth century, the rhubarb plant itself was unfamiliar to Europeans because only dried roots and rhizomes had been imported from the East. In England, apothecary and herbalist John Parkinson (1567–1650) received seeds from a friend, grew a few plants, and experimented with making a syrup from the leaves. Nothing came of his experiment but he gave rhubarb the scientific name of *Hippolapathum maximum rotundifolium exoticum*. Thank heavens for Linnaeus and his botanical naming system.

---

63. Quattrocchi, *CRC World Dictionary of Plant Names*, 2294.

When the cultivation of rhubarb began in Europe and Britain, garden rhubarb and Siberian rhubarb were the plants of choice, rather than the more medicinal Chinese species, most likely because of cost and availability. Nevertheless, herbalists John Gerard, Nicholas Culpeper, and others used the more mundane varieties for several ailments, including syphilis. Credited with many things, American founding father Benjamin Franklin is sometimes said to have been instrumental in rhubarb's hop across the Atlantic. Sources generally agree that the plant was being grown in North America by the end of the eighteenth century, but it was slow to catch on for the dining table most likely because memories lingered of its use as a laxative.

At the beginning of the nineteenth century, someone—it's not recorded who—discovered that rhubarb was more than a medicinal plant and that the stems were edible. Of course, the taste begged for something sweet to balance its tartness. Coincidentally, sugar was becoming more widely available and more affordable. It didn't take long before the rhubarb tart was born and, as they say, the rest is culinary history.

With the Victorian penchant for large, showy plants, rhubarb became de rigueur for any respectable garden and dessert tray. If it wasn't planted as an ornamental in an herbaceous border, it always had a place in the kitchen garden. Even though rhubarb is technically a vegetable, in the late 1940s a New York court declared it a fruit because it was most often eaten for dessert.[64] Although rhubarb's popularity faded for a while, it has made a comeback with a wider culinary repertoire.

Because of its phallic shape, rhubarb was believed to be an aphrodisiac in India as well as a cure for erectile problems. In English and American slang, the word *rhubarb* referred to genitals, usually male, and impotence. According to American folklorist Vance Randolph (1892–1980), in the Ozarks it came to be known as pieplant because the word *rhubarb* had too much of a sexual connotation.

Miscellany

What's old is new again and rhubarb has made a comeback in recent years in the kitchen (stalks only, of course) and the garden. There are many heirloom

64. Cumo, *Encyclopedia of Cultivated Plants*, 878.

and hybrid varieties to choose from. Whether or not you want to eat it, rhubarb can add a dramatic splash as an ornamental garden plant.

Some compounds in the root and rhizomes are being studied for use in fighting Alzheimer's and other diseases. Chinese rhubarb is used in Traditional Chinese Medicine and Ayurveda, as is the species *R. officinale*, which has the common names of *Chinese rhubarb* and *Indian rhubarb*.

Tansy

ANTITHESIS OF ITS NAME

Common Tansy, Garden Tansy (*Tanacetum vulgare* syn. *Chrysanthemum vulgare*); also known as bachelor's buttons, bitter buttons, golden buttons, hind heal, yellow buttons

Botanical Family: Asteraceae, formerly Compositae / Aster, Daisy

Growing from one to four feet tall, tansy is sometimes described as weedy because of its tendency to sprawl. Its deeply cut, fernlike leaves are highly aromatic and its clusters of flat, bright yellow flowers resemble buttons or daisies without white petals. Even when dried, the flower scent is strong. Tansy is native to Europe and Asia.

Toxicity and Cautions

All parts of the plant contain the monoterpene thujone, which can be neurotoxic. Ingesting a little over time or in large amounts can cause vomiting, diarrhea, stomach pain, dizziness, kidney or liver damage, convulsions, coma, and death. Handling the plant can cause dermatitis. Tansy is also an abortifacient.

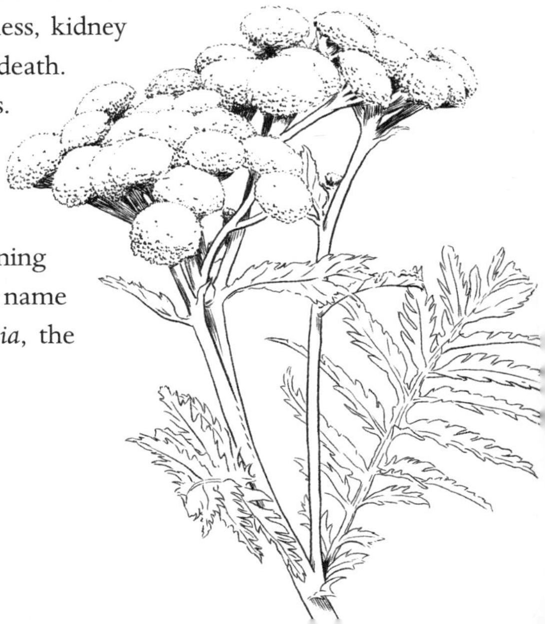

History and Lore

From the Greek word *athanatos*, meaning "undying" or "immortal," this plant's name evolved into the medieval Latin *athanasia*, the

Old French *atanasie*, and Middle English *tansaye*.[65] The significance of the name may have come from the long-lasting flowers and fragrance or the plant's use in funeral preparations. It was customary in medieval Europe to rub tansy on a corpse to preserve it before burial as well as to deter worms and other corruption afterward. Similar practices were followed in Scandinavia and the North American colonies. The flowers were sometimes tucked into funeral shrouds and coffins and wreaths placed on the dead, serving as decoration and helping to mask unpleasant odors. In New England, it continued to be used for funerals well into the nineteenth century. In Yorkshire, England little cakes made with tansy and caraway seeds were traditionally served at funerals.

In a somewhat similar vein for kitchen use before refrigeration was available, tansy was rubbed on meat to help preserve it as well as to deter flies. As an insect repellent, sprigs were placed or hung on windows. In Elizabethan England, it was a popular strewing herb because of its clean, camphoraceous scent that freshened the air and helped control pests. Tansy was widely used in public places during plague years, and at other times in Scandinavia and Britain, it was an insect repellant placed in bedding and in clothes chests. In America, it was even rubbed on dogs to rid them of fleas.

Almost every medieval home garden in German-speaking areas of Europe had a patch of tansy, which they called *wurmkraut*, meaning "worm herb." As in Britain, it was used medicinally to expel intestinal worms. In New England, a small bag of tansy was simply hung around a child's neck to get rid of worms. In the Faroe Islands, the flower buds were chewed for this purpose. Throughout England tansy pudding was a traditional treat at Easter, but its main purpose was, you guessed it, to get rid of worms.

Tansy became the name of a sweet dish, which was a milk pudding served with dinner. By the sixteenth century, a tansy evolved into a dish made with scrambled eggs and other ingredients but, oddly enough, not tansy. Used sparingly, the bitter taste of the plant found other culinary uses. In Oxfordshire, the flowers were mixed into custards and sometimes used to flavor cheeses and cakes. At various times, tansy was used as a substitute for sage or pepper. The buds were used along with hops to flavor beer in Denmark. Tansy leaf and

---

65. Watts, *Elsevier's Dictionary of Plant Lore*, 376; Skeat, *The Concise Dictionary of English Etymology*, 490.

sugar mixed into whiskey was a favorite of Tennessee entrepreneur Jack Daniel (c. 1848–1911).

Called tanazitam, tansy was one of the plants ninth-century Emperor Charlemagne noted as essential for the medicinal garden. Tansy flower tea was used for colds and fever in England; in America the leaf was used. In the Netherlands, wine flavored with tansy buds became a general medicine for children, and not just for worms.

According to Fenland lore, tansy aided fertility because it could always be found where there were wild rabbits. What better proof was needed? English physician Nicholas Culpeper advised women to eat tansy leaves to aid in pregnancy. Drinking beer that had been boiled with tansy was said to prevent miscarriage. Quite to the contrary, throughout the Middle Ages European women used tansy as an abortifacient. Even twelfth-century abbess and herbalist Hildegard von Bingen prescribed tansy and other herbs for obstructed menses.

During the nineteenth century in the United States, tansy was also commonly used as an abortifacient, which often led to poisonings as well as death. One such case was Louise Bunce (1843–1881) of Iowa who was said to have died by suicide, but it could have been an accidental overdose of the tansy oil she took to produce an abortion. Unmarried women were sometimes coerced into taking it by the men who got them pregnant. Intentionally or not, some of them died. In Indiana, Charles Howard McCaughey Jr. was convicted of causing the death of Eliza Dyer (d. 1899) by criminal malpractice. In Texas, Thomas Wilson was convicted of murdering his daughter Minnie Wilson (d. 1898). After getting her pregnant, he poisoned her with ergot and tansy oil when an attempted physical abortion failed.

Originally from England, Ann Lohman (1812–1878) had a rough start in life but made it to New York City and eventually set herself up as Madame Restell. It's not certain how she started her medicine business, but with her preventative powders and pills, some of which contained tansy, she helped women regulate their menstruation and, if necessary, abort a fetus. She also set up a boarding house where women could safely give birth and put their babies up for adoption. However, many people had a different opinion about her work. After years of ups and downs and legal cases, Lohman became known as the wickedest woman in New York. She died by suicide. It seems as though the words *undying* and *immortal* are the antithesis of this plant.

Miscellany

Despite the dangers, tansy is used in Ayurveda, Traditional Chinese Medicine, Western herbal remedies, and homeopathy. The plant was introduced into the American colonies in the early seventeenth century by John Winthrop Jr. (1606–1675), who later became governor of Connecticut. Tansy escaped cultivation and has become naturalized throughout most of North America. Although regarded as an invasive weed in some areas, it is frequently included in gardens and the dried flowers in potpourri.

PART 4
Ominous Others

As with the previous two categories, some of the plants listed here could fit into some of the others. For example, rue, wormwood, and savin juniper can be found in gardens today, but they do not rank amongst the more popular plants. Even though tobacco had widespread use in ancient times, it doesn't fit under Classic Killers because it was a ceremonial plant and not a murder weapon. Oddly enough, tobacco has become a classic killer of modern times. Plants such as darnel and corn cockle were a hidden threat centuries ago, but modern farming practices have rendered them mostly harmless. Even so, that doesn't mean we should let our guards down.

Broom

MARRIAGE AND A ROYAL NAME

Common Broom, Scotch Broom (*Cytisus scoparius* syn. *Sarothamnus scoparius, Genista scoparius*); also known as besom, broomstraw, brushes, English broom, European broom, green broom, Irish broom

Botanical Family: Fabaceae, formerly Leguminosae / Pea, Legume, Bean

Broom is a woody, multistemmed evergreen shrub that can reach up to eight feet tall and wide and often forms dense stands. The lower leaves consist of three leaflets, while the upper leaves are single. Its yellow and orange pealike flowers are fragrant. When mature, the silky gray-green seedpods turn black and snap open with a popping sound as they eject the small black seeds. Broom is native to the British Isles, Europe, and northern Africa. It has become naturalized in North America and Australia.

Toxicity and Cautions

All parts of the plant are toxic and can be fatal if ingested. Broom contains sparteine and cytisine, which are nicotinic alkaloids commonly found in tobacco plants. It also contains the glucoside scoparin, which is a gastrointestinal irritant. Ingestion can cause nausea, vomiting, dizziness, headache, and abdominal pain. Sparteine effects the heart and is known to cause uterine contractions.

Resembling small peas, the seeds can be a hazard because children find them attractive. Broom is easily confused with gorse (*Ulex europaeus*), which is not toxic.

History and Lore

This plant's species name *scoparius* comes from the Latin *scopae*, meaning "broom" or "besom."[66] Its long, flexible branches served as the original household broom, which consisted of a cluster of stems with tufts of small branches at one end. Broom branches were also used for roof thatching in northern England and Scotland. Before hops came into vogue for beermaking, the green stem tops of broom were sometimes used to bitter the flavor and make it more intoxicating.

Often associated with Romany weddings, jumping the broomstick was a fairly common form of marriage declaration in the British Isles and Europe. The custom was called "married over the broomstick" and sometimes used to indicate a trial marriage whereby a couple could live together without the stigma of living in sin. If the union didn't work out, the couple could jump backward over the broom to undo the union. In Warwickshire, the phrase "marriage over the broomstick" referred to a hasty marriage, and in Somerset, an unmarried woman stepping over a broom meant she was destined to have a child out of wedlock.

In traditional English and Scottish ballads, the term *going to the broom* referred to meeting amongst the dense bushes for a sexual liaison. In Brittany, matchmakers—who were often the village tailor—acted as go-betweens with the bridal couple's parents. A twig of broom was sometimes worn as a symbol of a tailor's office as marriage broker.

Broom was not mentioned medicinally until the thirteenth century in the Welsh text known as *The Physicians of Myddfai*, which was written by a number of physicians over a period of time in Myddfai, Carmarthenshire. A recipe to treat pain caused by a thorn stipulated that broom tops should be boiled in a boy's urine, and then applied to the wound. The entry also noted that the fat of a wild cat would work just as well instead of the urine.

---

66. Watts, *Elsevier's Dictionary of Plant Lore*, 46.

In sixteenth-century England, broom was used as a diuretic and a purgative. After his usual overindulgence, King Henry VIII was said to drink water distilled with broom flowers. The plant was also used in labor to hasten birth. Herbalist and physician John Gerard noted that it cleansed the liver and kidneys. He also suggested pickling the buds and young flowers in vinegar and salt so they could be eaten like capers (*Capparis spinosa*). Broom capers were also recommended by early eighteenth-century English doctor and medical author William Salmon who suggested their use in treating stomach issues. Billing himself as a Professor of Physick, Salmon created a brand of remedies that were sold well into the nineteenth century.

It has long been believed that broom is the *Planta Genista*, the plant from which the Plantagenets took their royal surname. It originated with the romantic notion that Geoffrey of Anjou (1113–1151) wore a sprig of flowers in his hat so his troops could spot him and easily follow him into battle, even though this would seem to make him a better target for enemy archers. At any rate, the name wasn't adopted until centuries later when Richard (1411–1460), Duke of York, wanted to emphasize his descendance from Count Geoffrey and several English kings when he tried to claim the throne.

What broom lacks in medicinal history, it makes up for in folklore. In Sussex and the Isle of Man, taking the flowers into the house was regarded as unlucky, but especially in May because it meant the father or mother of the house would soon die. In some areas, just picking the flowers were reputed to cause the death of a parent regardless of the month. In other parts of the British Isles, sweeping the house with green branches during the month of May would result in the head of the household's death. Also, beating a child with a stick of broom was said to halt their growth.

In Wales, broom was said to be a charm that could make someone sleep and that scattering dried leaves or flowers in a circle would cause all those within it to fall asleep. Italians burned broom in the belief that it would keep witches away. In Bohemia, farmers rode branches (à la hobbyhorse) around their fields on Good Friday to keep moles away. In Ireland, a solitary broom bush was often believed to be a dwelling or gathering place of the fairies. In *Tam Lin*, an old ballad from the Scottish borders, a broom bush was the home of the Faery Queen. However, according to other versions of the story, Tam

Lin, who was also known as Thomas the Rhymer, met the Faery Queen under a hawthorn or yew.

Miscellany

Scientific research is ongoing to determine if there are any medicinal applications for some of the plant's chemical constituents. Despite safety risks, broom is used in some herbal remedies.

Common broom was introduced into North America as an ornamental plant and is now regarded as a noxious weed in some areas. Other species in the *Cytisus* genus are used as ornamental garden plants.

Buttercup

CRAZY FOR CROWFOOT

Creeping Buttercup (*Ranunculus repens*); also known as butter and cheese, butterflower, crazy, crowfoot, crowtoe, elf goblets

Meadow Buttercup, Tall Buttercup (*R. acris*); also known as blister cup, butterflower, crazies, crowflower, fairy basins

Botanical Family: Ranunculaceae / Buttercup

The plants included here are two of the most common wild buttercups. They have cup-shaped flowers with five rounded, slightly overlapping petals that curve inward and reflect light into the center, giving them a shiny glow. They are, of course, the color of butter. Reaching less than a foot tall, the dark green leaves of creeping buttercup are deeply lobed, heavily veined, and rise from a hairy stalk that creeps along the ground. The meadow buttercup grows up to three feet tall. Its leaves are similar but have more of a feathery appearance with five to seven lobes. The flowers are solitary or grow in clusters. Both plants are native to Europe and naturalized in temperate regions worldwide; creeping buttercup is also native to Asia.

Toxicity and Cautions

Buttercup contains the glycoside ranunculin, which, when the plant is damaged, breaks down into the toxin protoanemonin. Touching the sap can cause blisters and a burning, itching rash. It is also a serious eye irritant. Ingestion can cause burning blisters in the mouth, stomachache, severe abdominal pain, vomiting, diarrhea, paralysis of the nervous system, and damage to the digestive system. Symptoms may sometimes include severe headache and dizziness. Death can occur by respiratory or cardiac failure. Although the plant has been used as food by boiling or drying it—which can expel some toxins—consuming it is not recommended.

History and Lore

Many of us played the childhood game of holding a buttercup flower under someone's chin to see whether they liked butter. The yellow reflection or shine meant they did. In eighteenth-century England, this was used as a form of divination to tell whether someone was telling the truth, jealous, or in love with the person holding the flower.

The genus name *Ranunculus* comes from the Latin *rana*, meaning "frog," and *unculus*, "small," and although Swedish botanist Carl Linnaeus is often credited with bestowing the name, it had been used by Pliny the Elder centuries earlier.[67] Pliny noted that buttercups were also known to the Greeks as batrachion. Until the eighteenth century in England and Europe, the plants were commonly called crowfoot because of the shape of the leaves. Their Irish name *fearbán* comes from the word *fearb*, meaning "welt," referring to the effect the sap often has on the skin.[68] The name *buttercup* didn't come into wide use until the late eighteenth century.

The bitter taste of the plant is its defense against being eaten, which is why cows generally avoid it. Despite this, there was a long-held belief in England that butter was yellow because cows snacked on the flowers. Buttercups were also believed to have magical power, and on Midsummer's Eve, garlands with buttercups were placed on cows to bless the milk. In Ireland, the flowers were picked on May Eve and placed in houses and barns for decoration and for protection from fairies and other supernatural entities that were said to be active at that time of year. The plant was rubbed on cows' udders to protect the animal from fairy meddling and to increase milk production. However, a nasty trick to play on someone was to pull up the buttercups from their field because it reputedly made their cows give less milk.

Printed in the late fifteenth century in Rome, a text known as the *Herbarium Apulei* is believed to have been compiled in the fifth century or earlier. In it, buttercups were recommended as a cure for lunacy. To achieve this, a wreath made

67. Austin, *Florida Ethnobotany*, 563.

68. Mac Coitir, *Ireland's Wild Plants*, 206.

from the plant and held together with red thread had to be worn around the neck during the waning moon of April or in early October. The tenth-century *Old English Herbarium* also echoed the use of buttercups for treating lunacy. While acceptance of this cure lingered for centuries, it was quite the opposite in the English Midlands where the odor of the meadow buttercup was said to cause madness. This belief is the source of the folk names *crazy* and *crazies*.

The celery-leaved buttercup (*R. sceleratus*) was known in the past as marsh crowfoot but most often as cursed crowfoot. It was described by first-century Greek botanist Dioscorides and its use was recommended by later physicians to remove tumors and other growths. The plant may have been called cursed crowfoot because it is especially potent; ingesting a small amount can cause blisters throughout the digestive tract. Another possibility for the name is that it has been frequently mistaken for hemlock water dropwort (*Oenanthe crocata*), which has a dark history of sinister use.

Called clufwyrt by the Anglo-Saxons, a tincture of buttercups was used to treat shingles and sciatica. In medieval England, where raising blisters was believed to rid the system of impurities, the caustic sap was used as a counter-irritant and rubbed on warts and chilblains. However, herbalist and physician John Gerard warned against the medicinal use of buttercups. He also noted that beggars rubbed the leaves on their skin to raise blisters so people would take pity and be more apt to give them money. Nevertheless, buttercups continued to be used through the eighteenth century, especially a leaf extract for arthritis and a poultice of the taproot for blisters and abscesses. In the twentieth century, an all-purpose ointment made by simmering buttercups in Vaseline became popular in Northumberland. In Ireland, rubbing the leaves on the temples was said to be a remedy for headache.

In North America, buttercups were used medicinally by the Cherokee, Iroquois, and Meskwaki to treat a range of ailments, including abscesses and snakebites. European settlers arrived with remedies from their homelands, which included the removal of warts, corns, and other growths. American botanist and explorer John Bartram (1699–1777) recommended buttercup for syphilis. One shudders to imagine how that treatment was administered.

Miscellany

The cultivated cousins of wild buttercups are common in gardens. Especially popular is the Persian buttercup (*R. asiaticus*), which looks more like a crepe paper peony. However lovely, keep in mind that all species of *Ranunculus* are poisonous.

Corn Cockle

SPARE THE WEED, SPOIL THE GRAIN

Common Corn Cockle (*Agrostemma githago* syn. *Githago segetum, Lychnis githago*); also known as cockleweed, corn campion, corn pink, corn rose, crown-of-the-field, gith, old-maid's-pink, pook-needle, puck needle, purple cockle

Botanical Family: Caryophyllaceae / Carnation, Pink

The name *corn cockle* is also spelled as one word or hyphenated.

Corn cockle is an upright annual with slender, silky-haired stems reaching one to three feet tall. The long narrow leaves are pointed at the tip and grow opposite on the stem. A single pink to purplish or red flower with a tubular base grows atop the long stalk. The flower is pale or white in the center of its five petals that have three thin dark stripes leading outward. Five narrow sepals protrude beyond the petals like radial spurs and give the flower a pinwheel appearance. The seedpods contain numerous rounded black seeds. Corn cockle is native to Europe and the Mediterranean and has been naturalized throughout North America.

Toxicity and Cautions

All parts of this plant are toxic and contain steroidal saponins and, in particular, the glycoside githagenin. The seeds have the highest concentration of toxins. Ingestion of the seeds can cause vomiting, diarrhea, severe abdominal pain, dizziness, and slow breathing. It can damage red blood cells and cause respiratory failure, as well as heart failure.

The name *saponin* for these compounds comes from the soap-like substance that some plants produce for protection against disease and, with a bitter taste, against herbivores.

History and Lore

The history of this plant is intertwined with grain agriculture dating back before the Romans; however, it became an unintended byproduct of their empire expansion, which aided corn cockle's introduction into new areas. Growing amongst cultivated grains, the seeds caused poisonings by being swept up in the harvest and contaminating the flour produced from it.

In England, the name *corn cockle* or just *cockle* was often applied to any noxious weed, including darnel, that grew in grainfields. While the word *corn* is used in North America for maize, in Europe it refers to cereal crops. The word *cockle* comes from the Old English *coccul* and medieval Latin *cocculus*, meaning "little berry," which refers to the seed's appearance.[69] The genus name comes from the Greek words *agros* and *stemma*, meaning "field" and "wreath" or "garland," respectively.[70] Even though corn cockle was considered a scourge, the flowers are charming and in many parts of Europe they were used as colorful decoration on festival wreaths. The folk names of *pook-needle* and *puck needle* come from Sussex and suggest an association with the mischievous hobgoblin Puck.

Although many animals avoid eating corn cockle because of the bitter taste, it has caused the death of domestic livestock when the seeds contaminate their feed, just as it has with milled flour for bread. Writing in the sixteenth century, English botanist John Gerard noted that corn cockle spoiled the taste and color of bread and made it unwholesome. In *Love's Labor Lost* (act 4, scene 3), Shakespeare put it simply, "Sowed cockle, reap no corn." Although bread made with contaminated flour often turned gray, the very poor had little choice but to consume the unpleasant food or go hungry.

In France, pulling up corn cockle from the fields was part of the *Fête des Brandons* (Festival of the Firebrands) held on the first Sunday in Lent, which traditionally marked the end of winter. The practice was a holdover from ancient

69. Barnhart, *The Barnhart Concise Dictionary of Etymology*, 136.

70. Coombes, *Dictionary of Plant Names*, 21.

purification rites to prepare the land and, as the growing season progressed, remove noxious weeds from the fields.

A similar custom called corn-showing was practiced in Herefordshire, England, until the late nineteenth century. On Easter, groups of villagers took to the fields to weed out the corn cockle from the spring wheat, which was also known as Lent grain. A picnic of cake, cider, and cheese was taken along, and whoever pulled the first or most corn cockle received the first or largest piece of cake. In addition to cake, a young man was often rewarded with a kiss from a pretty girl for his efforts. Guld-riding was another similar practice that took place in Lancashire on Easter Monday. It involved the perambulation of fields by the lord of the manor, or his representative, to examine the status of tenant lands. Although the practice was named for *carr-gulds*, a folk name for corn marigold (*Chrysanthemum segetum*), which was unwanted because it depletes the soil's nutrients, corn cockles were also a prime target in the search.

Despite its toxicity, corn cockle was used as a diuretic and expectorant in the traditional medicine of Turkey. In medieval Europe, the seeds were used as a laxative. In medieval Wales, it was part of an elaborate remedy for pneumonia, involving a mixture that included hemlock, which was taken for three days, followed by wine that contained corn cockle and about a dozen herbs. If that remedy didn't cure, it may have killed or in the least kept the patient in a state of oblivion and unaware of any discomforts.

Miscellany

With modern farming practices, corn cockle has become rare in grainfields, and in the contamination of flour, mostly nonexistent. Because it is an attractive flower, it is grown as an ornamental, especially in cottage-style gardens. Corn cockle is included in some seed mixes for creating wildflower meadows.

Cuckoopint

SEX AND SAINTS

Cuckoopint (*Arum maculatum*); also known as adam-and-eve, adder's-tongue, arrowroot, bloody fingers, cuckooflower, dog's dick, fairy lamps, jack-in-the-pulpit, lords-and-ladies, naked boys, snake's meat, stallions and mares, starchwort, wake pintel, wake-robin, wild arum

Botanical Family: Araceae / Arum

The name *cuckoopint* is often hyphenated.

Found along riverbanks, in woodlands, and in hedgerows, cuckoopint grows up to ten inches tall and has arrow-shaped leaves that are often speckled with purplish blotches. A pointed white or purplish structure called a spathe (a specialized type of leaf) rises on a separate stem above the leaves. The spathe forms a protective hood around a cylindrical spike of tiny flowers that are most often purple but sometimes yellow. The flowers develop into red berries. Cuckoopint is native to Europe, western Turkey, and the Caucasus region.

Toxicity and Cautions

All parts of the plant are toxic, especially the berries, and contain an acrid juice that can irritate the skin. Toxins include cyanogenic glucosides and calcium oxalate, which are tiny, sharp crystals that cause pain and swelling. Ingestion can cause a burning sensation in the mouth, swelling of the throat, vomiting, breathing difficulties, and possibly death. Cuckoopint is often mistaken for wild garlic (*Allium ursinum*).

History and Lore

First-century Greek physician Dioscorides recommended the plant as an antidote for snakebite and indicated that rubbing it on the hands was a preventative for getting bitten. Pliny the Elder noted that cuckoopint kept snakes away because it made them tipsy if they consumed it. He did not provide details on how to tell if a snake was tipsy. A connection with snakes continued into medieval Europe where it was believed that adders obtained their venom from eating the berries. By the fifteenth century, the plant's relationship with poison changed. According to the *Hortus Sanitatis*, an encyclopedia of natural history compiled by Jacob Meydenbach, eating the leaves with salt or the root boiled in honey could counteract any type of poisoning.

At various times in Europe, the root was used as a treatment for asthma, rheumatism, and jaundice. As a remedy for gout, seventeenth-century English herbalist Nicholas Culpeper suggested that the berries or roots could be combined with ox dung to make a poultice. He also noted that the plant juice could be used to heal plague sores or to burn off warts. For cosmetic skin issues in the eighteenth century, the sap was combined with distilled water to remove freckles as well as facial wrinkles. During the nineteenth century, cuckoopint continued to be used medicinally as a diuretic and stimulant.

The very starchy root had several other uses. One was to stiffen the elaborate ruffs and collars that were popular during the sixteenth and seventeenth centuries in England and Europe. However, English physician John Gerard warned that laundresses were paying the price with chapped and blistered hands. Cuckoopint also served a culinary purpose, and during the Victorian era it was cultivated on a grand scale on the Isle of Portland, located just off the southern coast of Dorset. The roots were boiled and made into a powder called Portland sago, which was a substitute for arrowroot, a popular thickener for soups and other dishes. Today the familiar powder comes from the arrowroot plant (*Maranta arundinacea*). When pale skin was the fashion rage in Europe—a suntan indicated that a person was a lowly outdoor laborer—the boiled root was made into Cypress Powder, a French cosmetic for the face.

Like other plants, the word *cuckoo* in the name indicates that it blooms in the spring around the time that the cuckoo bird returns to England. However, the plant's unusual flower attracted attention and gave rise to other lore. In his book *Vickery's Folk Flora*, English botanist Roy Vickery (b. 1947) lists over one hundred folk names for the plant. As you may have noticed from those mentioned here, many are sexual in nature because of the phallic shape of the flower spike and positioning in the spathe. Although nowadays we pronounce *pint* as in *pint of beer*, back in the day it would have rhymed with *mint* and was an abbreviation for *pintel* or *pintle*, an Old English word for penis.[71] Robin, in one of its names, comes from the Old French *robinet*, meaning "penis," and the word *wake* alludes to an erect penis.[72] In Dorset and other areas of southwest England, young girls were warned not to touch the plant because they would become pregnant. Cuckoopint appears as a symbol of fertility in the seventh of a series of unicorn tapestries, *The Unicorn Rests in a Garden*, which was created in the fifteenth century. In the late nineteenth century, the plant's reputation was somewhat rehabilitated as it became a genteel symbol of ardor and given the name *lords-and-ladies*.

Despite all the sexual connotations, a legend from Cambridgeshire gives cuckoopint a spiritual spin. In the tenth century, the relics of the abbess at East Dereham, St. Withburgh or Withburga (d. c. 743), were moved to the church in Ely approximately forty miles away. That church and abbey had been founded by her sister, who was also a saint, St. Etheldreda (d. c. 680). When the procession by boat with St. Withburgh's remains stopped to rest on the Little Ouse River before completing the journey to Ely, the nuns from Thetford Priory honored the abbess by strewing her coffin and barge with cuckoopint flowers. Legend has it that as the journey progressed, flowers fell into the water, quickly took root, and immediately spread as they bloomed, producing a soft glow that lit the riverbanks. Not all is complete fantasy. The Irish who immigrated to the Fenlands during the nineteenth-century famine called cuckoopint fairy lamps; the locals called them shiners. In fact, cuckoopint pollen is phosphorescent and gives off a faint light at dusk.

Miscellany

Although generally considered unsafe, cuckoopint is used in homeopathic remedies. In the garden, its close relative Italian Arum (*Arum italicum*) is used as an ornamental; however, it is considered invasive in some areas. The plant is often known as Italian cuckoopint and is very similar but a little larger and has yellow flowers. The leaves have white veining, sprout in the autumn, and stay through the winter.

---

71. Richardson, *Britain's Wild Flowers*, 170.

72. Watts, *Elsevier's Dictionary of Plant Lore*, 93; Hatfield, *Hatfield's Herbal*, 88.

Darnel

DIM, DRUNK, AND DOUBLE WHAMMY

Darnel (*Lolium temulentum*); also known as cockle, darnel ryegrass, poison darnel, poison ryegrass, tares

Botanical Family: Poaceae, formerly Gramineae / Grasses

Reaching up to three feet tall, darnel is an annual cereal grass that closely resembles wheat. In fact, the plants look so much alike that it is not until the ears (grain-bearing tops) develop that they can be easily distinguished. Wheat ears become heavy and droop downward; darnel is lighter and does not droop. Wheat ripens to brown, darnel to black. Native to the Mediterranean, darnel became widespread throughout temperate and tropical regions around the world.

Toxicity and Cautions

Although the plant itself is not to blame, toxins have occurred so often in the seeds that darnel has been regarded as a poisonous plant for thousands of years. Darnel is susceptible to a number of diseases; however, the endophytic ryegrass fungi *Epichloë occultans*, a symbiotic microorganism that infects the seeds, is the source of potent toxins that have physiological and psychological effects. Ingesting infected darnel can cause dizziness, headache, mental confusion, visual and speech difficulties, hallucinations, vomiting, tremor, general weakness, and coma. Occasionally, death can occur from respiratory failure.

History and Lore

More or less a forgotten plant, if anyone in this day and age has heard of darnel, it's usually through references in Shakespeare's work. Back in the Bard's day, darnel's effects were a well-known literary trope. However, long before the Globe Theatre existed, darnel was mentioned by Roman playwright Titus Maccius Plautus (c. 254–184 BCE). In one of his comedies, a character was told to eat less darnel because of its effect on his eyesight. In Roman poet Ovid's *Fasti*, a Book of Days for the Roman year, he bids that fields be cleared from darnel because it spoils the eyes. As for Shakespeare, in *King Lear* (act 4, scene 4), it is intimated that darnel might be the cause of Lear's erratic behavior and insanity. In *Henry VI Part 1* (act 3, scene 2) and *Henry V* (act 5, scene 2), darnel is a metaphor for betrayal and treachery. Representing subversion, it came to symbolize the Gunpowder Plot of 1605, and in its association with the move to reinstate Roman Catholicism, the derogatory name *popish darnell* was frequently used.[73] In late seventeenth-century England, the term *dim-sight* also meant "dim-witted," and saying that someone had eaten darnel meant the person wasn't the sharpest pencil in the box.

Various names for the plant point to the overall inebriated effect it has when consumed. The species name, *temulentum,* comes from the Latin *temulentus,* meaning "drunk." The English name for it comes from a northern dialect of Old French *darnelle,* which was derived from *darne,* meaning "dizzy."[74] Likewise, its Modern French name, *ivraie,* comes from *ivre,* meaning "drunk."[75]

The infection of wheat fields by darnel was well known, but not always regarded as a bad thing. For centuries, it was used to give beer an extra kick. Barley and darnel beer was a heady, narcotic intoxicant that was eventually prohibited in France. Most often, darnel ended up in flour. Although the term *dazed bread* initially meant bread that was not well baked, by the seventeenth century it referred to bread that contained darnel.[76] In earlier centuries, Pliny the Elder noted the plant as a pest to cereal crops and that any bread contain-

73. Lüttge et al., *Progress in Botany 72*, 96.

74. Skeat, *The Concise Dictionary of English Etymology*, 109.

75. Watts, *Elsevier's Dictionary of Plant Lore*, 101.

76. Camporesi, *Bread of Dreams*, 123.

ing it caused vertigo. Although the Greeks and Romans separated darnel from other grains, second-century physician Galen noted that when wheat was scarce such care wasn't always taken. Up until the nineteenth century in parts of Europe and England, ancient purification rites were preformed to prepare the land for planting and for the growing season. These practices included the removal of darnel, corn cockle (*Agrostemma githago*), and other noxious weeds from the fields.

Sowing darnel seeds in someone else's wheat field must have been a fairly common and sneaky act of revenge in ancient times because a Roman law in 533 CE declared it a crime. In the Bible, sowing evil seeds is the theme in a parable from Matthew (13:2 4–30), which Dutch painter and printmaker Abraham Bloemaert (1564–1651) depicted in his 1624 painting of the *Parable of the Wheat and the Tares* (*tares* is a folk name for darnel). Although the peasants he illustrated are usually described as lazy, their appearance of drowsiness may actually have been meant to show the effects of darnel.

Since it was believed to be poisonous, darnel was sometimes included in Mithridatium, a mixture combining poisons with antidotes that was used throughout Europe and England for immunity against intentional poisoning. Oddly enough, darnel had medicinal uses. First-century Greek physician Dioscorides recommended darnel meal as a type of poultice for gangrene and putrefied ulcers as well as for itchy skin diseases. He also recommended taking it in harsh red wine as a cure for diarrhea and bed-wetting. Despite noting that darnel caused drunkenness when eaten in hot bread and that it sometimes caused blindness or dim sight, seventeenth-century English herbalist John Gerard recommended it for several cures. One remedy to treat boils or hard lumps on the skin was made with darnel seeds, powdered linseed, olive oil, and pigeons' dung. Gerard also recommended darnel in wine for dysentery and menorrhagia.

Although darnel has been perceived as wheat's evil twin, we now know that the plant itself didn't cause the problems attributed to it. But alas, poor darnel is subject to a double whammy. In addition to the endophytic fungi that so frequently infects it, the plant is also susceptible to ergot. The combined effects of consuming doubly infected darnel are frightening, indeed.

Miscellany

Modern agricultural methods and food hygiene regulations have rendered the problem of darnel effectively extinct. Although darnel is still around mostly in northern Africa and parts of Asia and it does occasionally show up in Britain and Europe, it no longer finds its way into beer and bread.

Hemp

GALLOWS, HASHISH EATERS, AND ASSASSINS

Hemp, Marijuana (*Cannabis sativa*); also known as cannabis, gallow-grass, ganja, grass, hashish, industrial hemp, neckweed, weed

Botanical Family: Cannabaceae / Hemp

Hemp is a slender plant with cane-like stalks that can grow up to twelve feet tall. The leaves are arranged in a palm shape and heavily veined with toothed edges. The female plant produces small, greenish-yellow flowers that grow in a cone-like structure and are high in THC (tetrahydrocannabinol). Instead of flowers, male plants have small, round pollen sacs.

Toxicity and Cautions

While hemp and marijuana are the same species, they are differentiated according to the amount of THC, the psychoactive compound that provides a high. Laws distinguish which name applies. CBD (cannabidiol) is derived from both male and female plants.

Hemp has about sixty compounds known as cannabinoids, which can be found in all parts of the plant, with the highest levels in the female flowers and resins. THC is the most psychoactive cannabinoid that altars sensory experiences and perception. Acute cannabis toxicity can cause lethargy, slurred speech, and difficulty with coordination. Large amounts of THC can affect the heart and vascular system and can cause confusion, delusions, visual and auditory hallucinations, anxiety, and tachycardia.

History and Lore

Hemp is known by many names, including *hashish* (Arabia), *beng* (Persia), *kif* (Morocco), *dagga* (South Africa), and *gangha* or *bhang* (India). Mainly used in

Mexico and the United States, the name *marijuana* comes from the Portuguese *maran guango*, meaning "intoxication."[77] After being maligned and outlawed in the twentieth century, marijuana is becoming increasingly accepted and mainstream. Often associated with the counterculture of the 1960s and '70s, and those of us who were hippies, this plant has a long history that stretches back thousands of years.

Hemp is believed to have originated somewhere in central Asia and distributed by the Scythians, who took it with them when they migrated west. According to Greek historian Herodotus (c. 484–c. 430–420 BCE), the Scythians used it in sweat lodges by sprinkling water with hempseeds over hot stones.

Hemp fibers were widely used throughout the ancient world for rope, fishing nets, sacking, and much more. In fact, it has been used for fabric that is almost as fine as linen. In addition to hemp fabric, the Chinese used it medicinally for several ailments. By the third century in China and India, cannabis resin with wine served as an anesthetic. The plant was dedicated to the Hindu god Shiva and was believed to cure a wide range of physical issues and spiritual problems.

Hempseeds have been found at various sites throughout Neolithic Europe and in ceramic jars in Germany dating to approximately 5500 BCE. In archeological evidence from Bavaria, the remains of clay pipes indicate that it was smoked. The ancient Greeks and Romans used hemp mainly as a fiber and medicinal plant. Greek physician Dioscorides recommended it for pain as did Greco-Roman physician Galen, who also noted the sense of well-being it produced, but warned that too much caused intoxication and impotence.

In medieval Serbia, a piece of hemp rope or object made of hemp was believed to have strong protective powers and was often used as an amulet. The Slavs and Romanians used hemp shrouds for burials, and in the Balkans, a circle of hemp fibers burned over a fresh grave was believed to keep the deceased's spirit from wandering as a vampire. Cultivated for fiber in the Fenlands of Cambridgeshire, hemp was commonly used to make gallows rope. The plant became a symbol of hangings and placing a stem at someone's door meant they were wished dead. As for hemp nooses, in an eerie sort of coincidence,

77. Watts, *Elsevier's Dictionary of Plant Lore*, 189.

according to Kentucky folk belief, a string of hemp around the neck was a remedy for epilepsy.

Of course, getting high has been an important property of the plant. One of the stories told by Scheherazade in *One Thousand and One Nights*, a collection of folktales (author unknown) from the Middle East and India, was the "Tale of the Hashish Eater." The 1876 Centennial Exposition in Philadelphia included a Turkish Hashish Exposition where attendees could sample the wares, and by 1883 many major cities had fashionable hashish parlors. In mid-nineteenth-century Paris, Dr. Jean-Jacques Moreau (1804–1884) was fascinated by hemp intoxication because it was unlike the drunkenness of alcohol. Moreau founded a group of intellectuals, who called themselves *Le Club des Haschichins* (the Hashish Club) and used the gatherings as his laboratory for studying the effects of cannabis. Hashish was so commonplace during the nineteenth century that it was readily available from European and American pharmacists.

Despite its acceptance, there were prohibitions against the plant from time to time. In the early twentieth century, American states began to ban it and by the late 1930s, the Federal Bureau of Narcotics criminalized it. In a political move, marijuana became associated with violent crime and banned despite objections from the American Medical Association. During his campaign in Egypt, Napoleon Bonaparte tried to ban its use because of the effect it had on his troops. In the fifteenth century, use of cannabis in Europe was widespread enough to alarm the Church. Pope Innocent VIII (1432–1492) issued a papal bull against it as an unholy sacrament used by witches.

Prohibited in the Middle East due to the licentious behavior it was believed to cause, theologians also wanted it banned to prevent widespread access to mystical states of consciousness. Another major reason to ban it was to put down a sect called the Hashishins, also known as the Assassins. Founded by Hasan-ibn-Sabbah (1050–1124), the group was an antiauthoritarian, radically religious military order that carried out murders. Reputedly, members were intoxicated with hashish before being sent out on a hit. The word *assassin* traces back to the Old French *assassis*, meaning "hashish eaters who committed murder," which was derived from the Arabic *hashshashin*, "hashish eaters."[78]

78. Barnhart, *The Barnhart Concise Dictionary of Etymology*, 41.

Miscellany

Hemp is used medicinally for a range of ailments in Chinese and Ayurvedic practices. Medical use is slowly becoming legalized in more US states and countries in the European Union. Recreational use is being legalized more slowly; however, some US states and EU countries have decriminalized its possession.

CBD oil is widely available for use in pain relief, anxiety, and other disorders. Hempseed oil does not contain CBD or THC in significant quantities and is used medicinally for a range of skin conditions as well as for cooking. In an ironic echo of Kentucky folklore, CBD is being studied for potential therapeutic use in severe cases of epilepsy.

Mistletoe

MYSTIQUE AND DUNG

European Mistletoe (*Viscum album*); also known as allheal, golden bough, whiteberry, witches'-broom, witches' nest

Botanical Family: Santalaceae / Sandalwood

Mistletoe is a woody, semiparasitic evergreen shrub that grows in tangled clumps on a host tree. It has forking branches with thick, leathery leaves that are yellowish green. The tiny white or greenish-white flowers have four petals and mature into white or yellowish berries. It grows most frequently on apple trees, poplars, willows, and hawthorns but is somewhat rare on oaks. This species of mistletoe is not a serious threat to its host. It is native to Europe and parts of Asia.

Toxicity and Cautions

All parts of the plant are poisonous and contain the cardiotoxin viscotoxin and the toxic lectin glycoprotein viscumin. Ingesting mistletoe can cause headache, fever, chills, vomiting, bloody diarrhea, stomach pain, and slow heartrate. High amounts can result in seizures, coma, and, in some cases, death.

History and Lore

Growing atop trees and seemingly appearing out of nowhere, for centuries mistletoe was regarded as mysterious and magical. It was revered because of its liminal nature but even more so when it grew on an oak, a tree associated with the most powerful gods in Greek, Roman, Celtic, and Germanic cultures. There are numerous detailed and sometimes romanticized stories about how the Druids gathered mistletoe. However, British historian and Celtic scholar Peter Berresford Ellis (b. 1943) believes that Pliny the Elder's detailed description of the elaborate procedure may have been mistakenly attributed to Celtic

Druids of the British Isles instead of the Germanic tribes of Europe who inhabited areas near Gaul.[79] Both the Celts and Germanic peoples regarded mistletoe as a symbol of life force vitality and rebirth because it was green in winter and grew between the realms of heaven and earth. In Persia, mistletoe was also regarded as ethereal and not of this earth.

Of course, nowadays mistletoe is most famous for smooching underneath at Christmas, which may have originated in Great Britain where until the seventeenth century the plant was associated with fertility. It was said that sweethearts who kissed under it were destined to marry, but only if the mistletoe was burned on Twelfth Night. If it wasn't disposed of properly, there was a chance the couple would never marry, or at least not for a year.

Various guidelines provided the protocol for the romantic use of mistletoe. For example, after each kiss, the kisser or the kissee had to pluck one of the berries. Kissing could continue until there were no more berries. If a woman stood alone under the mistletoe, it was considered bad form for her to refuse a kiss. In County Armagh, Ireland, it was customary for a man to buy a Christmas gift for a woman who caught him unawares with a kiss under a sprig of mistletoe that she had hung. The French exchanged wishes under it at midnight on New Year's Eve. Regarded as a plant of peace in Scandinavia, enemies serious about reconciling their differences did so underneath mistletoe.

There is a great deal of folklore regarding mistletoe and its power to bring good fortune. In England, a sprig was hung in the home for a year and replaced with a fresh one each Christmas. In Wales, Yorkshire, and Worcestershire, a sprig was placed on the collar of the first cow that gave birth in the New Year in the belief that it would bring good health to the entire herd. According to dairy farmers, "No mistletoe, no luck."[80] Placed in the rafters under the roof in a home was believed to keep misfortune away in Germany, France, England, and Sweden. Children in seventeenth- and eighteenth-century England and Germany wore mistletoe amulets to keep them safe from witchcraft. In the Black Country of the West Midlands at the heart of industrial England, it was customary to wear a small bag of mistletoe around the neck for protection from witches and evil spirits. According to a Tyrolean blend of Pagan and Christian beliefs, mistletoe from an oak on which a crucifix was hung would provide pro-

79. Ellis, *A Brief History of the Druids*, 61.

80. De Cleene and Lejeune, *Compendium of Symbolic and Ritual Plants in Europe*, 415.

tection against witches. The Swedes gathered mistletoe on Midsummer's Eve and hung it in houses and barns to reduce the power of trolls.

Mistletoe was valued medicinally by Hippocrates who prescribed it for spleen problems. Greek physician Dioscorides recommended the leaves for boils and swellings. The Anglo-Saxons used it for epilepsy, stitch, and any sudden severe pain. In the sixteenth century, Flemish herbalist Rembert Dodoens noted it for ulcers and epilepsy as did English botanist Nicholas Culpeper almost a century later. In fact, mistletoe was used as a treatment for epilepsy until the mid-eighteenth century and often made into something wearable. In Sweden a finger ring was worn; for children in Normandy, mistletoe was made into a necklace or a chaplet for the head.

Being a versatile plant, mistletoe was used in a practice called liming, which was a common method for capturing birds in Europe and Great Britain from ancient times well into the nineteenth century. Pliny the Elder gave a recipe using the berries, which are generally sticky anyway, for making the substance called birdlime. Basically, it was a sort of glue that was smeared on tree branches to trap small birds. Although this method was usually used for food, it was sometimes done for sport, which is extremely cruel and not sporting at all.

While mistletoe's sudden appearance may have been a mystery early on, people figured out that it wasn't gods or supernatural beings distributing it, but birds excreting the seeds into the treetops. The word *mistletoe* evolved from Old High German *mistil* and Old English *mistiltān*, which may have meant "bird twig" in reference to the species of bird that fed on the berries.[81] The mistle or missel thrush is particularly fond of them. However, some etymologists refer back to the Old High German word *mist*, meaning "dung."[82] So actually, mistletoe may have been known as bird dung twig. Perhaps this is not something to think about next time you find yourself in a romantic situation under a sprig of it.

Miscellany

Mistletoe is used in a few cancer treatments in Europe and is being studied in the United States. It is used in some homeopathy treatments. Although dried plant material and extracts are widely available, there is little information about its safety.

81. Barnhart, *The Barnhart Concise Dictionary of Etymology*, 481.

82. Skeat, *The Concise Dictionary of English Etymology*, 288.

Rue

THE EYES HAVE IT

Common Rue, Wild Rue (*Ruta graveolens*); also known as garden rue, herb of grace, herbgrass

Botanical Family: Rutaceae / Rue, Citrus

Rue is a shrubby plant that reaches two to three feet tall and wide. It is an evergreen in warm regions. The oblong, bluish-green leaves are wider at the tips and give off a pungent odor when bruised. Growing in small clusters, the yellow or greenish-yellow flowers have four to five stemmed petals. The seedpod is a four-lobed capsule. Rue is native to southern Europe.

Toxicity and Cautions

All parts of the plant are toxic, especially the leaves, containing furocoumarins. Ingestion of large amounts can cause stomach pain, vomiting, exhaustion, confusion, and convulsions and can damage the liver. While it is potentially fatal, consuming dried plant material in small amounts is generally considered safe. Handling the plant may cause dermatitis and photosensitize the skin, making it burn easily and blister in sunlight. Rue is also an abortifacient.

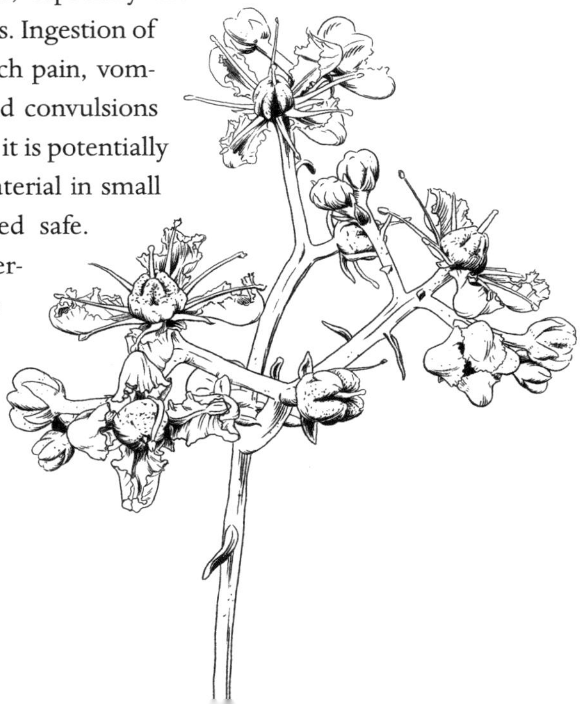

History and Lore

Rue is a plant steeped in centuries of wide-ranging folklore. During the Middle Ages in Europe, it was believed to cure ailments caused by enchantment. Washing the floors with rue was said to prevent a witch from entering a house. According to lore in Morocco, the plant could ward off abduction by the jinn or, if captured, help one escape from them. On the island of Jersey, through some unspecified means, rue was said to have the power to bestow second sight. In Venice, it was hung in a house as a charm for good luck. In other parts of Italy, bathing a newborn in a decoction of rue was believed to help the child grow up strong. If you wanted to keep on the straight and narrow, the thirteenth-century Welsh medical text *The Physicians of Myddfai* suggested eating rue in the morning to prevent unchaste desires.

For the ancient Romans, rue was a spice, and it is still used as such in various cuisines around the Mediterranean. In other parts of Europe, it was used to flavor beer and to jazz up mutton, eggs, and bread. Occasionally, it is still used in traditional recipes.

Medicinally, rue seemed to have been helpful for everything from coughs to the plague, but its use for the eyes was almost universal. The ancient Greeks used it to strengthen eyesight. Pliny the Elder noted that it was an aid to improve and maintain good eyesight as did the Anglo-Saxons centuries later. Tenth-century Arab physicians used it for eye diseases, especially cataracts. As it turns out, rue contains the glycoside rutin, which may be helpful in treating macular degeneration and other eye diseases.

The plant had many other medicinal applications. Pliny also noted that the bruised leaves of rue in wine was a cure for snakebite and wounds from all venomous beasts. In Lincolnshire, England, the plant served as a treatment for the bite of a mad dog. In the Fenlands of Cambridgeshire, a sleeping draught was made by boiling rue with common horehound (*Marrubium vulgare*) and then lacing it with poppy juice or laudanum. A woman known as Granny Gray who lived in the Fenlands offered pills with rue, hemlock, and pennyroyal as an abortifacient. Throughout England, rue was used as an ointment for headache, rheumatism, and warts. It was taken as tea to relieve coughs, improve appetite, and as a syrup for children with epilepsy. To treat an infant with epilepsy in Bulgaria, rue was rubbed on the back of its neck and behind its ears. In other areas of Europe, the plant was used to treat hysteria, vertigo, colic, and intestinal worms. In the Balkans, it was burned to fumigate homes after epidemics. In addition, veterinarians found rue useful in treating a range of horse ailments.

Seventeenth-century English herbalist John Gerard recommended rue as a counterpoison to wolfsbane, toadstools, and snakebites as well as a cure for the plague. It was common practice to hang bunches in windows to prevent the Black Death from entering the home. An east-facing window was regarded as the best location because the plague was said to come from that direction. Believing they could use it to their advantage, thieves wore rue to protect themselves when entering plague-stricken houses. Intended to warn people away, a red cross painted on the doors of afflicted homes in London during the plague of 1665 was like a neon sign for burglars. According to legend, during an outbreak in Marseilles, France, a concoction that became known as four thieves vinegar was rubbed on the hands and face in the belief that it would keep a person from catching the plague.

Rue was also used as a strewing herb, scattered on the floor to minimize smells, pests, and disease. In the mid-eighteenth century, the dock for prisoners in the Old Bailey criminal courthouse in London was strewn with it for protection against jail fever (typhus), which was raging in the Newgate prison. The practice lingered into the twentieth century with a ceremonial bouquet of rue placed on the judge's bench.

In addition to rue's medicinal use for the eyes, its most potent application was for protection from the evil eye. Originating in Naples, an amulet made with a sprig of rue called *cimaruta* from the term *cima di ruta*, meaning "a piece of rue," was believed to provide special protection for women during childbirth as well as for their infants.[83] The traditional cimaruta was fashioned from a leafy sprig with three short branches protruding from the stem. It eventually became an aggregated amulet with each branch end holding a charm or emblem such as a moon, key, fish, or rooster. Later, it was made of silver and became even more elaborate. The cimaruta as a combination charm was not a completely unique idea as somewhat similar Etruscan charms made of bronze have been discovered. Protecting children against the evil eye was not unique to Europe. The Maya of the Yucatan chewed leaves of rue and then rubbed it on their children's eyelids for protection.

---

83. Watts, *Elsevier's Dictionary of Plant Lore*, 74.

Miscellany

Rue is used in Ayurveda, homoeopathy, and herbal medicine, and is being researched in conventional medicine for its potential use in cancer treatments. The essential oil and dried plant material is widely available and often used as an insect repellant. Four thieves vinegar is now a name used for a do-it-yourself disinfectant and herbal remedy. Grappa, a grape-based alcoholic beverage of Italy, is sometimes flavored with rue. The plant is used in the garden as an ornamental.

Savin Juniper

A LONG TRAGIC LEGACY

Savin Juniper, Savin (*Juniperus sabina* syn. *Sabina vulgaris, S. officinalis*); also known as sabina

Botanical Family: Cupressaceae / Cypress

Savin juniper is an evergreen shrub that has two forms: upright from four to six feet tall with a five- to ten-foot spread or low growing and only three feet tall. The leaves on young plants are stiff and needlelike but become scalelike on mature ones. When crushed or broken, the foliage has an unpleasant odor. The bluish-black berries are actually fleshy seed cones. Savin juniper is native to parts of Europe and western Asia.

Toxicity and Cautions

All parts of the plant are toxic, containing the monoterpenes sabinene, sabinol, and thujone, and the hydrocarbons cadinene and terpinene. Thujone can be neurotoxic. Ingestion of savin juniper can cause irritation of the mouth, nausea, vomiting, diarrhea, stomach pain, difficulty breathing, convulsions, coma, and death. It is also an abortifacient. Handling the plant can cause skin irritation.

The berries of the common juniper (*J. communis*) are edible and used to flavor food and gin. Savin berries can be mistaken for them.

History and Lore

In medieval England, savin juniper was said to protect against witches because the unpleasant odor of its broken foliage was believed nasty enough to keep anything evil at bay. The story was a little different in Wales. There it was called devil's wort because it was thought that witches and magicians used the plant for spells; however, it was common juniper that had that distinction. Nevertheless, even though savin is highly toxic, it was used medicinally for thousands of years.

Roman historian and writer on husbandry management, Marcus Porcius Cato (234–149 BCE), recommended its veterinary use, especially for horses. As an equine contraception, it was believed in medieval England that the scent in a stable was enough to discourage amorous stallions from acting on their impulses. Into the nineteenth century, savin was used to rid a horse of worms and give it a shiny coat. For humans, first-century Greek physician Dioscorides recommended it for a range of issues from skin disorders to inducing menstruation or labor as well as anointing the genitals prior to sex to prevent pregnancy. He also noted that the plant could be used to repel wild animals.

The Old English name for the plant, *safine*, evolved from its Latin name, *sabina*.[84] For general pain relief, the Anglo-Saxons served savin as a drink with honey or wine; for headache, it was mixed with vinegar and oil, and then smeared on the head and temples. Seventeenth-century English physician John Gerard recommended the leaves mixed with honey to remove skin ulcers, spots, and freckles. He also noted that the leaves boiled in olive oil and rubbed on a child's belly would expel worms. How that was supposed to work is not clear.

As Dioscorides noted, savin juniper was a contraceptive and abortifacient, which has been its most widespread use throughout the centuries and its tragic legacy. Women died from complications in the abortion process because, quite often, a fetus died but was not expelled, which eventually killed the woman. Toxins from the plant made the process more harrowing and sometimes caused the woman's death outright. Savin was listed as an abortifacient in *The Trotula*, a tenth-century Italian book of women's medicine. In the early seventeenth century, John Gerard noted that drinking wine in which the leaves had been boiled would bring on menses, expel afterbirth, or induce an abortion. Later that century, English botanist and physician Nicholas Culpeper echoed the remedy and added that applying it to venereal sores would cure them. Savin was also commonly used throughout Europe for the same purposes.

The plant's use as an abortifacient was so common that a euphemism for it in Scotland was "giving birth under the savin tree."[85] English poet and play-

84. Pollington, *Leechcraft*, 153.

85. Hatfield, *Hatfield's Herbal*, 204.

wright Thomas Middleton (1580–1627) used it as a trope in his play *A Game of Chess* (act 1 scene 2), which was first staged at the Globe Theatre. Throughout Elizabethan England, savin acquired the folk names of *bastard killer* and *cover-shame*.

The use of the plant by pregnant girls was also a theme in some traditional English and Scottish ballads. A sixteenth-century ballad known variously as "The Queen's Maries" and "The Four Maries" tells a fictional story of Mary Hamilton, a lady-in-waiting to Mary Stuart, Queen of Scots (1542–1587). In this very dark tale, Mary became pregnant after an affair with the queen's second husband, Henry Stuart, Lord Darnley (1546–1567). Her use of savin was unsuccessful, she had the baby, drowned it, and was then executed for the murder. Although such ballads were the equivalent of Renaissance soap operas, they often had a grain of truth, and in this case, the widespread use of savin for abortion. Lord Darnley was known for infidelities, and although the queen had four ladies-in-waiting named Mary, none had the surname Hamilton. Mary Stuart's first husband was King Francis II of France (1544–1560), son of Catherine de Medici.

Savin's use as an abortifacient was a grim reality that continued into the nineteenth century in Great Britain, Europe, and North America. It was used for female problems in general and wasn't dropped from official pharmacopeias until the early twentieth century. Plying their trade outside the bounds of official medicine, charlatans were busy with their patent medicines and elixirs. Dubbed the Prince of Quacks, Ray Vaughn Pierce (1840–1914), who had a dubious medical degree, built an empire with a convalescent hospital, a factory that produced his concoctions (many contained opium), which he promoted in his book *The People's Common Sense Medical Advisor*. While he had a tonic for everyone, women were always a profitable target, and his almost magical elixir, called Dr. Pierce's Favorite Prescription, promised to cure female weakness, painful periods, menstrual irregularities, mental anxiety, and a host of other symptoms. You name it, his elixir seemed to cure it. The concoction reputedly contained savin, opium, and alcohol.

Miscellany

Despite the dangers, savin juniper is used in Traditional Chinese Medicine and homeopathic remedies. The plant, and several cultivars, are popular in the garden because of their hardiness and low maintenance.

Tobacco
PROFITS OVER PEOPLE

Common Tobacco (*Nicotiana tabacum*); also known as cultivated tobacco, sot-weed, Virginia tobacco

Wild Tobacco (*N. rustica*); also known as Aztec tobacco, rustic tobacco

Botanical Family: Solanaceae / Nightshade

Growing four to six feet tall, common tobacco has thick, hairy stems and large, broadly oval leaves. The tubular flowers can be white, pink, or red and widen at the end with pointed petals. They grow in a large cluster at the top of the stems. Wild tobacco is smaller and shrubbier, with lance-shaped leaves. Reaching up to five feet tall, it has whitish-yellow, funnel-shaped flowers.

Both plants are native to South America.

Toxicity and Cautions

All parts of the plant are toxic and contain the alkaloid nicotine, which is a stimulant to the nervous system and fatally toxic in large doses. Nicotine is highly addictive. Eating leaves or consuming them as tea can cause stomach cramps, difficulty breathing, severe weakness, seizures, and death. Smoking tobacco is the chief cause of lung disease, pulmonary diseases, and chronic bronchitis. Smoking or chewing tobacco is also a major cause of various types of cancer.

History and Lore

The modern commercial tobacco is a descendant from the common tobacco of South America. Both common and wild tobaccos were used by ancient Indigenous peoples and dispersed throughout North and South Americas. The word *tobacco* comes from the Spanish *tabaco*, which was the name of a smoking implement used by the Carib People of the Lesser Antilles and South America.[86] Made from a forked reed, the divided end was placed in the nostrils and the other held over a fire upon which tobacco leaves had been strewn.

Tobacco was used more than any other plant and known to most Indigenous societies. It was common from eastern Canada to southern Argentina and from the Atlantic to the Pacific. About eight thousand years ago, Indigenous peoples cultivated both species: wild tobacco in North America and common tobacco in Central and South America. The Pacific Northwest Haida and Tlingit peoples, who were mainly hunter-gatherers, also cultivated tobacco.

The Winnebago believed the plant to have mystical origins and power, as did the Chippewa, Pilaga of Paraguay, and Yecuana of Venezuela. Regarded as a blessing from the Creator, the Iroquois burn it at social and private ceremonies. Tobacco was a sacred herb in Peru and venerated for its stimulating effects.

While tobacco was usually smoked in rituals, it was ingested by shamans to produce an altered state of mind. Tobacco of the past had a much higher nicotine content than today's commercial plants. Some evidence suggests it could have contained hallucinogenic alkaloids that were made stronger by the accompanying nicotine.[87] And if that wasn't enough, tobacco was sometimes mixed with more potent substances such as datura.

Tobacco smoke symbolized the shaman's contact with the supernatural world. It was believed to strengthen their relationship with spirit helpers and to remove disease from a patient, especially if the illness was caused by a spirit or through witchcraft. People other than shamans who practiced medicine also used tobacco in a range of cures for common ailments and to stave off hunger. Brewed into a tea, the leaves were used to ease headaches, expel worms, and as a laxative and expectorant. The Iroquois used it to counteract poison and soothe insect bites, the Aztec to ease gout. The medicine bundles of most Plains tribes included tobacco and a pipe.

Christopher Columbus (1451–1506) took seeds back to Europe where it stirred interest, and by the sixteenth century, Brazil and many islands in the Caribbean were cultivating tobacco for the European market. In the early sev-

---

86. Watts, *Elsevier's Dictionary of Plant Lore*, 385.

87. Goodman, *Tobacco in History*, 23.

enteenth century, the colony of Virginia was exporting more and more of it as demand grew exponentially. Being an extremely labor-intensive crop, tobacco helped fuel the slave trade.

In Europe, tobacco was quickly adopted as a medicinal plant and believed to cure joint pain, migraines, and epilepsy. For protection against the plague, it was taken (form unknown) in the morning after fasting, followed by beer. The French called the plant *herbe a tous les maux*, meaning "the plant against evil, pains, and other bad things."[88] For first aid in Ireland and Scotland, a piece of tobacco leaf was bound to a cut or wound to staunch bleeding and aid healing.

French diplomat, scholar, and botanist Jean Nicot (1530–1604), whose name is the basis for the word *nicotine*, popularized tobacco smoking in France. He introduced it to the French Queen Mother Catherine de Medici, who preferred it as snuff to relieve her headaches. In those days, snuff was used by the more well-to-do people and kept in expensive decorative boxes. It didn't take long for European gardeners to discover what Indigenous people already knew. Tobacco was an effective insecticide; however, it is nondiscriminatory and toxic to earthworms and small animals.

Even though tobacco was known to be a narcotic in nineteenth-century America, it continued to be used medicinally as a sedative as well as a treatment for a host of common disorders. In addition to standard methods, the Europeans also adopted the questionable application from Central America of employing a tobacco smoke enema syringe. Initially used in the eighteenth century for a wide range of ailments, by the mid-nineteenth century it was only used to revive someone who had drowned. If that didn't cause a person to stir, nothing would.

Other questionable tobacco uses during the sixteenth and seventeenth centuries included potions that promised youth and vigor. Tobacco was even rumored to be an aphrodisiac. On a more mundane level, French fisherman believed it could attract fish by either spitting some chewed tobacco into the water or simply smoking a pipe. It's not clear why or how fish would be interested in pipe smoke.

The Spanish introduced the cigar into Europe during the early seventeenth century, but it wasn't until the 1880s that cigarettes entered the scene. The

88. Foster and Johnson, *Desk Reference to Nature's Medicine*, 258.

word *cigar* comes from the Spanish *cigarro*, which was derived from *sik'ar*, the Mayan word for smoking.[89] For well over a thousand years, Indigenous peoples of Mexico, Central America, and Brazil smoked bundles of tobacco leaves wrapped in corn husks.

Miscellany

Nonritual tobacco is no longer used medicinally, except to aid in breaking the addiction. The plant does not have significant use; however, because it is an enormously profitable commodity worldwide, it will continue to be marketed. It will also continue to kill people.

89. Keoke and Porterfield, *Encyclopedia of American Indian Contributions to the World*, 60.

Water Dropwort

DIE WITH A SMILE

Fine-Leaf Water Dropwort (*Oenanthe aquatica* syn. *O. phellandrium, Phelladrium aquaticum*); also known as fine-leaved water dropwort, horsebane, narrow-leaved celery, water fennel

Hemlock Water Dropwort (*O. crocata*); also known as cow hemlock, dead-man's-fingers, five-fingered root, horsebane, water celery, water lovage, yellow water dropwort

Botanical Family: Apiaceae, formerly Umbelliferae / Carrot, Parsley

As the name suggests, these plants grow in wetlands, damp meadows, and riverbanks. They reach three to five feet tall and have white flowers that grow in rounded, umbrella-shaped clusters. The flowers develop into seedheads of oblong, ridged fruits. The stems and roots contain a yellowish sap. The leaves of fine-leaf water dropwort are delicate, light green, and fernlike; the lower leaves are usually submerged in water. The roots resemble small white carrots. A yellow liquid from the fruits is called water fennel oil. Hemlock water dropwort has bright green leaves with fan-shaped lobes. It resembles parsley or celery. The lower stem joins with the fleshy tuber roots. Fine-leaf is native from Europe to Mongolia; hemlock is native to Europe, North Africa, and western Asia. Both have been naturalized in North America.

Although both dropworts are sometimes called water hemlock, they are not related to plants of that name in the *Cicuta* genus. However, both water hemlock (*C. maculata*) and water dropwort are regarded as amongst the most poisonous plants in North America and Great Britain.

Toxicity and Cautions

All parts of these plants are toxic with the highest concentration in the roots. They contain oenanthotoxin, which inhibits physiological responses and triggers convulsions. Ingesting hemlock water dropwort can cause nausea, vomiting, abdominal cramps, diarrhea, lowered blood pressure, convulsions, grand mal seizers, and death. Although fine-leaf water dropwort is less poisonous, it can produce many of the same ill effects and death if ingested.

Unlike other poisonous plants that often taste bitter, the roots of hemlock water dropwort are said to have a pleasant flavor and fragrant aroma. They are easily mistaken for wild parsnip (*Pastinaca sativa*).

History and Lore

Well into the nineteenth century, the fruits of the fine-leaf species were used for respiratory ailments such as bronchitis, consumption, and asthma in the British Isles, Europe, and the United States. The fruits have also been used for fever and ulcers and the roots as a treatment for hemorrhoids.

Cows and other livestock have been poisoned by eating the roots of hemlock water dropwort, as have people who mistook the plant for wild celery (*Apium graveolens*) or water parsnip (*Sium suave*). Nevertheless, the roots were made into poultices for people and cattle to treat certain conditions. In England, the roots were also used to poison rats and moles. The folk name *dead tongue* was applied to this species because ingesting even a small amount paralyses speech. Another characteristic is that it produces facial contortions resembling a smile.

According to Latin and Greek accounts, a plant called herba sardonia and sardónion was put to sinister use by the Nuragic people, the Indigenous pre-Roman occupants of Sardinia. Some sources note that it was the somewhat mysterious Phoenicians who arrived later around the eighth century BCE who used the plant for killing. At any rate, a drink or other mixture containing this toxic herb was given to inebriate and incapacitate criminals as well as the elderly or infirm who were regarded as societal burdens and no longer useful. After becoming sufficiently tipsy and unsteady, they were executed by being beaten to death or simply pushed from a high rocky precipice. Despite the violent end, their faces were said to show a terrible sort of grin as though they had been laughing. Greek author Homer made one of the earliest references to the plant's stupefying quality and is attributed with coining the word *sardonic* in reference to this effect.[90]

In describing the herb from Sardinia, first-century Greek physician and botanist Dioscorides observed that when eaten, it would make a person lose his senses and produce a particular spasm that could be mistaken for laughter. A generation later, information seems to have become scrambled about the symptoms. In his travelogue *Description of Greece*, Greek geographer and writer Pausanias (c. 120–180 CE) noted that the plant looked like parsley and caused anyone who ate it to die laughing.

The plant widely known as cursed crowfoot, now called celery-leaved buttercup, became associated with the lore of hemlock water dropwort, which it resembles. In the fourteenth century, Pietro d'Abano, a professor of medicine in Padua, Italy noted that the sardonic laughter was caused by drinking a draught of cursed crowfoot, which made a person go out of his mind and laugh nonstop. Sixteenth-century English herbalist John Gerard also thought the plant from Sardinia was a type of buttercup and identified it as Illyrian crowfoot (*Ranunculus illyricus*). Similar to Pausanias, he noted that it made a person appear to have died in laughter rather than in torment. On the subject of hemlock water dropwort, Gerard likened its appearance to poison hemlock and noted that it made people who ate it giddy in the head and to stagger as if drunk.

In the 1990s a suicide in Sardinia sparked the interest of a team of researchers at the University of Eastern Piedmont in Novara, Italy, because the grotesque facial expression of the person who died fit the accounts of the sardonic grin or laugh. For a decade they studied plants that were similar to the ancient descriptions, which included buttercups and water dropworts. In 2009, the team found the grin-producing compound and identified hemlock water dropwort as the plant responsible for the sardonic smile.

Miscellany

Although generally regarded as unsafe, both fine-leaf and hemlock water dropwort plants are used in homeopathic remedies. Cultivated for several thousand years, Java water dropwort (*O. javanica*) is native to Asia. Also known as water celery, Chinese celery, and Japanese parsley, it is edible and nontoxic. The stems

90. Barnhart, *The Barnhart Concise Dictionary of Etymology*, 684.

and leaves are used as a vegetable, either cooked or in a salad. It can be found in some specialty markets. Sometimes grown in water gardens, fine-leaf water dropwort has escaped cultivation and has naturalized in parts of North America. Both the fine-leaf and Java water dropworts are considered noxious weeds in some areas; check before planting.

Wormwood

TWO TYPES OF SPIRITS

Common Wormwood (*Artemisia absinthium* syn. *Absinthium officinale*); also known as absinthe, *absinthii herba,* felon herb, grand wormwood, green ginger, madderwort, motherwort, sagewort

Botanical Family: Asteraceae, formerly Compositae / Aster, Daisy

Wormwood is an erect, bushy plant that can reach up to five feet tall. Its lacy, deeply lobed leaves are silvery grayish green on top and whitish underneath, giving the plant a light, airy appearance. The leaves have a strong, sage-like odor when crushed. The small yellowish flowers are disc shaped and grow in clusters. The plant has an extremely bitter taste. Wormwood is native to parts of Europe, northern Africa, and Asia. It has become naturalized in North America.

Toxicity and Cautions

All parts of the plant contain the monoterpene thujone—*alpha*-thujone is the bad boy component—which can be neurotoxic. Consuming large amounts of wormwood or overuse can cause headaches, dizziness, and cramps. It can lead to nervousness, stupor, convulsions, coma, and potentially death. Small amounts can cause nervous disorders and handling the plant can cause dermatitis. Wormwood is an abortifacient.

History and Lore

Wormwood became known as *Grabkraut*, meaning "tomb herb," in medieval Silesia where it was used in funerals to help subdue odors by decorating biers and gravestones with it.[91] The plant was believed to have the power to summon spirits as well as provide protection from evil ones. Hanging a sprig of leaves on children's beds was said to protect them from bewitchment and elves.

It is no accident that this plant has *worm* in its name. The Egyptians mentioned it in the Ebers Papyrus for expelling intestinal worms, as did fifteenth-century English herbalist John Gerard. Roman philosopher Lucretius (fl. first century BCE) recommended smearing honey on the rim of a cup to get children to take their doses.

Pliny the Elder had other uses for it, noting that a little wormwood placed under the bed pillow relieved insomnia. Greek physician Dioscorides recommended it to relieve stomach and abdominal pains. Relieving digestive problems has been its most widespread use that continued well into the twentieth century. Dioscorides also noted that wormwood was effective against poisoning and helped relieve hangovers. For hundreds of years, it was used by many who celebrated too much with Dionysus.

Seventeenth-century herbalist Nicholas Culpeper suggested wormwood as an antiseptic for beestings, wasps, scorpions, and snakes. He also recommended placing it in the wardrobe to keep pests away from clothes and linens. Because it is so highly aromatic, it was used to keep vermin out of granaries and planted around crop fields to deter mice.

As with many pungent plants, wormwood was used to guard against the plague. According to one method, it was steeped in vinegar, and then the mixture carried in a covered pewter container that could be opened and the contents sniffed when passing through malodourous areas. In his pamphlet *The Wonderfull Yeare*, English dramatist Thomas Dekker (1572–1632) noted that some people put pieces of wormwood in their noses and ears, which made them look like a Christmas bore's head stuffed with sprigs of rosemary.

Wormwood was used by the ancient Greeks and Romans in wine making, and before hops entered the scene in England, it was sometimes used to flavor beer. In the eighteenth century, wormwood came into its own as the beverage

---

91. De Cleene and Lejeune, *Compendium of Symbolic and Ritual Plants in Europe*, 387.

absinthe. Also known as *la fée verte*, meaning "the green fairy," absinthe was emerald green and highly alcoholic. Drinking it entailed a preparation ritual called louching, which included sugar to soften the bitter tase. With a shot of absinthe in a glass, a spoon with sugar was placed across the top. Cold water was slowly poured over the sugar, and as the solution mixed with the absinthe, it turned from green to milky. The drink was highly addictive and said to have mind-altering effects. Combining absinthe with cognac, French painter Henri de Toulouse-Lautrec (1864–1901) called the drink *Atremblement de Terre*, meaning "earthquake."[92]

Containing five other herbs, absinthe started out in Switzerland as a medicinal tonic, especially for fatigue and fever. Production of it began in France during the early 1800s. Some versions of the drink also contained southernwood (*A. abrotanum*), a close relative of wormwood, which was believed to be an aphrodisiac. With that and the rumor that it was hallucinogenic, the avant-garde crowd enthusiastically embraced the drink and absinthe became all the rage. Despite some sordid bohemian associations, absinthe served as an artistic muse that fueled a great deal of Belle Époque creativity. It was promoted with risqué postcards and posters; one even featuring the actress and theater icon Sarah Bernhardt (1844–1923).

In England, unconventional Victorians were familiar with the green spirit. Irish poet Oscar Wilde (1854–1900) was known to occasionally indulge. In America, absinthe found a home in French-speaking cosmopolitan New Orleans. The famous Old Absinthe House in the French Quarter is now a landmark tourist attraction. Although American writer Ernest Hemingway (1899–1961) missed the height of the absinthe craze in Paris, he sipped the drink in Barcelona and procured bottles from Cuba when living in Key West during Prohibition. References to absinthe appear in *For Whom the Bell Tolls* and *The Sun Also Rises*.

Popular at the tail end of the industrial revolution, absinthe was medicine for the masses and available in all the cafés. As with any product, there were cheap knockoffs that anyone could afford. Following the mid-1870s blight in the vineyards and higher cost of wine, grain alcohol served as a substitute in absinthe. Instead of herbs, copper salts were sometimes used to produce the

92. Adamson and Segan, *Entertaining from Ancient Rome to the Super Bowl*, 392.

green color. By the early twentieth century, absinthe was regarded as a public health threat, and between 1905 and 1915, many countries banned it.

Miscellany

Today's versions of absinthe are regulated with lower amounts of thujone. Thujone is also regulated in the wormwood used to produce vermouth and other beverages. By the way, the term *wormwood* comes from the German name of the plant, *wermut*, as did the French word *vermouth*.[93] The jury is still out on whether *alpha*-thujone is psychoactive and causes hallucinations. After all, back in the day, the alcohol in absinthe ranged from 90 to 148 proof. Research is ongoing for potential medicinal applications of *alpha*-thujone.

While the dried herb is widely available, there are also many cautions about it. As for the garden, wormwood is sometimes included for its foliage; however, in some areas, it is considered an invasive weed.

---

93. Watts, *Elsevier's Dictionary of Plant Lore*, 435.

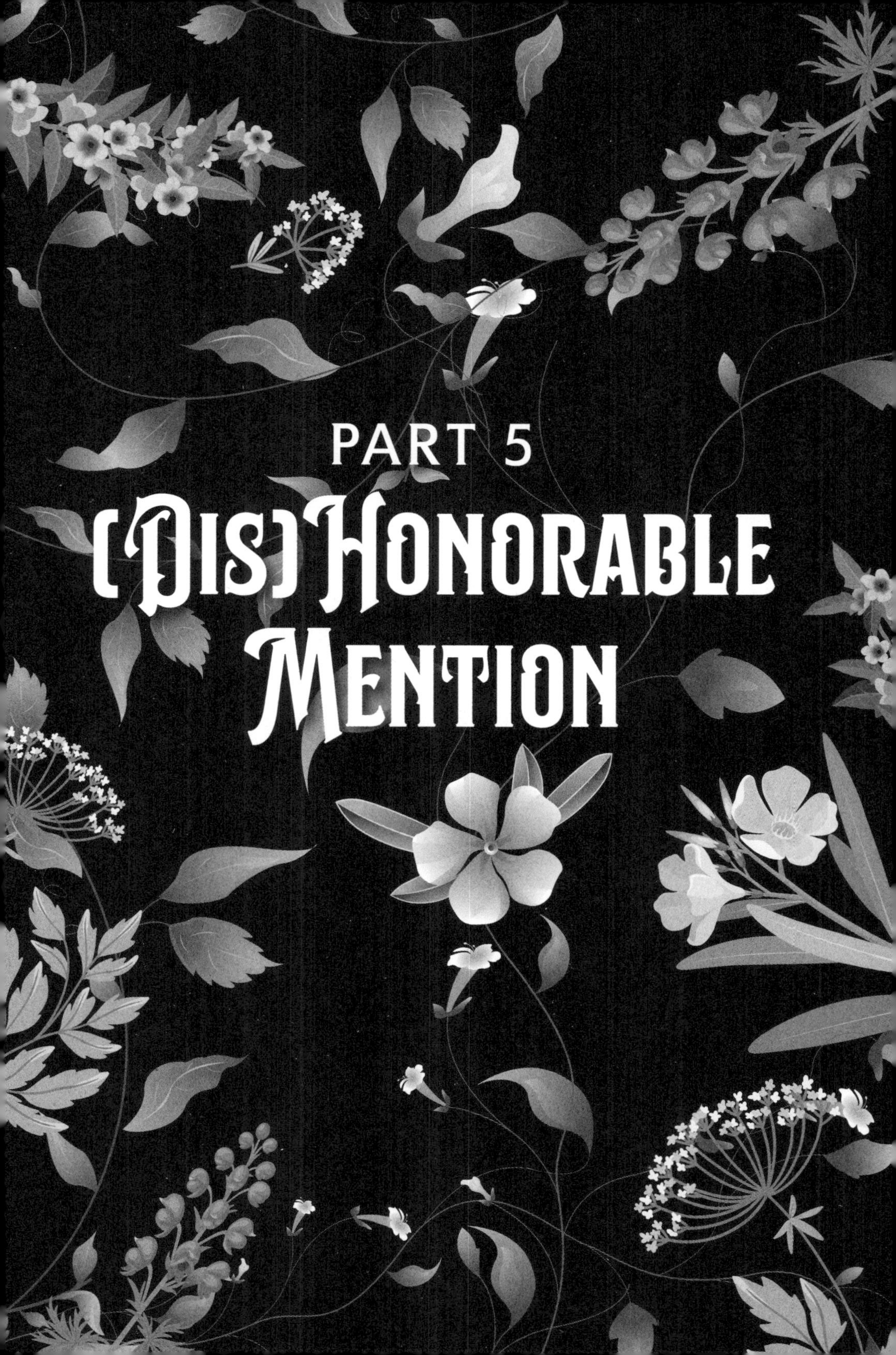

PART 5

(Dis)Honorable Mention

Apart from the houseplant dieffenbachia, the plants listed in this category are not exceptionally well known and have sparse, if any, folklore. Their stories may be short, but they are no less interesting than their poisonous brethren. Although you may have heard of the antiquated practice of trial by ordeal, did you know that a poisonous bean was sometimes used for it? While we all have our tastes in jewelry, there's one type you should never put in your mouth. We will also see why you should not park your car or stand under a certain tree when it rains.

Birthwort

TICKING TIME BOMB

Birthwort, European Birthwort (*Aristolochia clematitis*); also known as creeping birthwort, heartwort, pipewort

Botanical Family: Aristolochiaceae / Birthwort

The unbranched stems of birthwort grow upright or recline amongst neighboring vegetation. Its heart-shaped leaves are deeply veined. Growing in clusters of two to eight along the stems, the tubular, greenish-yellow flowers are S-shaped with elongated hoods. Birthwort is native from Europe to the Caucasus region and has been naturalized in Great Britain and parts of North America.

Toxicity and Cautions

The roots and stems of birthwort contain aristolochic acid, which is a nephrotoxin and carcinogen. The effects of ingestion are cumulative and lead to kidney disease and cancer. Birthwort is also an abortifacient.

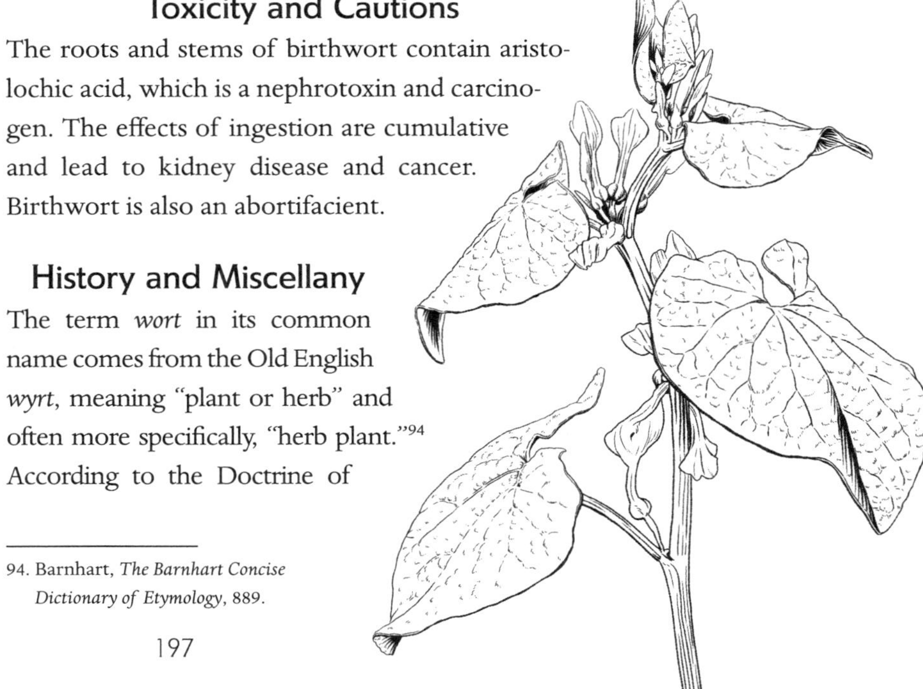

History and Miscellany

The term *wort* in its common name comes from the Old English *wyrt*, meaning "plant or herb" and often more specifically, "herb plant."[94] According to the Doctrine of

94. Barnhart, *The Barnhart Concise Dictionary of Etymology*, 889.

Signatures, the resemblance of the flower to the birth canal or a serpent was believed to indicate its use for childbirth and snakebites. From ancient Greece and Rome to medieval times and later, the juice from the stem added to wine was used to induce childbirth, ease the process, and expel the afterbirth or a dead fetus. It was widely used as an abortifacient.

Although Greek physician Hippocrates recommended it for uterine complaints, he also noted that it was useful for other ailments such as a pain in the side. The Anglo-Saxons used it to relieve fevers and as an antidote for snakebites. Early medieval Byzantium medical texts show that it was also a treatment for epilepsy and asthma.

In a story similar to darnel and ergot, birthwort in grainfields is a serious contaminant that took decades to figure out. During the 1950s, localized epidemics of multiple types of cancer and a unique kidney disease—later dubbed Balkan Endemic Nephropathy (BEN)—occurred in rural villages of present-day Bosnia-Herzegovina, Croatia, Romania, Serbia, and Bulgaria. Intensive research over the years ruled out genetic factors, environmental contaminants, and fungal toxins. Growing abundantly throughout the region, birthwort with its aristolochic acids were eventually found to be the culprit. To make matters worse, it is not only a matter of birthwort contaminating flour made from the grain, but decaying plant material releases the aristolochic acids, which contaminate the soil and are taken up by nearby food crops. Aristolochic acid is a ticking time bomb in the body and in agricultural fields.

Calabar Bean

BACK OFF, BELLADONNA

Calabar Bean (*Physostigma veneosum* syn. *Faba calabarica*); also known as chop nut, ordeal bean

Botanical Family: Fabaceae, formerly Leguminosae / Pea, Legume, Bean

Calabar bean is an evergreen climbing vine with woody stems that can reach up to fifty feet long. Its broad, oval leaves taper to a point, and pale pink or purplish flowers grow in pendulous clusters. The seedpods are about six inches long and contain two or three dark brown seeds that slightly resemble kidney beans. Native to tropical Africa, calabar bean was introduced into Brazil and India.

Toxicity and Cautions

Calabar seeds contain the highly toxic alkaloid physostigmine, which affects signals between the nerves and muscles. Ingestion can cause muscle weakness, increased sweating, nausea, vomiting, stomach pain, shortness of breath, and a slow heartbeat. Death can occur from respiratory failure or cardiac arrest.

History and Miscellany

The species name *veneosum* was derived from the Latin *venenum*, meaning "poison."[95] The common name comes from the Calabar region in what is now southern Nigeria. During the sixteenth century, the Portuguese, French, English, and Dutch established trading posts along coastal West Africa to access natural resources, which in their eyes included slaves. The area was then infiltrated by Christian missionaries bent on stamping out Indigenous practices.

95. Morwood, *Oxford Latin Desk Dictionary*, 202.

One such practice was trial by ordeal. Ironically ordeal by fire, water, and poison were also stock-in-trade methods used in Europe. British Army physician and botanist William Freeman Daniell (1818–1865) was one of the first outsiders to witness the botanical lie detector of the Efik people. A person accused of a serious crime or suspected of witchcraft was given a drink of milky white liquid made from calabar beans. Vomiting and surviving after consuming the beverage were considered proof of innocence. Of course, a guilty person died. Calabar was also used as a type of duel to settle disputes whereby two adversaries would ingest half a bean. It was winner-take-all if one survived… if.

Because the missionaries in Old Calabar were from Scotland, samples of the plant ended up at the Edinburgh Botanical Gardens. Affiliated with the city's medical school, the calabar bean was investigated and found to be of use to ophthalmologists and is still sometimes used for treatment of glaucoma. It was also discovered that the alkaloids physostigmine (from calabar bean) and atropine (from belladonna) were mutually antagonistic and could be used as antidotes to counteract one another.

Dieffenbachia

DON'T DITCH IT

Dieffenbachia (*Dieffenbachia seguine* syn. *Caladium seguinum*); also known as dumb cane, gold dieffenbachia, leopard lily, poison arum

Botanical Family: Araceae / Arum

Growing up to six feet tall, the broad shiny leaves of dieffenbachia are variegated or spotted. A greenish-yellow spathe (a specialized type of leaf) grows on a separate stem amongst the leaves and forms a protective hood around the cylindrical spike of tiny white flowers. Dieffenbachia is native to tropical Central and South America.

Toxicity and Cautions

All parts of the plant, especially the stalks, contain calcium oxalate, which are microscopic needles that irritate the skin and can cause blistering, burning, swelling, and itching. Sometimes just handling the plant can cause a reaction and blisters can last up to ten days. Ingestion is painful and can cause blistering and swelling of the mouth, throat, and vocal cords so much so that it can cause loss of speech and block the airways. The word *dumb* in *dumb cane* is a reference to the inability to speak and in the past was used as a slur. But wait, there's more. Dieffenbachia also contains proteolytic enzymes that break down proteins and can leave open sores in the esophagus and stomach.

History and Miscellany

First cultivated in Europe in the eighteenth century, the dieffenbachia became widely adored as a houseplant and still is. Most people who have one in their homes, know that it is poisonous, but may not know about its less-than-stellar past.

As if curare—a poison made mainly from the plants in the *Strychnos* genus and sometimes a few others—wasn't dangerous enough for arrow poison, Indigenous people in the upper Amazon region combined dieffenbachia sap with it to boost the effectiveness or perhaps to make it more painful. In the colonial plantations of Jamaica, dieffenbachia was used to produce granulation in sugar as well as to punish slaves by rendering them unable to speak.

The most pervasive use of dieffenbachia has a conflicting history about sexual impotence. Without providing much detail, many sources mention that it was used by Indigenous men in the Caribbean to induce temporary impotence as a means for contraception. However, in nineteenth-century American homeopathic medicine, a tincture of dieffenbachia was used as a treatment for frigidity and impotence. In the 1940s, it came to light during the Nuremberg Military Tribunal that the Nazis used an extract of dieffenbachia to torture concentration camp prisoners and conducted experiments to cause sterility in those they deemed undesirable.

While this plant's history leads down a dark rabbit hole, it's important to remember that the dieffenbachia isn't responsible for its abusive use. Often described as a delightful houseplant, it earns its keep by removing toxins from indoor air. So, don't ditch the dieffenbachia.

Giant Hogweed

STRIKING AND DANGEROUS

Giant Hogweed (*Heracleum mantegazzianum*)

Botanical Family: Apiaceae, formerly Umbelliferae / Carrot, Parsley

Looking like Queen Anne's lace on steroids, giant hogweed can grow ten to twenty feet tall with deeply incised, lobed leaves that can reach five feet wide. The stems are one to three inches in diameter with dark purplish blotches. Clusters of white flowers form flat-topped, umbrella-shaped heads that can be over two feet across. The winged, flattened, oval seeds are green and turn brown as they mature. Native to Asia and eastern Europe, it has become naturalized throughout western Europe and North America.

Toxicity and Cautions

Sap in the leaves, stems, and seeds is toxic and contains furocoumarins. Contact with the skin can cause significant irritation, itching, rashes, and open sores. The sap can also cause severe phototoxic dermatitis, which occurs when the skin is exposed to the ultraviolet rays of sunlight. It can cause severe sunburn, blistering, painful sores, and scars. Hypersensitivity to sunlight may last for several years. Getting sap in the eyes can cause temporary or permanent blindness.

Before it develops into a colossus, giant hogweed can be mistaken for cow parsnip (*Heracleum lanatum*) and angelica (*Angelica atropurpurea*).

History and Miscellany

During the nineteenth-century scientific zeal of exploration, professional and amateur botanists were collecting and carting home anything unfamiliar. Such was the case with giant hogweed, giving it a free ride into western Europe and

Great Britain where it was given as a gift to Kew Gardens for study. This ornamental curiosity made the jump across the pond to North America during the Victorian era craze for über-sized plants. Beekeepers liked giant hogweed for its oversized flowers that could feed many bees close to home. However, as in Europe and England, giant hogweed escaped cultivation and made itself at home in the American and Canadian landscape. Due to the potential public health hazard, it is on the federal noxious weed list in the United States and the invasive plant list of Ontario.

Its dangers were realized in Britain in the 1970s when physicians witnessed what seemed to be an outbreak of painful skin conditions that coincided with the rapid spread of the plant. After the event made headlines, the group Genesis included the song "The Return of the Giant Hogweed" on their *Nursery Cryme* album.

Manchineel

TREE OF DEATH

Manchineel Tree (*Hippomane mancinella*); also known as beach apple, death apple, manzanillo, poison guava

Botanical Family: Euphorbiaceae / Spurge

Manchineel is an evergreen tree that reaches about forty feet tall. It has reddish-gray bark and shiny, lance-shaped leaves. The small greenish-yellow flowers grow on short stalks at the end of branches. Sweet scented and apple-like, the fruit grows singly or in pairs. Manchineel is native to southern Florida, the Caribbean, Mexico, and Central America.

Toxicity and Cautions

The entire tree is poisonous with various toxins in different parts. The milky sap in the leaves and bark contain phorbol, which usually causes severe dermatitis and temporary blindless if it gets in the eyes. The sap can be carried by rain from the tree to an unsuspecting passerby. Other parts of the tree contain a cocktail of hippomanin, mancinellin, sapogenin, and physostigmine. Toxins can be ingested, inhaled, or absorbed through the skin. Physostigmine is found mostly in the fruit, which has a sweet taste, initially, but soon turns burning and painful. Ingestion can cause the throat to swell closed, high blood pressure, and severe gastroenteritis. Death can occur from heart or respiratory failure.

History and Miscellany

The Spanish first encountered this tree in Florida and named it *arbol de la muerte*, meaning "the tree of death."[96] This not only referred to eating the fruit,

96. Hammer, *Foraging in Florida*, 12.

but also the use of the sap by Indigenous people throughout the Caribbean to poison arrow tips. Spanish explorer and conquistador Juan Ponce de León (c. 1460–1521) was the first European to reach Florida in 1513. Although he is best known for his quest to find the legendary Fountain of Youth, he was also known for his ruthless treatment of Indigenous people and had a reputation for taking slaves. On his returned to Florida in 1521 to establish a Spanish colony, the Calusa people of the region defended their territory from takeover. Ponce de León was wounded with an arrow and taken to Cuba where he later died. It is generally believed that the arrow tip carried manchineel sap.

A little over a century later, English navigator, geographer, and buccaneer Basil Ringrose (c. 1653–1686) arrived in the Caribbean and recorded his encounter with the sap in his logbook. After standing under a manchineel tree during a light rain, he noted that his skin broke out in red spots where sap had dripped on him and that he was not well for about a week. That's no surprise as the sap has been known to eat through paint on cars parked underneath the tree.

Pokeweed
FROM INK TO PORT

Pokeweed, Pokeroot (*Phytolacca americana* syn. *P. decandra*); also known as American nightshade, coakum, crowberry, ink plant, inkberry, pigeonberry, pocan, pokeberry

Botanical Family: Phytolaccaceae / Pokeweed

Reaching between six to ten feet tall and sometimes a little more, poke has one or more reddish stems and bright green, oval- to lance-shaped leaves that give off an unpleasant odor when crushed. Pinkish stems hold elongated clusters of small greenish-white flowers that develop into dangling clusters of purple-black berries. Pokeweed is native to a large area of North America and is now found in parts of Europe.

Toxicity and Cautions

All parts of the plant are poisonous with the roots being most toxic and the ripe berries the least. Pokeweed contains the alkaloid phytolaccine and the saponin phytolaccagenic acid. While few deaths have been attributed to this plant, serious poisoning can occur. Symptoms appear about six hours after ingestion and can include nausea, vomiting, stomach pain, diarrhea, headache, and convulsions. Handling the plant can cause contact dermatitis, plus, toxins can be absorbed through abrasions in the skin.

History and Miscellany

Although regarded as edible, the use of pokeweed can be a game of toxic roulette because preparing it can be tricky. Referred to as poke salad, the young shoots have to be boiled twice using fresh water each time. Although double boiling reputedly destroys the toxins, people have had gastrointestinal problems after eating pokeweed prepared this way. Up until 2000, a company in Arkansas removed the risk by selling canned poke greens.

The name *poke* comes from the Algonquian word for the plant, *pocan*.[97] Poke was used medicinally for a range of ailments by the Algonquian, Iroquois, Delaware, and Mi'kmaq. The Iroquois used it for love medicine; however, the directions were vague: "Tie in a poplar tree, then place amongst roots."[98] Pokeweed was taken to Europe in the seventeenth century and cultivated as a dye plant. It escaped the farm and now grows throughout western and central Europe. In addition to dye, the berry juice was used as a substitute for ink by the Pennsylvania Dutch and by soldiers during the Civil War. For a time, the berries were used in Portugal to enhance the color of port, but the practice was discontinued because it hindered the taste.

97. Small, *North American Cornucopia*, 539.

98. Moerman, *Medicinal Plants of Native America*, 337.

Rosary Pea

PRAY CAREFULLY

Rosary Pea, Jequirity Bean (*Abrus precatorius*); also known as crab's-eyes, Indian licorice, paternoster pea, precatory bean, Seminole beads, wild licorice

Botanical Family: Fabaceae, formerly Leguminosae / Pea, Legume, Bean

This plant is a slender, woody vine that tends to climb over and cover neighboring vegetation. Growing in clusters, the pealike flowers range from lavender pink to pale red. The leaves consist of eight to fifteen pairs of leaflets. The seedpods are flat and contain shiny, scarlet-red peas that have one black spot. Native to India and tropical Asia, rosary pea is now widely naturalized throughout the tropics and subtropics around the world.

Toxicity and Cautions

All parts of the plant are poisonous with the highest concentration in the seeds. It contains the toxalbumin (toxic protein) abrin, which is similar to ricin from the castor bean plant and one of the deadliest plant toxins. Poisoning can occur through ingestion, inhalation of crushed seeds, or absorption through the skin. Symptoms can occur after several hours or days and include abdominal pain, vomiting, diarrhea, stupor, convulsions, and death.

History and Miscellany

In India, the leaves were used medicinally as tea to treat fever, colds, and coughs. With a licorice flavor, the roots were also included in some remedies. Because the peas have an almost perfect uniform weight, they were used as a unit of measure called ratti for weighing gold. Their uniform size also made them attractive for jewelry. Called gunja in Sanskrit, gunja mala are prayer beads made from the seeds. Westerners found them attractive for rosary beads. However, making the seeds into jewelry is risky business as breaking or piercing the outer shell releases the toxins. Wearing rosary pea jewelry may also be unsafe as toxins can be absorbed through the skin.

The rosary pea entered the West Indies and Florida through the slave trade. In the West Indies, as in parts of Africa, people wore the beads as a charm for protection against evil spirits. Grown as an ornamental plant in Florida, rosary pea escaped the garden and is considered an invasive, noxious species. Rosary pea seeds and jewelry are widely available.

SPURGE

OUCH!

Caper Spurge (*Euphorbia lathyris*); also known as mole plant, gopher spurge, myrtle spurge, paper spurge

Sun Spurge (*E. helioscopia*); also known as cat's milk, madwoman's milk, wartweed

Botanical Family: Euphorbiaceae / Spurge

Caper spurge has narrow, triangular leaves and yellow-green flowers with wide, arrow-shaped bracts (modified leaves) underneath. Each flower holds a three-lobed seed capsule. Sun spurge has distinctive red stems and serrated oblong leaves that are wider at the ends and taper at the base. The cup-shaped flowers are light green to pale yellow with a seed capsule in the middle and rounded bracts underneath. Caper spurge is native to the Mediterranean; sun spurge, to most of Europe and northern Africa. Both plants were introduced into North America.

Toxicity and Cautions

The sap and fruits (seed capsules) are toxic, containing diterpene esters and caustic alkaloids. The milky white latex sap can cause mild to severe contact dermatitis and blistering. In addition, sun spurge can cause photosensitivity, which makes the skin vulnerable to severe sunburn. Contact with the eyes can cause temporary to permanent damage to the cornea. Ingestion can cause swelling of the mouth, difficulty swallowing, nausea, vomiting, abdominal pain, and diarrhea.

History and Miscellany

The common name *spurge* comes from the Latin *expurgare*, meaning "to purge," because of the plant's strong laxative properties.[99] Both plants were used internally as such and externally the caustic sap was applied to the skin for removal of warts and other types of blemishes. The Anglo-Saxons used spurge to cure leprosy and treat snakebites. Caper spurge was so named because the green fruits were a substitute for capers, the unripe green buds of the caper bush (*Capparis spinosa*) that is used as a seasoning and garnish. Of course, one too many spurge capers could turn an enjoyable dish into a precarious experience.

Sun spurge had a wider medicinal use in medieval and Renaissance England. As a plaster or mixed with oil (or even bear's grease) it was used to relieve aching joints and sciatica, and to restore lost hair. However, English herbalist Nicholas Culpeper warned that when used internally as a purge it would scorch the entrails. He also noted that it "provokes lust and heals numbness and stiffness of the privities proceeding from cold, by anointing."[100] Now that's a thought that gives one pause.

99. Barnhart, *The Barnhart Concise Dictionary of Etymology*, 751.

100. Culpeper, *The English Physician*, 188.

Upas Tree

TALL TALES

Upas Tree (*Antiaris toxicaria* syn. *A. macrophylla*); also known as bark cloth tree, poison arrow tree, sacking tree

Botanical Family: Moraceae / Mulberry, Fig

Reaching up to a stately one hundred fifty feet and sometimes taller, the upas has smooth, pale gray bark. The heavily veined leaves are oblong to oval with a rounded base and pointed tip. The small (less than an inch) round fruit ripen to red or purplish and grow on the branches underneath the leaves. The upas is native to tropical regions from Africa through Southeast Asia to Australia.

Toxicity and Cautions

The milky latex sap contains the highly toxic cardiac glycosides cardenolides and antiarin, which have a digoxin-like effect, similar to foxglove, on the heart. Ingestion can cause convulsions, extreme diarrhea, unconsciousness, and death by cardiac arrest.

History and Miscellany

About as tall as the tree itself, tales began circulating in England during the early 1780s with a sensational account about a poisonous tree in Indonesia. According to legend, the upas emitted vapors so deadly that no other plants or animals could live within ten miles of it. Skeletal remains of man and beast were said to be scattered across the landscape. Of course, this begs the question: Who lived to tell the tale? But never mind the details, people were fascinated so much so that by the early nineteenth century, the notorious tree had become a meme in political cartoons. English poets Samuel Taylor Coleridge (1772–1834) and William Blake used the tree as a metaphor for false friendship.

Even Erasmus Darwin (1731–1802)—English physician, botanist, sometimes poet, and grandfather of Charles—mentioned it in his poem "The Loves of Plants." But alas, the eyewitness report that appeared in *London* magazine in 1783 and attributed to a Dutch or German surgeon N. P. (or J. N.) Foersch turned out to be false. It was a hoax perpetrated by English Shakespearean scholar and editor George Steevens (1736–1800), who was a well-known serial literary and scientific prankster.

While upas trees are not surrounded by a ten-mile radius of skeletal remains, the toxic sap has been put to deadly good use for poisoning the tips of arrows and blow darts throughout the islands of Southeast Asia. For good measure, it was sometimes combined with the sap of strychnine trees. Other parts of the upas were used for medicine and fibers from the bark for making cloth. If you are interested in growing one, seedlings are available for purchase online.

Water Hemlock

DEADLY TOYS

Common Hemlock, Spotted Water Hemlock (*Cicuta maculata*); also known as beaver poison, poison parsnip, muskrat weed, spotted cowbane

European Water Hemlock, Cowbane (*C. virosa* syn. *C. mackenzieana*); also known as children's-bane, Mackenzie's water hemlock, northern water hemlock

Botanical Family: Apiaceae, formerly Umbelliferae / Carrot, Parsley

Both plants have hollow stems with purple streaks or splotches. The leaves are oval- to lance-shaped and coarsely toothed. Small white flowers grow in loose dome-shaped, umbrellalike clusters. Common water hemlock is native to most of North America, the European species is native to northern Europe, Asia, Russia, Canada, and Alaska. They both have wider ranges today.

Toxicity and Cautions

All parts of water hemlock contain cicutoxin, a potent neurotoxin, with the highest concentration in the roots, swollen lower stems, and new growth. Ingestion can cause nausea, vomiting, abdominal pain, convulsions, delirium, seizures, tremors, and death. Symptoms may occur within an hour, death by respiratory failure within a few hours. Common hemlock is regarded as one of the most poisonous plants in North America and Great Britain.

The water hemlocks are easily mistaken while foraging for the edible Queen Anne's lace or wild carrot (*Daucus carota*), water parsnip (*Sium suave*), and wild parsnip (*Pastinaca sativa*).

History and Miscellany

Although risky, the Cherokee used water hemlock roots as a contraception and sometimes to cause permanent sterility. To poison their arrows for warfare, the Klamath people of the American northwest mixed the plant juice with rattlesnake venom and the decomposed liver of a deer or other animal after it had been buried in the ground for a few days. Even if an arrow missed its target, perhaps the odor was enough to make an enemy retreat.

Well into the nineteenth century, water hemlock was used in Europe and America to treat migraines. Despite the dangers, the European species is still used in homeopathic remedies. The common water hemlock is available for gardens.

In both America and Europe, these plants were responsible for the loss of livestock, as the folk name *cowbane* suggests. They also caused the death of children who found the hollow stems attractive for peashooters and whistles. In Sweden, water hemlock had the folk name *näckrot*, meaning "neck-root," because it grew at the edges of ponds and lakes, which were said to be the habitat of the näcken.[101] The näcken were said to be dangerous shape-shifting water spirits that usually appeared in human form. Called the necks in England, they are more widely known by their German name *nixies*.

101. Thorpe, *Northern Mythology*, 82.

White Snakeroot

POISONOUS MILK

White Snakeroot (***Ageratina altissima*** **syn.** ***Eupatorium rugosum, E. ageratoides***)**;** also known as deerweed, richweed, white sanicle

Botanical Family: Asteraceae, formerly Compositae / Aster, Daisy

White snakeroot ranges from two to four feet tall. Its leaves are rounded at the base and sharply pointed at the tip with coarsely serrated edges. The showy flowers consist of small bright white florets in clusters that grow at the ends of the stems and from the axils of the upper leaves. The plant is native to eastern and central North America but is now found in a wider area.

Toxicity and Cautions

All parts of the plant contain the toxic alcohol tremetol, which includes the ketone tremetone. These produce a deadly condition known as the trembles in livestock that eat the plant. It causes an illness known as milk sickness in people who consume milk, butter, or meat from effected animals. Symptoms of milk sickness include nausea, vomiting, weakness, muscle tremors, difficulty breathing, inactivity, and depression. Death can occur within a few days.

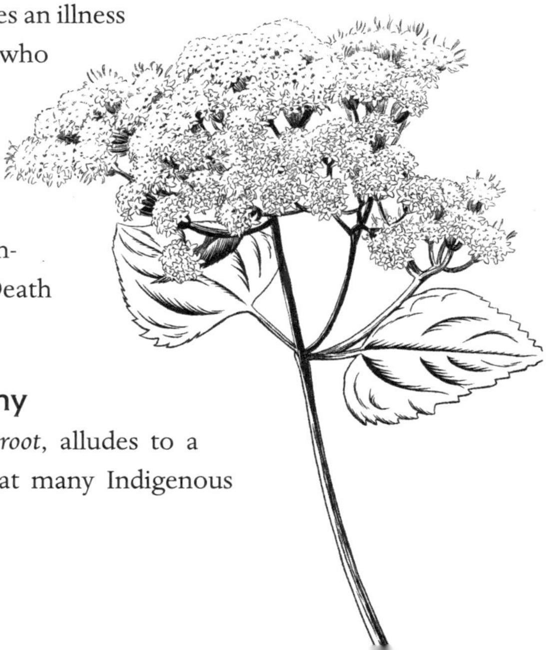

History and Miscellany

The common name, *white snakeroot*, alludes to a remedy made from the roots that many Indigenous peoples used for snakebites. The Iroquois also used a decoction of the root for gynecological issues and venereal disease; the Chickasaw and Choctaw chewed it for toothache. Although European settlers adopted medicinal uses, they did not understand the toxicity of the plant.

Since colonial times, there were occasional outbreaks of milk sickness, but in the early nineteenth century, epidemics of the disease swept through the Midwest, killing thousands and leaving people perplexed for decades. Nancy Hanks Lincoln (1784–1818), the mother of Abraham Lincoln (1809–1865), is believed to have died of it. Yes, American actor Tom Hanks (b. 1956) is a descendent of hers.

Midwife and frontier doctor Anna Pierce Hobbs Bixby (1802–1869) was equally baffled by the outbreaks until a Shawnee woman helped her piece the puzzle together. Through her work in raising awareness, Dr. Bixby was able to reduce the outbreaks in her area of Illinois by 1834. Despite this, her attempts to alert a wider population were not taken seriously. Even though over the years farmers and others came to the same conclusion, it wasn't until the early twentieth century when white snakeroot was fully recognized as the culprit.

Yellow Jessamine

UNTOWARD SYMPTOMS

Yellow Jessamine (*Gelsemium sempervirens* syn. *G. nitidum*); also known as Carolina jasmine, Carolina jessamine, evening trumpet flower, false jasmine, wild woodbine

Botanical Family: Gelsemiaceae

Yellow jessamine is an evergreen vine that twists and climbs ten to twenty feet long. It has reddish-brown stems, shiny lance-shaped leaves, and milky sap. The sweetly scented, funnel-shaped flowers are canary yellow and grow in clusters or solitary. The plant is native to the southern United States, Mexico, and Central America.

Toxicity and Cautions

All parts of the plant contain the toxic alkaloids gelsemine and gelseminine, including the sap and nectar. The flowers and roots have the highest concentrations. Ingestion can cause nausea, vomiting, diarrhea, dizziness, blurred vision, muscle weakness, convulsions, and death by respiratory failure.

History and Miscellany

Yellow jessamine came into medicinal use in the early nineteenth century by followers of the eclectic herbal movement, which was a populist approach to herbal medicine in America. By mid-century, the plant had entered conventional medicine in the Pharmacopoeia of the United States and remained there until the early twentieth century. Yellow jessamine was included in the British Pharmacopoeia for a time, too. Arthur Conan Doyle had been taking it for neuralgia and wrote a letter to the *British Medical Journal* about his experience with the plant. In true Sherlock Holmes fashion—inquisitive but a tiny bit reckless—he experimented on himself, slowly increasing the dosage. At one point he reported that it produced giddiness, at another dosage, headache and diarrhea. It was the extremeness of the latter symptom at yet a higher dose that prompted him to conclude his research.

The plant was used for its sedative and antispasmodic properties to treat fevers and coughs, but it was most widely used for pain and neuralgia. Tinctures for headache were available into the 1930s in the United States. *The Pharmaceutical Journal Formulary* in London listed a tincture of gelsemium in several mixtures for neuralgia; one mixture also included tincture of nux vomica, the seed of the strychnine tree. *The National Formulary* from the American Medical Association of 1924 listed its use for migraine, neuralgia, and uterine pain. The entry also noted: "Efficiency uncertain. Untoward symptoms sometimes result from comparatively small doses."[102] Despite the dangers, yellow jessamine is used in homeopathic remedies.

102. Hewlett et al., *Epitome of the Pharmacopeia of the United States and the National Formulary*, 86.

PART 6

Frightful Fungi

From the classic mushroom to some weird, alien-like shapes, fungi have been used by people for thousands of years. Mushrooms were amongst the items in the satchel of the corpse known as the iceman found in a glacier in the Alps who died approximately 5,300 years ago. He may have carried them for medicinal use. While cultural background generally determined whether a person is a mycophile (loves mushrooms) or a mycophobe (fears them), times have changed and more people worldwide are finding them a delectable dish. Foraging for them is another matter and often where people have sometimes gone wrong, terribly wrong.

Brown Roll-Rim

FATAL ERROR

Brown Roll-Rim (*Paxillus involutus* syn. *Agaricus involutus*); also known as common roll-rim, naked brimcap, poison pax

Fungi Family: *Paxillaceae*

The common name *roll-rim* is also spelled *rollrim* and *roll rim*.

Initially, the cap of this mushroom has a quintessential rounded shape but over time it flattens out and sometimes becomes funnel shaped. The cap has a downward rolled edge and often a bump in the middle. It is two to four inches wide, pale to reddish brown, and turns darker with age. The gills are thick, pale yellow, and turn brown. They bruise easily and turn reddish brown when touched. About three inches tall, the stem is the same color as the cap. It also bruises easily. This mushroom grows singly or in groups on rotting wood. It can be found in Great Britain, Europe, North America, Asia, and Australia.

Toxicity and Cautions

Although some people can eat this mushroom for months or years without a problem, or experience only mild gastrointestinal discomfort, they can have a sudden, extreme reaction. The symptoms may appear within an hour to a few hours after ingestion and include stomach cramps, nausea, vomiting, diarrhea, coma, and death.

The cause is as yet an unidentified antigen that stimulates an autoimmune reaction and causes

the breakdown of red blood cells. Ingestion can also cause kidney damage and liver failure. As if that isn't bad enough, species in the *Paxillus* genus tend to accumulate mercury from the soil.

History and Lore

The genus name *Paxillus* is Latin, meaning "wooden peg" or "small stake," because it sometimes looks like a wooden fastener.[103] Up until the early twentieth century, the brown roll-rim was popular for foraging and eating throughout central and eastern Europe. In Poland, it was traditionally pickled and salted. This mushroom was commonly believed to be safe to eat when thoroughly cooked—a point still made by some sources today. While that may rid it of some toxins, this mischievous mushroom holds on to others.

A high-profile and rather sad case of poisoning occurred in 1944 when German mycologist Julius Schäffer (1892–1944) made the fatal error of mistaking a cluster of brown roll-rims for a similar-looking milk cap mushroom (*Lactarius* spp.). He fell ill and the day after eating them was admitted to the hospital but died of renal failure seventeen days later. Schäffer was known for developing a chemical test to help identify mushrooms in the *Agaricus* genus. Several species were named in his honor, including *Agaricus schaefferianus* (now *Agaricus urinascens*), *Cortinarius schaefferianus*, and others. He is the only mycologist in modern times known to have died from eating mushrooms. Rather ironically, Schäffer is more widely known today for his watercolor studies of fungi; reproductions of his work sell for hundreds of dollars. While other deaths in eastern Europe have been attributed to this mushroom, scientists believe that there are probably more that have gone unnoticed because the cumulative toxic effects were not previously understood.

Miscellany

Although the exact antigen in this mushroom that effects people is unknown, studies are finding that it may inhibit some growth receptors of cancer cells. This mischievous mushroom may hold promises that warrant further biomedical research.

103. Morwood, *Oxford Latin Desk Dictionary*, 134.

Dead-Man's-Fingers

JUST PLAIN CREEPY

Dead-Man's-Fingers (*Xylaria polymorpha* syn. *X. obovate, X. corrugate, Hypoxylon polymorphum, Sphaeria polymorphia*); also known as dead-man's-toes

Dead-Moll's-Fingers (*X. longipes syn. Xylosphaera longipes*); also known as dead-man's-fingers

Fungi Family: *Xylariaceae*

Growing up to four inches tall, dead-man's-fingers have an uneven cylindrical, club, or spindle shape, which is usually curved. When young, they are pale grey or bluish with a whitish tip but mature to a brown or black, charred appearance. Dead-moll's-fingers are very similar but slightly smaller with a narrow stem at the base. Both fungi can grow solo but are most often found in clusters. Although their shapes vary, overall, they resemble swollen, gnarly fingers, and it doesn't take a vivid imagination to envision a corpse trying to claw its way out of a grave.

Spookiness aside, these are wood-rotting fungi that feed on dead and dying trees or buried wood, breaking them down for nutrients that also feed little creepy-crawlies. They can be found in Great Britain, Ireland, Europe, and North America.

Toxicity and Cautions

According to some sources, dead-man's-fingers are not poisonous but not edible, either; others say they are edible in their early development. The thing is, while poisonings may not have been linked to these fungi, there has not been any rigorous research into their toxicity. However, research into the

Xylaria genus in general suggests that all members of it contain some level of amatoxins and phallotoxins. These toxins are found in some of the deadliest mushrooms, including death cap. They affect blood cells, damage the liver and kidneys, and cause death. Ingesting these forest floor morsels is another instance of fungi roulette, but with a dead man's finger on the trigger.

Although dead-man's-fingers may make a nice macabre touch to Halloween decorations, be careful if they grow in your backyard or garden because they will attach to any damaged tree or shrub root and eventually kill it. In apple trees, they can cause black root rot.

History and Lore

One might expect a plethora of morbid folklore to be connected with these fungi, but alas, only in Lithuania. According to legend, they were the fingers of the Baltic god Velnias, who was associated with death, reincarnation, and ancestral worship. He was generally regarded as benevolent, but under Christianity his reputation suffered and he became linked with the devil.

The genus and species name for dead-man's-fingers comes from the Greek *xylos*, meaning "wood," and *polymorpha*, meaning "many forms," in reference to its variety of shapes.[104] The origin of the common name is self-explanatory, but it got me wondering about the name *dead-moll's-fingers* because I couldn't trace the source. Why not call it dead-woman's-fingers or dead-lady's-fingers? In the sixteenth and seventeenth centuries, the term *moll* meant "prostitute" but by the early nineteenth century it referred to the female companion or accomplice of a thief.[105] By the early twentieth century, the familiar phrase *gun moll* meant "the companion of a gangster." Did this mean that the fingers of the larger fungi were supposed to have belonged to a criminal? Or perhaps the word *moll* in the name was simply a whim.

Miscellany

A related species, Wu Ling Shen (*Xylaria nigripes*), has been used in Traditional Chinese Medicine for centuries and is being researched for possible applications in treating epilepsy.

---

104. Woehrel and Light, *Mushrooms of the Georgia Piedmont and Southern Appalachians*, 88.

105. Barnhart, *The Barnhart Concise Dictionary of Etymology*, 484.

Death Cap
RENDER UNTO CAESAR

Death Cap (*Amanita phalloides* syn. *Agaricus phalloides, Hypophyllum virosum*); also known as death cup
Fungi Family: *Amanitaceae* / Amanita

Death caps are usually about as wide as they are tall, ranging from two to six inches, and sometimes a little larger. The cap can be greenish bronze, olive yellow, yellow, or brown and often appears darker in the middle with faint radiating streaks. It is domed at first but flattens as it matures. The gills are white but turn cream or slightly pink. The stem is white to pale yellow, darker at the base, and usually has a remnant of the membranous veil near the top. Death caps can produce fairy rings. It is native from Europe to western Russia and northern Africa. It was introduced into North America and grows on both coasts.

Toxicity and Cautions

All parts of this mushroom contain the amatoxins alpha-amanitin and gamma-amanitin, which causes liver cells to burst, and the phallotoxin phalloidin, which destroys red blood cells. Eating as little as half a mushroom can kill an adult. Symptoms can appear ten to twenty-four hours after ingestion and include diarrhea and cramps, which often subside, giving false hope. After about five days, the liver and kidneys begin to fail. By the tenth day, coma, respiratory failure, and death occur. Those who survive suffer permanent kidney and liver damage.

Death caps closely resemble several edible mushrooms of the *Amanita* genus as well as a few others. Sources vary slightly but most indicate that this mushroom is responsible for 90 percent of deaths by mushrooms worldwide.

History and Lore

Like most mushrooms, death cap has a phallic shape, especially midway in its development. Its species name was derived from the Greek *phallos*, meaning "phallus."[106] The ancient Romans were quite fond of mushrooms but preferred them in their early stage of development when they are small and covered with a veil that gives the immature fungus an egg-like appearance. At that stage it can be particularly difficult to discern the species, especially for the untrained eye, which can be deadly.

Caesar's mushroom (*Amanita caesarea*) was so named in the eighteenth century because it was known to have been a favorite of many Roman emperors and, like many upper-class Romans, Emperor Claudius absolutely loved them. While he may have enjoyed mushrooms, according to Roman historians Tacitus and Dio Cassius, a feast of fungus caused his departure from this world. Although some sources note that he ate mushrooms laced with aconite, adding poison wasn't necessary. It would have been much easier to mix death caps with his usual mushrooms before the plate was rendered unto Caesar. His wife, Agrippina, is generally believed to have carried out the deed, or she hired the assassin Locusta to do it.

Like their poisonous counterparts in the plant world, mushrooms have served as murder weapons for novelists. Of course, writers are free to use artistic license for a good story, and besides, many of us are only familiar the mushrooms available in the supermarket. But that's not always the case. Mycologist R. Gordon Wasson gave American novelist Anne Parrish (1888–1957) kudos for getting the details right in her 1925 book *The Perennial Bachelor*. In 1973, this deadly mushroom had top billing in British author June Thompson's (c. 1930–2022) novel *Death Cap*.

Death cap was also used for real-life (or perhaps real-death is more accurate) murder by the Paris Poisoner, Henri Girard (1875–1921). His life of crime had a conventional start with low-level convictions such as fraud relating to the lottery and theft. Although trained as a druggist, he eventually found that being an insurance broker could be far more lucrative, but not for selling insurance. He persuaded people to take out life insurance policies, and when that didn't work, he took them out secretly using the alias Emile Ramon as

106. Stevenson, *Oxford Dictionary of English*, 1332.

the beneficiary. He first dabbled with typhus bacteria (*Salmonella typhi*) but upped his game with death caps. In all, Girard killed two clients and attempted to dispatch six others. When he was arrested, police found a diary where he recorded the how and when for some of his activities, including his victims' symptoms. Four accomplices were also arrested: his wife, mistress, chauffeur, and wine merchant. His wife was sentenced to life with hard labor, the mistress got twenty years, and the others, two years. A swindler to the end, Girard cheated the justice system by committing suicide with some type of bacteria he smuggled into prison.

Death cap may have also claimed the life of the Holy Roman Emperor Charles VI (1685–1740) of Austria. Although some sources say his death was brought on by a chill he caught while hunting, others note that it was more likely the mushrooms he consumed on his hunting trip in the mountains. He was said to have complained of indigestion after eating them but then seemed to be fine. Ten days later he suddenly died. Charles was known for his overly lavish lifestyle and excessive spending habits, which his family and state financial advisors were unable to restrain. In the end, it was a fungus that curtailed his extravagance.

Much more recent murder by death cap occurred in Australia in 2023. Erin Patterson (b. 1974), who served her guests a special beef Wellington, was charged with three counts of murder and five attempted murders. Despite the widespread belief, poisonous mushrooms do not provide a warning via foul taste. In fact, death caps are said to have a pleasant, somewhat sweet flavor. Christina Hale (1955–2012) of Bridgewater, England, tragically discovered this after making soup with the ones she picked in her backyard. According to the West Somerset coroner, it was a case of death by misadventure.

Another incident that could have been a misadventure involved French physician Pierre Bastien (1924–2006) in 1981. To prove that his special treatment that included vitamin C injections, two types of antibiotics, and a diet of carrot soup had been the reason several of his patients survived death cap poisoning, he demonstrated on himself by eating one. He survived. However, in addition to being regarded as an irresponsible experiment, many in the medical community believed it was without merit because he may have started the antidote before eating the mushrooms. No one but Bastien recommended the treatment.

Miscellany

Perhaps the only bright side is that a pharmaceutical company in Germany has been working with the alpha-amanitin from death caps to develop drugs for treating tumors.

Destroying Angel

BEWARE THE WOLF

Destroying Angel, European Destroying Angel (*Amanita virosa*); also known as death angel

Eastern American Destroying Angel (*Amanita bisporigera*); also known as death angel, destroying angel

Fool's Mushroom (*Amanita verna* syn. *Agaricus verna*); also known as destroying angel, spring amanita

Western American Destroying Angel (*Amanita ocreata* syn. *Amanita bivolvata*); also known as death angel, destroying angel

Fungi Family: *Amanitaceae* / Amanita

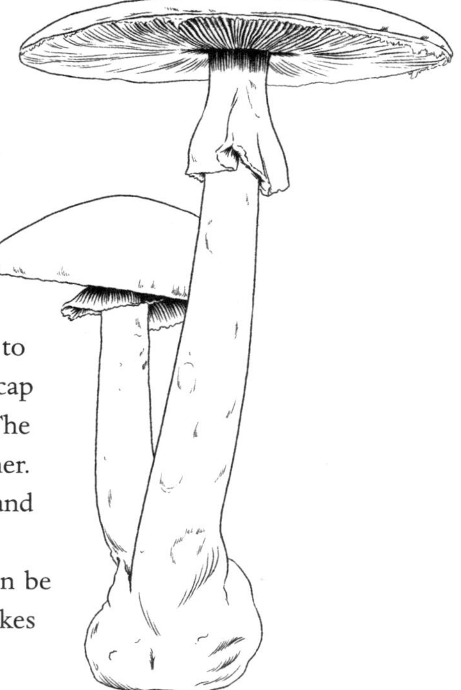

In addition to sharing the common name *destroying angel*, these four closely related species also have strikingly similar appearances. Their caps are initially egg shaped, develop into a bell shape, and then occasionally flatten out with a bump in the center. They are pure white but sometimes dull to beige and often turn tan with age. The cap is sometimes slightly tilted on the stem. The gills are white and arranged closely together. The stem is white, often slightly curved, and sometimes has a bulbous base.

The species *A. virosa* and *A. verna* can be found in Europe and Great Britain. It takes an expert to distinguish the two; however, they appear at different times of year—*A. verna* (vernal) can be found in the spring. As noted in their common names, *A. bisporigera* and *A. ocreata* grow in different areas of North America.

Toxicity and Cautions

Like their cousin the death cap (*Amanita phalloides*), the destroying angels contain the amatoxin alpha-amanitin, which causes liver cells to burst, and the phallotoxin phalloidin, which destroys red blood cells. Symptoms include diarrhea, vomiting, nausea, and abdominal pains that occur from five to twelve hours after ingesting. The initial onset of symptoms is usually followed by a lull that lasts for several hours or a day or two, giving a false sense of hope that the danger has passed. Not so. The symptoms usually return with a vengeance, and by that time, the liver and kidneys are already damaged. Without treatment, coma and death follow.

History and Lore

The species name for one of the European mushrooms, *A. virosa*, comes from the Latin *virosis*, meaning "poisonous," which is also the basis for the word *virus*.[107] This should be no surprise as it usually makes the list of the top eight or ten most deadly mushrooms. For foragers who know how deadly they are, the stark white of these mushrooms against the backdrop of nature's colors can seem eerily beautiful and inviting.

The destroying angels are often mistaken for the wood mushroom (*Agaricus sylvicola*) and the field mushroom (*Agaricus campestris*) as well as the common puffball (*Lycoperdon perlatum*). That was the case with William Hickman (b. 1968) of Ohio in 2022 who gathered what he thought were puffballs growing in his yard. Taking a picture with his smartphone and using an app to identify them, he thought he was good to go, but they were not puffballs. Although he said they were delicious, about eight hours after eating them he thought he was going to die and nearly did. Hickman was fortunate that his local emergency room had him transported to the University Hospital in Cleveland where they had experience with treating mushroom poisonings. Luckily, an experi-

107. Editorial Staff, *Webster's Third New International Dictionary*, 2556.

mental treatment that doesn't work for everyone worked for him. According to Hickman, it took about six months for him to get back to feeling normal.

Miscellany

Massachusetts artist Michelle Vigeant, who has a degree in biology, created an interesting print called "Pawprints of Death." It shows a wolf walking into the distance with a path of pawprints turning into a trail of destroying angel mushrooms behind him. I don't know what the artist's intent was, but to me it symbolizes the proverbial wolf in sheep's clothing: the innocent-looking, pearly mushrooms beckon, but their bite is deadly.

Ergot

FROM PLAGUES TO THE COUNTERCULTURE

Ergot, Rye Ergot (*Claviceps purpurea*); also known as horn seed, mother of rye, rye smut, spurred rye

Fungi Family: *Clavicipitaceae* / Ergot

Ergot is a parasitic fungus that thrives in damp conditions on cereal grains. It is most common and severe on rye. Infection results in growths called sclerotium that look like large, purplish-black kernels protruding from the heads of grain. It was named ergot from the Old French *argot*, meaning "cock's spur," because the shape of the diseased grain resembles the spur on a rooster's foot.[108] Ergot is found worldwide.

Toxicity and Cautions

Ergot contains seventy alkaloids including ergotamine, ergocristine, and lysergic acid. Ergotism, or ergot poisoning, has two forms with different symptoms. Convulsive ergotism symptoms include hallucinations, hysteria, twitches, spasms, a crawling sensation on the skin, and erratic behavior. The other, gangrenous ergotism, is characterized by a loss of sensation in the extremities, infection, and gangrene. This form can be fatal. Ergotism is caused by eating contaminated bread.

History and Lore

Ergot is well known because it has been a leading candidate for the spark that ignited the Salem witch panic and trials of 1692 in Massachusetts. The earliest potential mention of ergot dates back thousands of years to an Assyrian tablet

108. Barnhart, *The Barnhart Concise Dictionary of Etymology*, 250.

that noted oddities on ears of grain. The Greeks seemed to have no interest in rye and apparently did not experience ergot contamination of other grains. Although the Romans cultivated rye along the Rhine and Danube Rivers, Pliny the Elder mentioned it as a famine food and fodder for cattle.

Bread was a dietary staple for people in medieval Europe and, grown is large quantities, rye was a staple for peasants and the poor. Ergot on rye crops had become so commonplace that it was thought to be a normal part of the plant and, in some cases, the larger kernels were rumored to be better. Even early botanical drawings of rye included ergot sclerotia. The fungus was harvested along with the grain and baked into bread. It wasn't until the late seventeenth century that ergot poisoning was recognized as a disease. Although less well known than bubonic plague, outbreaks of ergotism were common and just as scary, especially with the often accompanying psychosis. Sometimes entire villages fell victim to it.

An early documentation of a gangrenous ergotism outbreak can be found in the text *Annals of Xanten*, or *Annales Xantenses*, a chronicle written by the monks at Xanten Abbey, not far from present-day Düsseldorf, Germany. The memorable entry for the year 857 details a plague that caused people's limbs to rot and fall off. A documented epidemic also occurred in the years 944–945 that affected Paris and the Aquitaine region of France, where nearly twenty thousand people perished.

The disease was called St. Anthony's fire and *ignis sacer*, meaning "holy fire," because of the tingling, burning sensations in the limbs and the belief that praying to St. Anthony could cure it.[109] The Antonines, Hospital Brothers of St. Anthony who cared for the afflicted, was founded in the late eleventh century near the church La-Motte Saint-Didier in southeastern France, where the saint's relics were held. The religious hermit St. Anthony of Egypt (c. 251–356) was said to have had visions and suffered psychic attacks from demons, the description of which is not unlike a bout of ergotism.

Repeated outbreaks of ergotism swept across Europe for centuries and even put its mark on the art world in the work of some Renaissance masters. The numerous amputees and bizarre, hallucinatory scenes in the work of Flemish painter Pieter Bruegel the Elder (d. 1569) and Dutch painter Hieron-

109. Marcello, *The Psychopharmacology of Herbal Medicine*, 334.

ymus Bosch show a vision of hell that may have been stoked by the disease. In addition, American anthropologist James Wood (b. 1949) has noted that perhaps not all instances of the plague may have been the Black Death, but ergotism instead. Just as ergot is believed to have been the catalyst in Salem, it's interesting to note that witch trials in sixteenth-century Scotland occurred mainly in rye-growing areas.

Although in the late seventeenth century botanists in France and Germany had figured out that the ergot sclerotia had to be cleaned from the grain, it took a long time for that knowledge to be widely dispersed. Meanwhile, outbreaks continued. In 1722 during the Russo-Persian War, Tsar Peter the Great (1672–1725) had a setback on his way to Constantinople (now Istanbul) when his army, both soldiers and horses, were hit with ergotism.

In sixteenth-century Germany, botanist and physician Adam Lonicer (1528–1586) made the first written reference concerning the use of weirdly shaped rye grains to hasten childbirth. Already in use by midwives long before Lonicer discovered it, ergot rye was known as *mütterkorn*, meaning "mother's grain." Of course, dose is everything. Just the right amount brings on labor, too much or given at the wrong time and it's an abortifacient. Midwives also discovered that just the right amount prevented excessive bleeding during and after childbirth. Powdered ergot called *pulvis ad partum*, meaning "powder of birth," was used by midwives and doctors.[110] By the second half of the nineteenth century, ergot was being used for the treatment of migraine. The fungus continued to be studied and its alkaloids isolated and analyzed for beneficial uses.

In 1938 at Sandoz Pharmaceuticals in Switzerland, chemist Albert Hoffman (1906–2008) unintentionally produced a semisynthetic ergot alkaloid, lysergic acid diethylamide (LSD). As scientists sometimes do, he ingested it to find out its effects and initiated a new avenue of research into hallucinogenics. Although it showed promise for treating alcoholism and use in psychotherapy, some warned that it was too alluring for abuse and too dangerous. American psychologist Timothy Leary of Harvard University begged to differ. In addition to its use in psychology, Leary believed that it was something that the general public should have, especially young people. LSD caught on, big time, with the

---

110. Chamberlain, *From Witchcraft to Wisdom*, 115.

counterculture of the 1960s, and the psychedelic era began as people turned on, tuned in, and dropped out.

Miscellany

The alkaloid ergotamine is still used in childbirth and to prevent postpartum hemorrhage. Clinical interest in the therapeutic potential of ergoline hallucinogens is beginning to emerge again for potential use in the treatment of autism and palliative care. The name *St. Anthony's fire* is still used in describing intense inflammation of the skin from ergotism and erysipelas (a skin infection).

False Morel

AN EVIL TWIN

False Morel (*Gyromitra esculenta* syn. *Helvella esculenta, Physomitra esculenta*); also known as beefsteak mushroom, brain mushroom, elephant ears, turban fungus

Fungi Family: *Discinaceae*

The false morel does not have the quintessential umbrella-shaped cap and gills of mushrooms; in fact, it looks like a mishappen blob on a stubby pedestal. The cap is an irregular shape with wrinkles or rounded lobes that resemble the folds of a brain. It is brownish red and darkens to almost black as it ages. The cap can be about four inches tall, five or six inches wide, and perched on a wide stem that is about two inches tall. The stem is lighter reddish brown, tan, or creamy white. False morel is found throughout Great Britain, Europe, and North America.

Toxicity and Cautions

False morels can send a person out of this world and into the grave. All parts of this mushroom contain the toxin gyromitrin, which is unstable, and when cooked or broken down in the body after ingestion, it turns into monomethylhydrazine, a compound that is used in rocket fuel. Ingestion can cause stomach pain, vomiting, dizziness, and sometimes coma and death. Except in severe cases, symptoms usually do not appear for several hours or even a day or two. Gyromitrin affects the central nervous system and damages the liver, the gastrointestinal tract, and possibly the kidneys. It also destroys red blood cells. In a mild case of poisoning, a person can recover within several days; a severe case can cause death within a week.

Gyromitrin is a cumulative carcinogen and eating false morels repeatedly may build up toxins in the body. The hooded false morel (*G. infula*) is also deadly, but oddly enough, while the snow morel (*G. gigas*) and false brown morel (*G. fastigiata*) also contain gyromitrin, no documented poisonings have been attributed to them.

History and Lore

False morel is like an evil twin, ready and waiting to deceive the unwary forager because it is easily, and often, confused with the highly prized common (true) morel (*Morchella esculenta*). The outer surface of the true morel cap has narrow, flattened ridges and a slight honeycombed appearance. True morels are the most expensive mushrooms because they are notoriously difficult to cultivate, which is why foraging for them is so popular. However, true morels are not without their own problems. Because they contain the toxin hydrazine, they can cause poisoning if eaten raw or if not thoroughly cooked. There is a widespread and erroneous belief that cooking any type of mushroom removes all toxins.

Although much more toxic, the false morel has been and is still regarded as an edible mushroom and a delicacy in Scandinavia, parts of Europe, as well as in some areas of North America. Like the true morel, it is not safe to eat raw and can be fatal if consumed that way. Preparation techniques, such as parboiling, are said to reduce its toxicity, and recipes from many sources note to parboil them at least twice, using fresh water each time. Although instructions are often provided on how to prepare false morels, they should be regarded as a don't-try-this-at-home demonstration. Also, while gyromitrin may be evaporated out of the mushrooms during the boiling process, it ends up in the air and inhaling gyromitrin can be just as bad as ingesting it. In addition, even after cooking, enough of the toxin can remain in the mushrooms and cause illness.

Many people have eaten false morels for years without a problem but some people have gotten very sick or died after eating them only once. But here's where it gets even weirder: two people can eat from the same plate of prepared false morels and one will be fine while the other, not so much. It really is a situation of fungi roulette. Ironically, the species name for the false and common morels comes from the Latin *esculentus*, meaning "edible."[111]

Miscellany

False morels are sold in public markets in Poland, Bulgaria, and Finland; however, it is required by law in Finland to sell them with a warning about their toxicity along with a legal description for their preparation. Czechia, Spain, Germany, Switzerland, Sweden, and Norway have banned the sale of them. The debate continues amongst foragers and on websites about consuming them. To eat or not to eat? That is the question, but to be safe, just say no.

111. Harrison, *Latin for Gardeners*, 81.

Fly Agaric
SANTA AND SOMA

Fly Agaric (*Amanita muscaria* var. *muscaria* syn. *Agaricus muscarius*); also known as deadly amanita, fairy tables, fly mushroom, pixie stools, red cap, wart caps

Fungi Family: *Amanitaceae* / Amanita

Fly agaric is the classic fairy-tale mushroom with a red or sometimes slightly orangish cap studded with white flakes. The cap can measure four to eight inches in diameter. The off-white stem is often shaggy and has a slightly bulbous base. A prominent ring near the top of the stem is the remnant of the veil that encased the mushroom when it first emerged from the ground. Usually growing in dense groups and occasionally rings, fly agaric is mostly found in forests, especially near birch or spruce trees. This mushroom is found throughout the Northern Hemisphere.

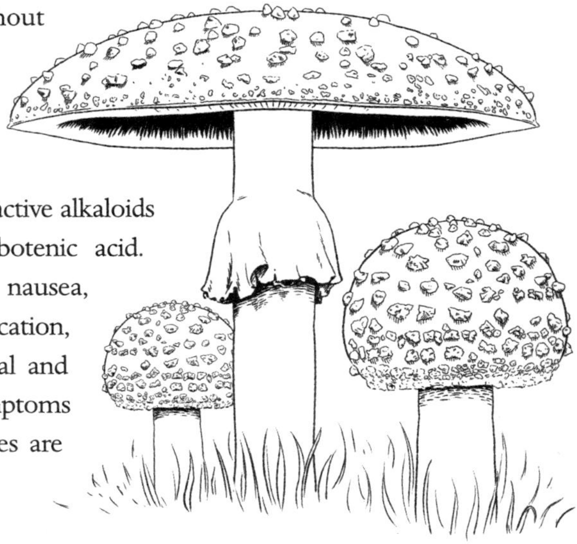

Toxicity and Cautions

Fly agaric contains the psychoactive alkaloids muscarine, muscimol, and ibotenic acid. Ingestion can cause dizziness, nausea, delirium, drowsiness, intoxication, low blood pressure, and visual and auditory hallucinations. Symptoms can be intense and experiences are highly variable. Ingesting large amounts can cause severe illness, coma, and sometimes death.

While this mushroom is poisonous, it is also edible; however, it requires a lengthy and very specific preparation. Those who write about its culinary use usually include the caveat to do so at your own risk, which means, don't do it.

Yellow fly agaric (*A. muscaria* var. *guessowii*) in North America and (*A. muscaria* var. *formosa*) in Europe are varieties of the classic species and contain the same psychoactive compounds. The only difference is that they have yellow to orange caps instead of red. Fly agaric has several more lethal cousins: death angel (*A. verna*), destroying angel (*A. virosa*), and death cap (*A. phalloides*).

History and Lore

Although this mushroom is named for the mundane use of killing flies, it is most widely associated with a different sort of flying: shamanic flight. Fly agaric has been important to shamans in Siberia and the Baltic region for communicating with unseen realms as well as deceased people and gods. It was one of the hallucinogens that allowed the shaman to leave their body and enter the spirit world, retrieve souls, or discover why someone was ill. During initiation, fly agaric was taken by drinking the urine of a shaman who had eaten the mushroom. The alkaloid muscarine remains active and has the same effect as firsthand consumption of it. Following the ecstatic journey phase that is often experienced after ingesting fly agaric, the final phase as it wears off has been likened to mental derangement.

Within Indigenous populations, mainly shamans consume the mushroom; however, it found more widespread use in Europe as an intoxicant. In Hungary it became known as the mad mushroom. In parts of Scandinavia, the water that the mushrooms were cooked in was sometimes used as a holiday drink. Fly agaric was a popular inebriant in Russia until the cheap and more easily obtainable vodka replaced it.

Fly agaric was sometimes included in Mithridatium formulas that were employed as preventative remedies for protection against intentional poisoning. Like most things poisonous, it was regarded as a witch's plant and sometimes cited as an ingredient in their magical flying ointment. Although the suggestion has been made, it is hotly debated whether Viking berserkers partook of it to produce a state of battle frenzy.

Referring to it as the divine mushroom of immortality, American author and ethnomycologist R. Gordon Wasson was the first to suggest that fly agaric was the mysterious, unidentified plant called soma in ancient texts. Soma is both a plant and a god described in the *Rigveda* (c. 1000 BCE), a text containing hymns of the Aryan or Indo-Iranian peoples who migrated from central Asia into the Indus Valley. The Hindu-Vedic god Soma was the Master of Plants, a healer, and bestower of riches. The plant soma was believed to have come from heaven and was described as an inebriant that produced visions. Said to provide strength and immortality, its juice was made into a drink that was offered as libation to deities and used in ritual ceremonies. Although Wasson's theory received acclaim, it was also highly criticized.

Theories regarding the use of psychedelics in early Christianity have been controversial and raging for decades. Some of the speculation has been fueled by a thirteenth-century fresco in the Plaincourault Chapel in Mérigny, France. It shows Adam and Eve standing beside the Tree of the Knowledge, which is not an unusual subject for a medieval painting; however, the tree is red and depicted with a mushroom-like top sporting an array of white dots and strongly reminiscent of fly agaric. The branches of the tree also resemble the mushroom.

During the psychedelic heyday of the 1960s/70s, fly agaric was one of the substances of experimentation. Better known for his novels such as *Even Cowgirls Get the Blues*, American author Tom Robbins (b. 1932) wrote about his experiences with it in *High Times* magazine. A century earlier, English author Lewis Carroll seems to have modeled some of Alice's experience in Wonderland on fly agaric, perhaps from reading contemporary accounts by the likes of English botanist and mycologist Mordecai Cubitt Cooke. While dealing with shifting realities, Alice changes size and encounters a prophetic hookah-smoking caterpillar ensconced on a large mushroom.

Known as *Glückspilz*, meaning "happiness mushroom," in Germany, during the nineteenth century fly agaric became a common theme in Christmas decorations throughout Europe.[112] It appeared on holiday cards along with symbols of good luck such as four-leaf clovers and horseshoes and became a good luck charm in its own right in central and northern Europe. Scandinavian Christmas

112. Marley, *Chanterelle Dreams, Amanita Nightmares*, 149.

cards commonly depicted fly agaric with gnomes cavorting amongst them. Frequently found beneath firs and spruces, fly agaric is like a candy apple beacon in the drab winter landscape and became firmly associated with Yule celebrations.

In addition, the night flight of Santa Claus has been compared with the Siberian and Lapp shamans who used the psychotropic properties of fly agaric for their travels. It has been suggested that Santa's red and white costume may have been inspired by the mushroom's colors. As for Rudolf and his cohorts, reindeer are fond of fly agaric and seek it out amongst their usual fare of lichen as well as in the urine from other reindeer or humans who have consumed it. Perhaps Santa's reindeer really know how to fly.

Miscellany

Fly agaric is used in homeopathy remedies for a range of ailments and is sometimes referred to as aga. In conventional medicine, the alkaloid muscimol is being studied for potential neuropharmacological applications.

Funeral Bell

DON'T LET IT TOLL

Funeral Bell (*Galerina marginata* syn. *G. autumnalis, Agaricus marginatus*); also known as autumn skullcap, deadly galerina, deadly skullcap

Fungi Family: *Hymenogastraceae*

The bell-shaped cap of this mushroom is tawny to orangish brown and flattens with age. It occasionally appears two-toned. The gills are tan to brownish and the whitish stem sometimes has a ring or zone around it that disappears with age. The funeral bell is about two inches wide and tall but sometimes a little taller. It grows singly but more often in clusters, which are also called a troop. Funeral bell can be found in Europe, North America, Asia, and Australia.

Toxicity and Cautions

Amongst the toxins found in the funeral bell, many are the same as the infamous death cap: the amatoxins alpha-amanitin and gamma-amanitin, which cause liver cells to burst, and the phallotoxin phalloidin, which destroys red blood cells. Ingestion may cause abdominal pain, nausea, vomiting, diarrhea, dizziness, and hypothermia. Symptoms can begin six to twenty-four hours after eating the mushrooms. While the situation may improve after three days, in serious cases it is a false remission. The toxins can severely affect the liver and kidneys and can cause coma and death within seven days.

History and Lore

One would think that the common names for this mushroom should be like a neon sign warning of its danger, but like many other mushrooms, ingestion is usually accidental. The main reason is that funeral bells fit into the informal category that mycologists call LBMs, Little Brown Mushrooms. Many types of LBMs look amazingly similar and are notoriously difficult to identify. For example, the funeral bell looks a lot like the sheathed woodtuft (*Kuehneromyces mutabilis*) and it is often confused with the honey mushroom (*Armillaria mellea*); both of these are edible and widely foraged. Funeral bell is also a lookalike with some of the hallucinogenic magic mushrooms in the *Psilocybe* genus. Mistaking these would send a thrill-seeking shroomer on a trip to the ER instead of a psychedelic wonderland. In addition, the funeral bell disproves a long-held belief that any mushroom growing on wood is edible.

Miscellany

In 2023, passionate mushroom forager in Hertfordshire, England, Marina Muttik posted a jaw-dropping TikTok video showing her taking a bite of a funeral bell. Even though she immediately spit it out, she raised a lot of eyebrows. Daring or dumb, this modern-day equivalent to the circus stunt of sticking one's head in a lion's mouth is not a trick anyone should try.

Ink Cap

TIPPLER BEWARE

Common Ink Cap (*Coprinopsis atramentaria* syn. *Coprinus atramentarius, Agaricus atramentarius*); also known as alcohol inky, smooth ink cap, tippler's bane

Fungi Family: *Psathyrellaceae*

Also known as inky caps, the name *ink cap* is also spelled as one word or hyphenated.

After emerging from the ground in the shape of an egg, the white, tan, or grayish-brown cap expands into a bell shape as it grows. The stem is a white to dingy buff and can be almost five inches tall. The gills are also white, initially. The mushroom lasts only a day before committing the fungus equivalent of suicide. The gills turn gray and then black, the cap darkens, and the rim curls up as the whole thing seems to melt, dripping black goo onto the ground. A dark puddle surrounds the base of the stem that is left standing.

Called deliquescing, this weird event is the result of enzymes that liquefy the gills for the purpose of distributing spores (seeds). The common ink cap can be found in the British Isles, Europe, and North America. It mostly grows in clusters but is occasionally solitary.

Toxicity and Cautions

While the common ink cap is edible, all parts of it contain the amino acid coprine, which interferes with the body's metabolism of alcohol. All is well and good as long as you haven't had any alcohol at least three days before eating any ink caps. Otherwise, you can end up with the equivalent of alcohol poisoning. However, like other things in the weird world of fungi, this mushroom is unpredictable and consuming it with any proximity to alcohol has no effect on some people.

For those who are affected, symptoms can occur thirty minutes to an hour after ingestion and include sweating, nausea, vomiting, dizziness, headache, and rapid heartrate. The symptoms can reoccur up to five days after eating the mushrooms if alcohol is consumed. The effects are sometimes severe.

History and Lore

Roman Emperor Claudius was rather fond of mushrooms and alcohol and was notorious for his intemperance. Although it has been suggested that his wife Agrippina did him in by serving him a plate of ink caps, consuming them with alcohol would have given him a rough time but would not have killed him. The notorious and extremely potent death cap is widely believed to have delivered the coup de grâce.

In medieval England, the common ink cap was regarded with suspicion and believed to be poisonous because of its unworldly transformation into a dark, smelly puddle. It was customary to kick the mushrooms to pieces when they first poked their little caps from the egg-shaped veil that encased them. This act was believed to prevent them from doing any evil in the world. British poet Percy Bysshe Shelley (1792–1822) joined the fray with several lines in his poem "The Sensitive Plant." Following a stanza about other fungi, the lines are commonly believed to be a description of an ink cap during its self-demise: "Their mass rotted off them, flake by flake, Till the thick stalk stuck like a murderer's stake."[113] In 1839 the stanza was omitted from the poem at the request of his wife, writer Mary Wollstonecraft Shelley (1797–1851). Why the author of the gothic novel *Frankenstein* objected to the stanza is unknown, but it was later reinstated. The ink cap's reputation was redeemed in the late nineteenth century when it was noted that large clumps of them were strong enough to lift paving stones in the Hampton Road, London, and in the town of Dunstable. An impressive feat for a mushroom.

French physician, botanist, and mycologist Jean Baptiste Francois Bulliard (1742–1793), more commonly known as Pierre Bulliard, wrote the first scientific description of this mushroom and described how it had been made into

---

113. Donovan et al., *The Poems of Shelley 1819–1820*, 311.

and used as ink. Bulliard found that boiling the ink caps in water with clove oil preserved the ink and prevented it from getting moldy. He used it as a background wash for his botanical drawings. Reproductions of his work are popular and fetch several hundred dollars. Following in Bulliard's footsteps, Jean-Louis Émile Boudier (1828–1920), a French pharmacist and mycologist, used ink cap ink to write his manuscripts. After allowing the mushrooms to melt down on their own in a jar, he decanted the liquid and added gum Arabic. Previously, during the seventeenth and eighteenth centuries, carbolic acid was the preservative. The species name comes from the Latin *atramentum*, meaning "blacking and writing ink."[114]

The ink cap has been used medicinally in Sweden to treat burns. The Swedes also regarded it as a natural alternative to the drug Antabuse to help alcoholics break the cycle. However, research showed that the coprine in the ink cap interfered with sperm count, so obviously not a good alternative for men. In Traditional Chinese Medicine, ink caps are used for dermatitis and sores and to improve digestion.

Miscellany

Ink made from the ink cap has been rediscovered and is used as an artistic novelty. Like Boudier, modern ink makers usually allow the caps to dissolve on their own for a week or longer for thicker ink. Because the smell of the liquified remains can be a deterrent to its use, a drop or two of essential oil is usually added. The illustrations for the book *Entangled Life*, which is about the world of fungi, by English biologist Merlin Sheldrake (b. 1987), were drawn using ink from the shaggy mane ink cap (*Coprinus comatus*).

---

114. Morwood, *Oxford Latin Desk Dictionary*, 19.

Jack-o'-Lantern

TRICK NO TREAT

Eastern American Jack-o′-Lantern (*Omphalotus illudens* syn. *Clitocybe illudens*)

European Jack-o′-Lantern (*O. olearius* syn. *Agaricus olearius*)

Western American Jack-o′-Lantern (*O. olivascens*)

Fungi Family: *Omphalotaceae* / formerly in *Marasmiaceae*

All these species are also known as false chanterelle, foxfire mushroom.

Jack-o'-lantern mushrooms grow in large clumps on the stumps or buried roots of trees. The cap is initially the quintessential umbrella shape with downward-rolled edges, but it becomes flattened with a shallow depression in the middle or a funnel shape at maturity. Often four inches wide or larger, the cap is bright brownish orange to yellowish orange. The long gills run down and attach lower on the stem than most other types of mushrooms. The stem is thick, tapers to the base, and is often curved. Both the gills and the stem are also orange.

The European and eastern American jack-o'-lanterns are practically indistinguishable and, for centuries, thought to be the same species. The European species grows in central and southern Europe, the eastern American species grows in central and northern Europe as well as east of the Rockies in North America. The species name *olearius* refers to olive trees, which the European mushroom favors. The western American species name *olivascens* refers to the olive hue in its orange color. The eastern American jack-o'-lantern is especially fond of oaks.

Toxicity and Cautions

All parts of the jack-o'-lantern mushrooms contain the toxic terpenes illudin S and illudin M and cause considerable gastric upset. Ingestion can cause vomiting, stomachache, diarrhea, headache, and nausea. The onset of symptoms usually occurs within one to three hours and can last for several days. Although eating these mushrooms is not fatal, it is said to be an extremely unpleasant experience.

Jack-o'-lanterns are frequently mistaken for two of the highly sought-after chanterelles, the smooth chanterelle (*Cantharellus lateritius*) and the golden chanterelle (*C. cibarius*) as well as the honey mushroom (*Armillaria mellea*), which is also bioluminescent.

History and Lore

Orange by day but luminescent and ghostly at night, no it's not Halloween; jack-o'-lantern mushrooms are bioluminescent. In the dark, the gills and root-like strands called mycelium, which grow in the soil and into decaying wood, give off a bluish-green glow. Luminosity on decaying wood was first documented by Greek philosopher and writer Aristotle (384–322 BCE). He noted it as a cold fire glowing on wood, as did Pliny the Elder centuries later when he saw the base of several olive trees aglow. Light without heat was a remarkable occurrence to the ancients and it stumped scientists for more than a millennium. Through the centuries, the phenomenon played into the widespread folklore of the will-o'-the-wisp, fairies, and other things that go bump in the night or at least glowed.

Bioluminescence occurs when the enzyme *luciferase* oxidizes the organic pigment *luciferin*, producing light. Although scientists worked for centuries to understand how it functioned, French physician and pharmacist Raphaël Dubois (1849–1929) unlocked the secret of glowing things. He discovered the two substances and named them from the Latin *lucifer*—no not the devil, it means "bringer of light" and "morning star."[115] Even after the body of the mushroom is gone, the mycelium often remains and continues producing light. Pieces of the glowing wood were called touchwood and foxwood.

115. Morwood, *Oxford Latin Desk Dictionary*, 108.

Although the term *foxfire* is often believed to have originated in the Appalachian region of North America, it was first recorded in England in 1483.[116] In addition to referring to the animal itself, in Old and Middle English the word *fox* also meant "cunning" as well as "fake." As a verb, *foxing* indicated a clever deceit.[117]

Northern lights are not only seen in the sky. Swedish writer and cartographer Olaus Magnus (1490–1557) noted how people in Scandinavia placed pieces of foxwood at intervals in the forest to light a path and find their way at night. A similar practice occurred in the battlefields of World War I. To avoid drawing attention from the other side of no-man's-land, soldiers attached small pieces of foxwood to their helmets. Walking below ground level through the trenches, it provided just enough light so they could see where they were going. Plus, using the glowing wood was safer than having an open flame around piles of munitions.

Of course, mushroom picking during daylight hours doesn't reveal the jack-o'-lantern's bioluminescence and they continue to be misidentified. In 2018, seven women attending a conference in Alstead, New Hampshire, became sick and several were hospitalized after adding what they thought were chanterelles to their dinner. In the autumn of 2023, jack-o'-lanterns were so prevalent in the Chicago area that in the nearby town of Palos Park local police warned people to stay away from them.

Miscellany

The toxins illudin S and illudin M are also toxic to tumor cells and are being studied for possible cancer treatments. The drug Irofulven, a semisynthetic derivative of illudin S, is in preclinical trials. The jack-o'-lanterns have a cousin down under in Australia, a white mushroom known as ghost fungus (*O. nidiformis*). It is also bioluminescent.

116. Hendrickson, *The Facts on File Encyclopedia of Word and Phrase Origins*, 319.

117. Barnhart, *The Barnhart Concise Dictionary of Etymology*, 297.

Liberty Cap

SYMBOL OF FREEDOM

Liberty Cap (*Psilocybe semilanceata*)

Fungi Family: *Hymenogastraceae*

This mushroom has a conical to bell-shaped cap that ranges from a creamy color to yellow or brown with radial striations. It usually has a distinctive knob on the top. The liberty cap is about an inch in diameter and two to four inches tall. Its slender stem is the same color or slightly lighter than the cap, often wavy, and sometimes has a bluish tinge at the base. The gills are initially cream colored before turning purple to black as the spores mature. This mushroom is found in Europe, the British Isles, and North America.

Toxicity and Cautions

All parts of the liberty cap contain the hallucinogenic neurotoxins psilocybin and psilocin. Of the more than one hundred eighty psychotropic wild species worldwide, the liberty cap is regarded as the most potent of magic mushrooms. The mushroom known as cubes *(P. cubensis)* is the most widely cultivated species. Various types of psilocybin mushrooms usually cause different types of psychedelic effects.

Ingesting liberty caps and other psilocybin shrooms can cause a change in sensory perception and consciousness as well as visual and auditory hallucinations and time distortions. An experience, or trip, can last from two to six hours or more. Bad trips, or negative experiences, also occur, as does losing touch with reality, which can be a serious risk to life. Some people have required hospital treatment. Ingesting these mushrooms can also cause vomiting, stomach pains, and anxiety attacks.

History and Lore

The earliest documented case of the psychedelic effects of mushrooms was in a letter written by physician and apothecary Everard Brande (1746–1834) and published in the *London Medical and Physical Journal* in 1799. Brande had attended a family who had prepared a stew with mushrooms that the father, identified only as J. S., had picked in central London's Green Park. He and his four children had eaten the stew. In addition to dilated pupils, Brande noted that the family experienced vertigo, stupor, and fits of laughter. The doctor was able to obtain a few samples of the mushrooms from Green Park, which he sent to a friend and botany professor at Oxford. The culprits were identified as liberty caps.

This mushroom's common name stretches back to ancient Rome. Slaves were given a conical, brimless felt cap called a pileus to mark their change in status when they were freed; slaves were not permitted to wear caps. The cap was similar to the pilos worn by Greek sailors and travelers. At any rate, the pileus was a mark of liberation. Fast-forward to the eighteenth century. As is sometimes the case, the past seems fascinating, and the classical world of the Romans and Greeks were of great interest to people on both sides of the Atlantic. As a result, the pileus became a political fashion statement and symbol of liberty. The caps that were worn became an emblem for the American and French Revolutions.

As often happens, the past can be blurred and the pileus became synonymous with a cap from Phrygia, an area of present-day Turkey, that was commonly illustrated throughout Greek art. Although the Phrygian cap is longer than the pileus and has a forward curl, the sentiment and symbolism of liberty stuck. In 1675, the people of Brittany donned red Phrygian caps (bonnet rougue) in protest against the taxation of King Louis XIV. Similarly, American Revolutionaries wore red knitted caps as a symbol of liberty. Flagpoles known as liberty poles flew a special flag or were topped by a liberty cap. Even today, both cap and poles are used on some American state and federal emblems. The bonnet de la Liberté became common headgear for French revolutionaries, and as a form of humiliation, King Louis XVI (1754–1793) was forced to wear one when he was arrested.

At this point, you may be wondering how the term *liberty cap* jumped from revolution to mushroom. Simple. Two English poets who were familiar with history, James Woodhouse (1735–1820) and Samuel Taylor Coleridge, noted that a certain little mushroom resembled the pole and cap of liberty. English botanist and mycologist Mordecai Cubitt Cooke apparently read poetry. In his 1871 *Handbook of British Fungi,* he called this mushroom Liberty-cap. Also of note, by the time he wrote his book, the caps of all mushrooms were referred to as pileus by mycologists. The name of this mushroom is regarded as particularly suitable by many who partake of it and feel that their minds are liberated. And if you are thinking that the Phrygian cap is somewhat familiar, Punch (of Punch and Judy fame) wears one, as does Papa Smurf.

Miscellany

Ongoing clinical trials have shown that psilocybin has the potential for treating depression, obsessive-compulsive disorder, anorexia nervosa, post-traumatic stress disorder, and substance abuse. Its use is becoming legal in some US states. Although the tide may be turning, in the UK it is still classified as a Schedule 1 substance along with drugs such as heroin and ecstasy.

WEBCAP

WICKED DEADLY

Deadly Webcap (*Cortinarius rubellus* syn. *C. speciosissimus, C. orellanoides*)

Fool's Webcap (*C. orellanus* syn. *Dermocybe orellana*); also known as sorrel webcap

Goldband Webcap (*C. gentilis* syn. *Agaricus gentilis*); also known as conifer webcap, deadly cort

Fungi Family: *Cortinariaceae*

Webcap mushrooms are so named for the common characteristic where the gills of young ones look like they are covered with cobwebs. The caps start out in a rounded umbrella shape but flatten as they mature and usually have a gentle bump in the center. Webcaps are especially symbiotic with trees and provide them with boosts of nutrients.

The cap of deadly webcap is tawny brown to orange with the edges rolled under. The gills are pale yellow but turn rusty brown. Often slightly bowed, the stem is usually paler than the cap with a red or yellowish mottled pattern. It is found in Europe, Asia, and North America. Fool's cap is tawny brown to reddish orange with pale yellowish gills that turn red. The mottled stem is slightly bowed and generally paler than the cap. It is found in northern Europe. The cap and gills of goldband webcap are yellowish brown. The gills darken to reddish brown. The yellow stem sometimes has remnants of a veil, giving it a banded appearance. It is found in Europe and North America.

Toxicity and Cautions

All parts of these mushrooms are poisonous, containing the nephrotoxin orellanine, which is similar in chemistry to the weedkiller paraquat. Like the death cap, symptoms are delayed, which gives the toxin time to make its way to the kidneys before poisoning is even suspected. It causes irreversible kidney damage and the need for dialysis or transplant. Symptoms may seem flu-like at first, along with headache, vomiting, diarrhea, and sometimes gastrointestinal upsets. The symptoms may occur days or up to three weeks after eating the mushrooms.

History and Lore

Perhaps due to their rarity, folklore seems to have ignored these mushrooms. The first documented case of webcap poisoning occurred during the early 1950s in what at first seemed like an epidemic that sickened about one hundred people in a small Polish town. Eleven people died. The cause was eventually determined to be the fool's webcap mushrooms consumed at the village fête. It was from the investigation of this incident that led Polish doctor Stanislaw Grzymala (1907–1966) to eventually isolate and name the orellanine toxin. A similar incident occurred in 1990 in France where twenty-six young men had taken ill. The cause was webcap soup. Luckily, none of them died.

The most famous case took place in 2008. British journalist and author of *The Horse Whisperer* Nicholas Evans (1950–2022) and his wife were visiting her brother in Scotland and had gathered what Evans thought were the edible chanterelle mushrooms. At least two or three of the four people who partook of the deadly dish needed kidney transplants. Sadly, the 2008 incident apparently wasn't famous enough. In 2017, a hiker on Dartmoor in England mistook the deadly webcap for an edible mushroom. Same outcome: he was hospitalized and needed a kidney transplant.

As we have seen, like their poisonous plant counterparts, mushrooms have their place in crime fiction. The literary phenomenon Sherlock Holmes is immortal in the minds of many and has been reimagined and reinterpreted by numerous authors as well as fans. One such book by Australian author Paul Ashton, *Practical Handbook of Bee Culture*, is imagined as a sort of diary kept by Holmes in his retirement. In a reminiscence about his pre-Watson days, Holmes mentions the use of the fool's webcap in a particular case. The deadly webcap also has a foothold in literary crime as the weapon in *The Colours of Murder* by Scottish author Ali Carter (b. 1983) and it is even mentioned in the kid's book *Pippa Parvin and the Mystery of the Missing Corgi Puppy*, by American author Emily Mah Tippetts (pen name D. Z. Mah).

Miscellany

Although they look different when compared side by side, the webcaps mentioned here are often mistaken for the much sought-after golden chanterelle (*Cantharellus cibarius*) and trumpet chanterelle (*Craterellus tubaeformis*). Expertise is important. A curious thing about these webcaps is that the orellanine toxin makes them fluorescent when exposed to ultraviolet light. That said, making a deuterium lamp part of your foraging gear is probably not worth the expense or effort because most experts recommend staying away from webcaps even though some species are edible.

Conclusion

While I was researching this book and following the trail of poisonous plants through the history of medicine, I was amazed that enough people lived to tell the tale. I also became fascinated with Catherine de Medici. There is no way of knowing how many poisonings she had a hand in, but one incident that most scholars note as wrongfully attributed is the death of the Queen of Navarre, Jeanne d'Albret (1528–1572). As the story goes, Catherine gave her a pair of gloves infused with opium, belladonna, henbane, and other herbs. While the use of poisoned gloves were her style, Catherine had nothing to gain from this death, especially just prior to the marriage of her daughter to Jeanne's son, which she believed would bring harmony between the Protestants and Catholics of France.

There were enough intrigues and machinations in the French royal court to keep Catherine busy; after all, she had learned from the best. The famous, or infamous, Florentine diplomat and philosopher Niccolò Machiavelli (1469–1527) dedicated his political treatise *The Prince* to her father, Lorenzo II de Medici (1492–1519). Catherine and her children were said to have kept copies at hand.

As the saying goes, the apple doesn't fall far from the tree. Catherine's daughter Margaret or Margot (1553–1615) who had married Jeanne d'Albret's son Henry (1551–1589) tried to have someone poison him for being unfaithful. Because Margot was believed to be going off the deep end, Catherine held her basically under house arrest to keep her out of trouble. Concerned about what her mother might do, Margot employed a food taster for safety. In later years, Henry Navarre reported that the Queen Mother had offered to get rid of her daughter.

Even though part of the history of poisonous plants and fatal fungi includes a trail of carnage, I hope you have enjoyed this excursion through their distinctive botanical world. Intertwined with the human story, albeit some of it dark, most of these plants are also associated with the better angels who have sought to bring comfort and healing. If anything, instead of ditching your gardening gloves, I hope this book has brought more awareness about the power of plants and fungi and the importance of learning about them, especially those you bring into your garden, home, and kitchen. Not every plant is a killer, and many that are can be handled safely. Knowledge and commonsense are key. After all, what a drab place this world would be without interesting gardens and uniquely fascinating plants and fungi.

Selected Bibliography

Adamson, Melitta Weiss, and Francine Segan, eds. *Entertaining from Ancient Rome to the Super Bowl: An Encyclopedia*. ABC-CLIO, 2008.

Aggrawal, Anil. *Textbook of Forensic Medicine and Toxicology*. 2nd ed. Avichal Publishing Company, 2017.

Amar, Zohar, and Efraim Lev. *Arabian Drugs in Early Medieval Mediterranean Medicine*. Edinburgh University Press, 2017.

Ando, Clifford, and Jörg Rüpke, eds. *Religion and Law in Classical and Christian Rome*. Franz Steiner Verlag, 2006.

Austin, Daniel F. *Florida Ethnobotany*. CRC Press, 2004.

Balick, Michael J., and Paul Alan Cox. *Plants, People, and Culture: The Science of Ethnobotany*. 2nd ed. CRC Press, 2021.

Barceloux, Donald. *Medical Toxicology of Natural Substances: Foods, Fungi, Medicinal Herbs, Plants, and Venomous Animals*. John Wiley & Sons, 2008.

Barnhart, Robert K., ed. *The Barnhart Concise Dictionary of Etymology*. HarperCollins, 1995.

Bastien, Joseph W. *Healers of the Andes: Kallawaya Herbalists and Their Medicinal Plants*. University of Utah Press, 1987.

Bäumler, Siegfried. *Heilpflanzenpraxis Heute: Arzneipflanzenporträts*. Elsevier GmbH, 2021.

Bechtel, Stefan, and Laurence Roy Stains. *Through a Glass, Darkly: Sir Arthur Conan Doyle and the Quest to Solve the Greatest Mystery of All*. St. Martin's Press, 2017.

Bingham, Eula, and Barbara Cohrssen, eds. *Patty's Toxicology*. 6th ed. Vol. 1. John Wiley & Sons, 2012.

Blyth, Alexander Wynter. *Poisons, Their Effects and Detection*. 3rd ed. Charles Griffin and Company, 1895.

Brevan-Jones, Robert. *Poisonous Plants: A Cultural and Social History*. Windgather Press, 2009.

Britten, James, and Robert Holland. *A Dictionary of English Plant-Names*. Trübner & Co., 1886.

Brown, Michael. *Death in the Garden: Poisonous Plants & Their Use Throughout History*. Pen & Sword Books, 2021.

Camporesi, Piero. *Bread of Dreams: Food and Fantasy in Early Modern Europe*. Translated by David Gentilcore. The University of Chicago Press, 1996.

Carlson, Kit. *The Book of Killer Plants: A Field Guide to Nature's Deadliest Creations*. Cider Mill Press Book Publishers, 2022.

Carod-Artal, F. J. "Hallucinogenic Drugs in Pre-Colombian Mesoamerican Cultures." *Neurologia* (Jan–Feb 2015). Epub September 3, 2011. NIH National Library of Medicine. https://pubmed.ncbi.nlm.nih.gov/21893367 / accessed 7/28/2023.

Carus, W. Seth. *Bioterrorism and Biocrimes: The Illicit Use of Biological Agents Since 1900*. Fredonia Books, 2002.

Castle, Frederick A., and Charles Rice, eds. *New Remedies: An Illustrated Monthly Trade Journal of Materia Medica, Pharmacy and Therapeutics*. Vol. VII. William Wood & Company, 1878.

Chamberlain, Geoffrey. *From Witchcraft to Wisdom: A History of Obstetrics & Gynaecology in the British Isles*. RCOG Press, 2007.

Chevallier, Andrew. *The Encyclopedia of Medicinal Plants*. Dorling Kindersley, 1996.

Clarke, Robert C., and Mark D. Merlin. *Cannabis: Evolution and Ethnobotany*. University of California Press, 2013.

Cooke, M. C. *Handbook of British Fungi*. Macmillan and Co., 1871.

Coombes, Allen. *Dictionary of Plant Names*. Timber Press, 1985.

Culpeper, Nicholas. *The English Physician*. B. & R. Crosby & Co., 1814.

Cumo, Christopher, ed. *Encyclopedia of Cultivated Plants: From Acacia to Zinnia*. ABC-CLIO, 2013.

De Cleene, Marcel, and Marie Claire Lejeune. *Compendium of Symbolic and Ritual Plants in Europe*. Man & Culture Publishers, 2003.

Dobelis, Inge N., ed. *Magic and Medicine of Plants: A Practical Guide to the Science, History, Folklore, and Everyday Uses of Medicinal Plants*. The Reader's Digest Association, 1986.

Donovan, Jack, Cian Duffy, Kelvin Everest, and Michael Rossington, eds. *The Poems of Shelley 1819–1820*. Vol. 3. Routledge, 2014.

Drysdale, John James, R. E. Dudgeon, and Richard Hughes, eds. *The British Journal of Homoeopathy*. Vol. 33. Henry Turner and Co., 1875.

Dutton, Joan Parry. *Plants of Colonial Williamsburg*. The Colonial Williamsburg Foundation, 1979.

Editorial Staff. *Webster's Third New International Dictionary, Unabridged*. Encyclopedia Britannica, 1981.

Editors. "The Powerful Solanaceae: Henbane." US Forest Service. Accessed August 2, 2023. https://www.fs.usda.gov/wildflowers/ethnobotany/Mind_and_Spirit/henbane.shtml.

Finger, Stanley. *Doctor Franklin's Medicine*. University of Pennsylvania Press, 2006.

Folkard, Richard. *Plant Lore, Legends, and Lyrics: Embracing the Myths, Traditions, Superstitions, and Folklore of the Plant Kingdom*. 2nd ed. Sampson, Low, Marston, & Company, 1892.

Foster, Steven, and Rebecca L. Johnson. *National Geographic Desk Reference to Nature's Medicine*. National Geographic Society, 2008.

Foust, Clifford M. *Rhubarb: The Wondrous Drug*. Princeton University Press, 2014.

Freeman, Margaret B. *The Unicorn Tapestries*. E. P. Dutton, 1983.

Frost, Louise, and Alistair Griffiths. *Plants of Eden*. Alison Hodge Publishers, 2001.

Garrod, Alfred Baring. *The Essentials of Materia Medica and Therapeutics*. 2nd ed. Walton and Maberly, 1864.

Gerald, Michael C. *The Poisonous Pen of Agatha Christie*. University of Texas Press, 1993.

Gerard, John. *The Herball or Generall Historie of Plantes*. John Norton, 1597.

Gomez, Julie. *A Guide to Deadly Herbs*. Hancock House Publishers, 1997.

Goodman, Jordan. *Tobacco in History: The Cultures of Dependence*. Routledge, 2005.

Gordon, R. Michael. *Murder Files from Scotland Yard and the Black Museum*. Exposit, 2018.

Grell, Ole Peter, Andrew Cunningham, and Jon Arrizabalaga, eds. *"It All Depends on the Dose" Poisons and Medicines in European History*. Routledge, 2018.

Grieve, Margaret. *A Modern Herbal*. Vols. 1 and 2. Dover Publications, 1971.

Hammer, Roger L. *Foraging Florida: Finding, Identifying, and Preparing Edible and Medicinal Wild Foods in Florida*. Globe Pequot, 2023.

Hammond, Claudia. "Would Shakespeare's Poisons and Drugs Work in Reality?" BBC Future, April 15, 2014. https://www.bbc.com/future/article/20140416-do-shakespeares-poisons-work.

Hanson, Glen R., Peter J. Venturelli, and Annette E. Fleckenstein. *Drugs and Society*. 11th ed. Jones & Bartlett Learning, 2012.

Hargreaves, Tony. *Poisons and Poisonings: Death by Stealth*. Royal Society of Chemistry, 2017.

Harrison, Lorraine. *Latin for Gardeners: Over 3,000 Plant Names Explained and Explored*. The University of Chicago Press, 2012.

Hatfield, Gabrielle. *Hatfield's Herbal: The Curious Stories of Britain's Wild Plants*. Penguin Group, 2009.

Hayes, A. Wallace, and Tetyana Kobets, eds. *Hayes' Principles and Methods of Toxicology*. 7th ed. CRC Press, 2023.

Hendrickson, Robert. *The Facts on File Encyclopedia of Word and Phrase Origins*. 4th rev. ed. Facts on File, 2008.

Hewlett, A. W., Torald Sollmann, M. I. Wilbert, and W. A. Puckner, eds. *Epitome of the Pharmacopeia of the United States and the National Formulary*. American Medical Association, 1924.

Hoblyn, Richard D. *A Dictionary of Terms Used in Medicine and the Collateral Sciences*. Blanchard and Lea, 1859.

Hodge, Matthew, and Elizabeth Kusko, eds. *Exploring the Macabre, Malevolent, and Mysterious: Multidisciplinary Perspectives*. Cambridge Scholars Publishing, 2020.

Hollingsworth, E. Buckner. *Flower Chronicles: The Legend and Lore of Fifteen Garden Favorites*. University of Chicago Press, 2004.

Humphrey, John, ed. *The Pharmaceutical Journal Formulary*. The Pharmaceutical Journal, 1904.

Husen, Azamal, ed. *Exploring Poisonous Plants: Medicinal Values, Toxicity Responses, and Therapeutic Uses*. CRC Press, 2023.

Huish, Robert, ed. *The Female's Friend and General Domestic Adviser*. George Virtue, 1827.

Inkwright, Fez. *Botanical Curses and Poisons: The Shadow-Lives of Plants*. Liminal 11, 2023.

Janick, Jules, ed. *Horticultural Reviews*. Vol. 34. John Wiley & Sons, 2008.

Kang, Lydia, and Nate Pedersen. *Quackery: A Brief History of the Worst Ways to Cure Everything*. Workman Publishing, 2017.

Kaplan, Matt. "Slivers of Science in Homer's *The Oddessey*: Modern Science Could Explain Mythic Tales of Transformation." *Discover Magazine*, January 19, 2015. https://www.discovermagazine.com/planet-earth/slivers-of-science-in-homers-the-odyssey.

Keoke, Emory Dean, and Kay Marie Porterfield, eds. *Encyclopedia of American Indian Contributions to the World*. Checkmark Books, 2003.

Kiple, Kenneth F., and Kriemhild Coneè Ornelas, eds. *The Cambridge World History of Food*. Vol. 1. Cambridge University Press, 2000.

Kowalchik, Claire, and William H. Hylton, eds. *Rodale's Illustrated Encyclopedia of Herbs*. Rodale Press, 1998.

Knight, Anthony P. *A Guide to Poisonous House and Garden Plants*. Teton New Media, 2007.

Lawrence, Sandra. *The Magic of Mushrooms: Fungi in Folklore, Superstition and Traditional Medicine*. Welbeck, 2022.

Lawrence, Sandra. *Witch's Garden: Plants in Folklore, Magic and Traditional Medicine*. Welbeck, 2020.

Lee, Sidney, ed. *Dictionary of National Biography, vol. 60 Watson–Whewell*. Smith, Elder, & Co., 1899.

Lewis, Walter H. *Medical Botany: Plants Affecting Human Health*. 2nd ed. John Wiley & Sons, 2003.

Lüttge, Ulrich, Wolfram Beyschlag, Burkhard Büdel, and Dennis Francis, eds. *Progress in Botany 72: Genetics, Physiology, Systematics, Ecology*. Springer, 2011.

Mac Coitir, Niall. *Ireland's Wild Plants: Myths, Legends and Folklore.* The Collins Press, 2015.

Macinnis, Peter. *Poisons: From Hemlock to Botox and the Killer Bean of Calabar*. Arcade Publishing, 2005.

Maitland, Karen. *The Dangerous Art of Alchemy*. Headline Publishing Group, 2015.

Marley, Greg. *Chanterelle Dreams, Amanita Nightmares: The Love, Lore, and Mystique of Mushrooms*. Chelsea Green Publishing, 2010.

Marren, Peter. *Mushrooms: The Natural and Human World of British Fungi*. Bloomsbury Publishing, 2018.

Martin, Deborah J. *Baneful! 95 of the World's Worst Herbs*. The Herb Lady, 2013.

Mayer, Adrienne. *Greek Fire, Poison Arrows, and Scorpion Bombs: Unconventional Warfare in the Ancient World*. Princeton University Press, 2022.

McCrery, Nigel. *Silent Witnesses: The Often Gruesome but Always Fascinating History of Forensic Science*. Chicago Review Press, 2014.

McGrath, Carol. *Sex and Sexuality in Tudor England*. Pen & Sword Books, 2022.

McQueen, Charlene A., ed. *Comprehensive Toxicology*. 3rd ed. Vol. 1. Elsevier, 2018.

Millar, James, ed. *Encyclopaedia Britannica*. 4th ed. Vol. XIII. Scotland: 1810.

Millman, Lawrence. *Fungipedia: A Brief Compendium of Mushroom Lore*. Princeton University Press, 2019.

Moerman, Daniel E. *Medicinal Plants of Native America*. Vols. 1 and 2. The University of Michigan Press, 1986.

Money, Nicholas P. *Mushroom*. Oxford University Press, 2011.

Nashe, Thomas. *The Works of Thomas Nashe*. Vol. I. Edited by Ronald B. McKerrow. A. H. Bullen, 1904.

Omissi, Adrastos, "Liberty Cap: The Surprising Tale of How Europe's Magic Mushroom Got Its Name." The Conversation, November 27, 2020. https://theconversation.com/liberty-cap-the-surprising-tale-of-how-europes-magic-mushroom-got-its-name-130668.

Owen, James. "Ancient Death-Smile Potion Decoded?" National Geographic News, June 5, 2009. https://web.archive.org/web/20090605063408/http://news.nationalgeographic.com/news/2009/06/090602-smiling-death-potion.html.

Pauwels, Ivo, and Gerty Christoffels. *Herbs*. Translated by Milton Webber. Struik Publishers, 2006.

Pereira, Jonathan. *The Elements of Materia Medica: The Natural History, Preparation, Properties, Composition, Effects, and Uses of Medicines*. Part II. Longman, Orme, Brown, Green, and Longmans, 1840.

Phaneuf, Holly. *Herbs Demystified: A Scientist Explains How the Most Common Herbal Remedies Really Work*. Hachette Books, 2022.

Phillips, Henry. *Flora Historica: Or the Three Seasons of the British Parterre*. Vol. 1. E. Lloyd and Son, 1824.

Pliny the Elder. *The Natural History of Pliny*. Vols. IV and V. Translated by John Bostock and H. T. Riley. Henry G. Bohn, 1856.

Pollington, Stephen. *Leechcraft: Early English Charms, Plantlore and Healing*. Anglo-Saxon Books, 2008.

Porter, Enid. *Cambridgeshire Customs and Folklore*. Vol. 4. Routledge, 2015.

Potterton, David, ed. *Culpeper's Color Herbal*. Sterling Publishing Co., 2007.

Pratt, Christina. *An Encyclopedia of Shamanism*. Vol. 1, A–M. The Rosen Publishing Group, 2007.

Quattrocchi, Umberto. *CRC World Dictionary of Plant Names: Common Names, Scientific Names, Eponyms, Synonyms, Etymology. R–Z*. Vol. 4. CRC Press, 2000.

Rätsch, Christian. *The Encyclopedia of Psychoactive Plants: Ethnopharmacology and Its Applications*. Translated by John R. Baker. Park Street Press, 2005.

Rätsch, Christian. *Marijuana Medicine: A World Tour of the Healing and Visionary Powers of Cannabis*. Translated by John Baker. Healing Arts Press, 2001.

Richardson, Rosamond. *Britain's Wild Flowers: A Treasury of Traditions, Superstitions, Remedies and Literature*. National Trust Books, 2017.

Roberts, Margaret F., and Michael Winks, eds. *Alkaloids: Biochemistry, Ecology, and Medicinal Applications*. Springer Science+Business Media, 1998.

Roberts, Nicole F. "The Science of Scare: Why We Love the Thrill of Being Afraid." Forbes, October 23, 2023. https://www.forbes.com/sites/nicoleroberts/2023/10/22/the-science-of-scare-why-we-love-the-thrill-of-being-afraid/?sh=7af7810574f2.

Rodin, Alvin E., and Jack D. Key. *Medical Casebook of Doctor Arthur Conan Doyle: From Practitioner to Sherlock Holmes and Beyond*. Robert E. Krieger Publishing, 1984.

Runkel, Sylvan T., and Dean M. Roosa. *Wildflowers and Other Plants of Iowa Wetlands*. 2nd ed. University of Iowa Press, 2014.

Ryan, John Charles. *Plants in Contemporary Poetry: Ecocriticism and the Botanical Imagination*. Routledge, 2018.

Sanders, Jack. *Secrets of Wildflowers: A Delightful Feast of Little-Known Facts, Folklore, and History*. Globe Pequot Press, 2014.

Scott, Susan, and Craig Thomas. *Poisonous Plants of Paradise: First Aid and Medical Treatment of Injuries from Hawai'i's Plants*. University of Hawai'i Press, 2000.

Sédir, Paul. *Occult Botany: Sédir's Concise Guide to Magical Plants*. Translated and edited by R. Bailey. Inner Traditions, 2021.

Skeat, Walter W. *The Concise Dictionary of English Etymology: The Pioneering Work on the Roots and Origins of the Language*. Wordsworth Editions, 1993.

Small, Ernest. *North American Cornucopia: Top 100 Indigenous Food Plants*. CRC Press, 2014.

Small, Ernest. *Top 100 Exotic Food Plants*. CRC Press, 2011.

Small, Ernest, and Paul M. Catling. *Canadian Medicinal Crops*. NRC Research Press, 1999.

Spinella, Marcello. *The Psychopharmacology of Herbal Medicine: Plant Drugs That Alter Mind, Brain, and Behavior*. The MIT Press, 2001.

Stephenson, John, and James Morss Churchill. *Medical Botany: Illustrations and Descriptions of the Medicinal Plants*. Vol. 3. Edited by Gilbert T. Burnett. John Churchill, 1837.

Stephenson, Steven L. *The Kingdom Fungi: The Biology of Mushrooms, Molds, and Lichens*. Timber Press, 2010.

Stevenson, Angus, ed. *Oxford Dictionary of English*. 3rd ed. Oxford University Press, 2010.

Stewart, Amy. *Wicked Plants: The Weed That Killed Lincoln's Mother & Other Botanical Atrocities*. Algonquin Books of Chapel Hill, 2009.

Storl, Wolf D. *The Herbal Lore of Wise Women and Wortcunners: The Healing Power of Medicinal Plants*. North Atlantic Books, 2012.

Stuart, David. *Dangerous Garden: The Quest for Plants to Change Our Lives*. Harvard University Press, 2004.

Suchard, J., Greb, A. "Negligible Oleandrin Content of Hot Dogs Cooked on Nerium Oleander Skewers." *Journal of Medical Toxicology* 17 (2021): 57–60. https://doi.org/10.1007/s13181-020-00805-4.

Tabor, Edward. "Plant Poisons in Shakespeare." *Economic Botany* 24, no. 1 (January–March 1970): 81–94.

Teuscher, Eberhard, and Ulrike Lindequist. *Natural Poisons and Venoms: Plant Toxins: Terpens and Steroids*. Walter de Gruyter GmbH & Co., 2023.

Thompson, C. J. S. *Poison Mysteries in History, Romance, and Crime*. The Scientific Press, 1923.

Thoreau, Henry D. *I to Myself: An Annotated Selection from the Journal of Henry D. Thoreau*. Edited by Jeffrey S. Cramer. Yale University Press, 2007.

Thorpe, Benjamin. *Northern Mythology: Popular Traditions and Superstitions of Scandinavia, North Germany, and The Netherlands*. Vol. 2. Edward Lumley, 1851.

Tsoucalas, Gregory, and Markos Sgantzos. "The Death of Cleopatra: Suicide by Snakebite or Poisoned by Her Enemies?" *History of Toxicology and Environmental Health: Toxicology in Antiquity*. Vol. 1. Edited by Philip Wexler. Academic Press, 2014.

Turner, Patricia, and Charles Russell Coulter. *Dictionary of Ancient Deities*. Oxford University Press, 2000.

Vickery, Roy, ed. *Vickery's Folk Flora: An A–Z of the Folklore and Uses of British and Irish Plants*. Weidenfeld & Nicolson, 2019.

Vitebsky, Piers. *Shamanism*. University of Oklahoma Press, 2001.

Watts, D. C. *Elsevier's Dictionary of Plant Lore*. Academic Press, 2007.

Watts, D. C. *Elsevier's Dictionary of Plant Names and Their Origin*. Elsevier, 2000.

Wexler, Philip, ed. *Toxicology in the Middle Ages and Renaissance*. Academic Press, 2017.

Williams, John, ed. *The Physicians of Myddfai*. Translated by John Pughe. Longman & Co., 1861.

Woehrel, Mary L., and William H. Light. *Mushrooms of the Georgia Piedmont and Southern Appalachians*. The University of Georgia Press, 2017.

INDEX

A

B

C

D

E

F

G

H

I

J

K

L

M

N

O

P

Q

R

S

T

U

V

W

Y-Z

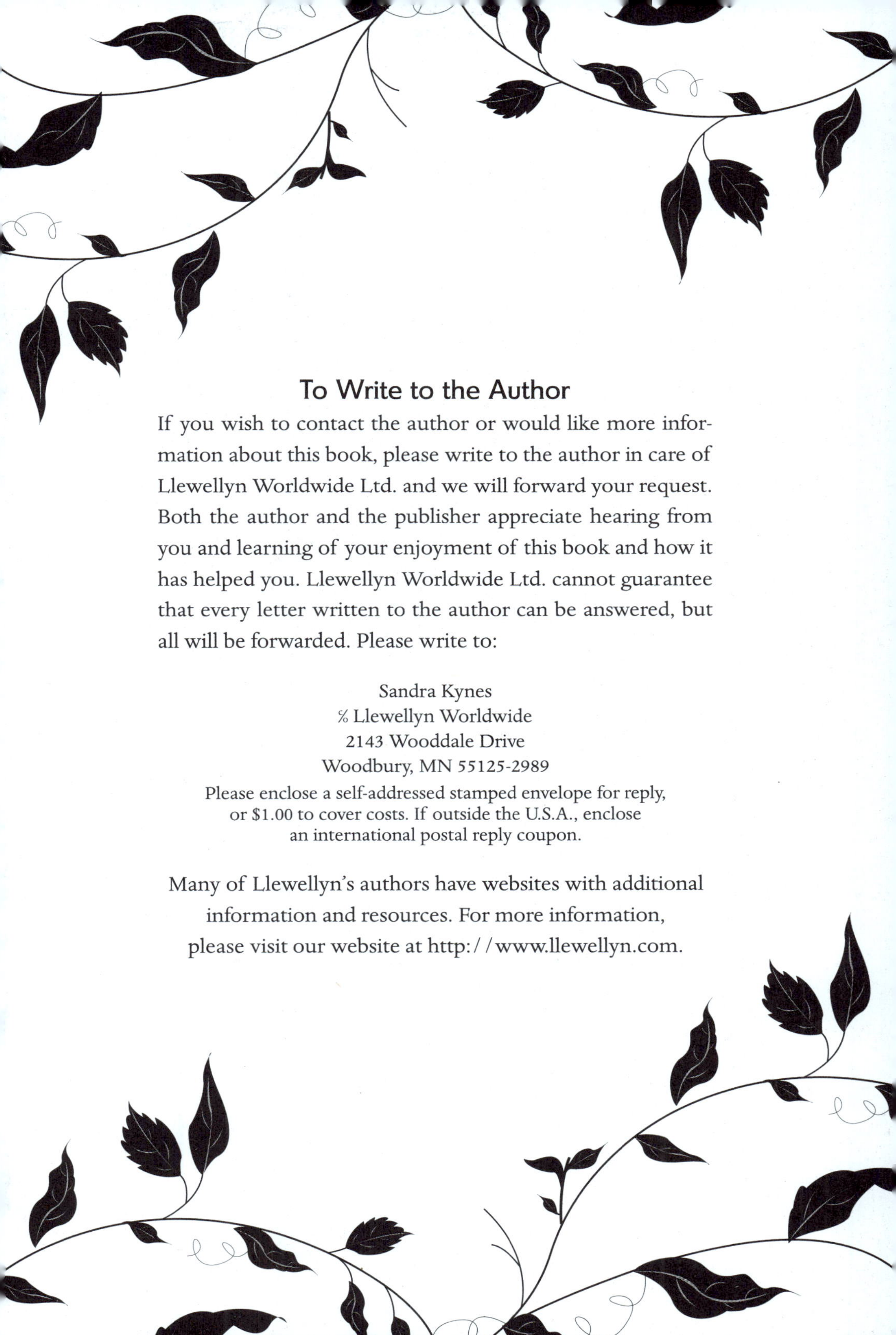

To Write to the Author

If you wish to contact the author or would like more information about this book, please write to the author in care of Llewellyn Worldwide Ltd. and we will forward your request. Both the author and the publisher appreciate hearing from you and learning of your enjoyment of this book and how it has helped you. Llewellyn Worldwide Ltd. cannot guarantee that every letter written to the author can be answered, but all will be forwarded. Please write to:

Sandra Kynes
℅ Llewellyn Worldwide
2143 Wooddale Drive
Woodbury, MN 55125-2989

Please enclose a self-addressed stamped envelope for reply, or $1.00 to cover costs. If outside the U.S.A., enclose an international postal reply coupon.

Many of Llewellyn's authors have websites with additional information and resources. For more information, please visit our website at http://www.llewellyn.com.